th
bre

National Institute of Economic and Social
   Research
Policy Studies Institute
Royal Institute of International Affairs
Joint Studies in Public Policy 1

BRITAIN IN EUROPE

National Institute of Economic and Social
    Research
Policy Studies Institute
Royal Institute of International Affairs
Joint Studies in Public Policy

STEERING COMMITTEE

National Institute of Economic and Social
   Research
Policy Studies Institute
Royal Institute of International Affairs
Joint Studies in Public Policy 1

BRITAIN IN EUROPE

Edited by
WILLIAM WALLACE

Heinemann · London

Heinemann Educational Books Ltd
LONDON EDINBURGH MELBOURNE AUCKLAND TORONTO
HONG KONG SINGAPORE KUALA LUMPUR NEW DELHI
NAIROBI JOHANNESBURG IBADAN
KINGSTON

Cased edition   ISBN 0-435-83919-5
Paper edition   ISBN 0-435-83920-9

First published 1980

Published by Heinemann Educational Books Ltd
Filmset by Northumberland Press Ltd
Gateshead, Tyne and Wear
Printed in Great Britain by Richard Clay (The Chaucer Press) Ltd
Bungay, Suffolk

Foreword

The papers in this volume were prepared for the first of a new series of conferences jointly sponsored by the three institutes listed on the title page. The model for this new enterprise has been the series of conferences and published volumes on economic policy organized by the National Institute of Economic and Social Research in 1978–9, which in turn draw on the experience of the Brookings Panel Conferences in the United States. The Steering Committee is responsible for the selection of themes of direct relevance to public policy, on which expert advice and discussion may help to broaden the public debate. Papers and comments are circulated in advance to all the participants in a working conference. Immediately afterwards, they are revised in the light of the conference exchanges, and published with a report of the proceedings as rapidly as possible.

We chose for our first theme a difficult and controversial subject which is at once highly topical and long standing. We did not discover any easy solutions, but we did examine the details of Britain's European predicament and explore some ways to escape from it. The conference itself witnessed some lively debates among participants with differing views. Views round the table shifted a little as the conference proceeded. We did not reach any unanimous conclusions, but we did discover some unexpected areas of common ground.

We are grateful to the Social Science Research Council for underwriting the cost of launching this new series. The second topic chosen is 'Wage Bargaining', for which papers are currently being prepared; further topics are now being considered by the Steering Committee. Our intention, in future conferences as in the one which has led to this volume, will be to throw fresh light on contentious issues of importance to British policy. I hope readers will agree that this first volume has fulfilled that objective.

Croham

London
January 1980

Contents

Contributors and Other Participants

Chairman
Lord Croham

Contributors
Laurens Brinkhorst, Member, Second Chamber, Netherlands Parliament

Professor A. J. Brown, School of Economics, University of Leeds

Miriam Camps, Senior Fellow, Council on Foreign Relations, New York

Hugh Corbet, Director, Trade Policy Research Centre

Elizabeth Dakin, Economist, National Farmers' Union

J. C. R. Dow, Executive Director, Bank of England

M. Emerson, Commission of the European Communities

Wynne Godley, Director, Department of Applied Economics, University of Cambridge

Bryan Gould, current affairs journalist, Thames Television

Professor Sir Bryan Hopkin, Department of Economics, University College, Cardiff

Daniel T. Jones, Senior Research Fellow, Sussex European Research Centre, University of Sussex

Professor David Marquand, Department of Politics and Contemporary History, University of Salford

Stephen Milligan, Brussels correspondent of *The Economist*

Ann D. Morgan, Senior Research Officer, National Institute of Economic and Social Research

John Pinder, Director, Policy Studies Institute

Professor Christopher Ritson, Department of Agricultural Marketing, University of Newcastle-upon-Tyne

D. K. Stout, Economic Director, National Economic Development Office

Carsten Thoroe, Research Fellow, Institut für Weltwirtschaft, University of Kiel

William Wallace, Director of Studies, Royal Institute of International Affairs

Other participants
Graham Avery
Frank Blackaby
Simon Broadbent
Ian Byatt
Martin Fetherston
Michael Jenkins
Sir Arthur Knight
Sir Ronald McIntosh
Roger Morgan
J. M. C. Rollo
T. M. Rybczynski
Helen Wallace
David Watt

1 Introduction and Comment on the Discussion

by William Wallace

Seven years have passed since the United Kingdom joined the European Community but the issue of its relationship with the Community as an entity and with the other member states remains unsettled. British opinion remains confused about the objectives of membership and deeply divided over its desirability. Successive governments have attempted to renegotiate the terms of entry, and later to persuade Britain's partners to alleviate the immediate adverse impact on the national economy of its contributions to the Community budget. If the Community remains a 'problem' for Britain, 'the British problem' also remains a preoccupation of the Community: a central issue at summits and European Councils in 1969, 1972, 1975 and 1979, a recurring source of contention ever since the first application in 1961.

The *acquis communautaire* among the original six members, outlined during the negotiations and developed during the 1960s, represented a rough balance of interests, from which all expected to benefit. For Britain, however, it had from the outset structural disadvantages, arising out of Britain's distinctive position as a highly urbanized industrial society with a small but efficient agricultural sector whose production is supplemented by substantial imports. The difficulties of adjusting the *acquis* to accommodate Britain's interests contributed much to the breakdown of the first negotiations for entry in 1962–3. Thereafter British governments accepted that they would have to negotiate only the principles of membership and the transitional arrangements for entry, and to rely upon the continuous process of negotiation within the Council of Ministers after accession to alter the balance of policies. British ministers and officials were to find after entry that their partners were far less willing to change established policies or to entertain requests for different priorities than they had hoped. Moreover, Britain had the misfortune to join the Community at the end of a long period of growth in the international economy. Its first years of membership were accompanied by economic recession and heightened inflation throughout the industrial world; this wrecked the Community's first attempts to move beyond the initial *acquis* towards an Economic and Monetary Union, gave other member states less room for generosity, and further damaged Britain's already fragile economy.

While most observers would recognize that these British, European, and international economic difficulties have complicated the process of mutual adjustment between the United Kingdom and the European Community, one simple explanation for failure is that Britain has not tried hard enough to make a success of membership. It is an explanation that finds much support in other member states, not least within their governments. The argument is advanced that British governments have become bogged down in attempts to gain immediate and short-term benefits, preoccupied with swaying their doubting domestic public to a more favourable view, and bent on mitigating the narrowly conceived budgetary costs of membership. If their thinking had been broader and more far-sighted their conception of the costs and benefits of membership would have been different, their approach to Community bargaining more positive, and the response of other member states more sympathetic. Thus Britain itself is largely responsible for the continuing dispute over conditions of membership and the continuing ambivalence or indifference of its citizens. Over the course of seven years a more positive strategy ought surely to have produced better results.

An alternative explanation, which commands support both in Britain and within some other member states, is that there is a fundamental and unalterable incompatibility of interests between the United Kingdom and its continental partners. The needs of the British economy, it is argued, are qualitatively different from those of the French, German, or Dutch. The economic importance and the political weight of domestic interests diverge sharply. There is too little sense of common interest and of shared loyalties, either in Britain or on the continent, to bridge the resulting gulf. Britain is thus condemned to remain for the foreseeable future on the fringes of the

European Community, associated with some of its political aims but never part of its central core.

The papers collected in this volume and the discussions at the Joint Studies conference on 11 and 12 December 1979 at Chatham House sought to go beyond such simple explanations to examine the roots of the continuing debate over Britain's relations with the Community. The conference began by examining the economic impact of Community membership on Britain, and the implications for Britain of the current balance of Community policies, drawing on the papers published here in chapters 3, 4, and 5. It moved on to discuss the potential costs and benefits for Britain of further developments in Community policies in areas already on the European agenda, starting from the papers published in chapters 6, 7, 8, and 9. The conference concluded by re-examining the question of British objectives within the Community and the related question of what kind of Community policies would be most advantageous to Britain. The interaction between economic and political objectives was raised and argued throughout these discussions.

The British Problem
A remarkable degree of consensus emerged. Participants who had taken sharply different views in the earlier argument over British entry were now drawn together on a number of issues. Our conclusions, briefly, took us beyond the dichotomy between maximalism and minimalism, set out in David Marquand's opening paper, to an acceptance that Britain's interests are not well served either by the current balance of Community policies or by a drift towards dissociation from the central *acquis*; that to further British interests through the Community, significant changes in Community priorities and policies are necessary; that these changes can be achieved only within a much wider framework of economic and political bargaining than is allowed by the immediate dispute between Britain and its partners over budgetary contributions and agricultural prices; and that this in turn requires fresh consideration of national strategy towards the Community and of the long-term development of the Community itself, not only by the United Kingdom but also by other member states.

Participants found their widest consensus when discussing the underlying criterion against which the Community's advantages or disadvantages for Britain should be assessed: the degree to which Community policies and obligations help or hinder the attempt to reverse our relative industrial decline. The conference, indeed, was from the outset much more preoccupied with Britain's industrial decline, and the interaction between domestic and international factors in that decline, than with the exact balance of budgetary contributions or the operations of the Common Agricultural Policy. It was readily accepted that the pattern of industrial decline was set long before Britain entered the Community, and that the coincidence of Community entry with a further downturn in Britain's international competitiveness did not imply any causal connection between the two. Britain's export performance in Community markets since entry has been quite creditable; it has been the continuing increase in imports, from Japanese and other extra-European sources as much as from the rest of the Community, that underlines the essential weakness of the British economy. The dynamic effects on domestic investment and production which it was hoped would follow from Community entry have not materialized; but this has been due to domestic factors and to the impact of international recession rather than to the workings of the Community market or the constraints of Community policies. It is therefore fruitless to spend much time debating the nature of the record in macro-economic terms. The available statistics are too unreliable, and the influences at work too diverse, to permit any convincing answers. It is far more important to concentrate on the question of what economic and industrial policies will most help to reverse this decline, and how far the Community might help or hinder such policies, without being distracted by the temptation to use the Community as a scapegoat for Britain's past failures.

It is nevertheless clear that in several specific areas Community membership has imposed significant additional burdens on the British economy. The established pattern of Community expenditure benefits member states which are net agricultural exporters, with a large proportion of their working population in agriculture. Britain, as a net importer with an agricultural sector that is small and relatively efficient, is condemned to remain a net contributor until either the framework of the Common Agricultural Policy is radically altered or the Community develops a different pattern of revenue and expenditure. The government White Papers of 1970 and 1971 estimated not inaccurately the scale of the budgetary costs of membership at the end of the five-year 'transition period' after entry, on the basis of Community policies then prevailing. British negotiators, however, expected that the dynamic effects of entry on the British economy would to some extent offset these costs, and that during the period of transition changes in the pattern of Community policies would begin to alter the distribution of expenditure. These hopes have been largely disappointed. Indeed, the real cost of the CAP has risen faster than the White Paper calculations allowed for, while our ability to pay has fallen.

Representatives of other member states argue that the distribution of costs and benefits through the Community budget is merely an incidental result of Community policies that bring general benefits to all its members. That argument is misplaced. The reality is that the current *acquis* distributes benefits, in varying degrees, among all its original members; and of those who joined in 1973, the two with large agricultural sectors benefit in the same way. Britain, alone among the present member states, is at a positive disadvantage – though Italy also now derives less evident benefits than its partners, and suffers from the current distribution of Community expenditure. Britain's disadvantage is not trivial. The estimates for its net contribution to the Community budget for 1980 amount to nearly 10 per cent of national income tax, under a government which came to office committed to economic regeneration through lightening the burden of direct taxation. It is equivalent to more than half Britain's projected deficit on the balance of payments for 1980 – in an economy which has been repeatedly constrained over the past twenty years by balance of payments considerations.

The pattern of transfers in terms of agricultural trade, including the benefit to Community exporters and the cost to Community importers of trading at prices fixed artificially high within a protected market (as discussed in chapter 4), highlights the imbalance between Britain's position and that of its Community partners. Some representatives of other member states have argued that the burden of Britain's contributions would be alleviated, and the dynamic benefits for Britain's economy increased, if only the overall pattern of our overseas trade were to shift further towards the Community. This argument is also misplaced. The analysis of chapter 3 demonstrates that Britain's overseas trade *has* adjusted significantly towards the Community since entry. Any reduction in contributions to the budget through a reduction in customs duties and agricultural levies on extra-Community imports would be of marginal significance to the overall balance; Britain's budgetary problem comes from the expenditure side far more than from the Community's sources of revenue. The benefits to Britain's economy from access to a wider 'home market' are shared by all other members of the Community; only Britain suffers the offsetting burden of budgetary and trade costs arising from the Common Agricultural Policy.

The criticism that Britain has made no real effort to help itself by using the Community's institutions and practices to its best advantage and by attempting to present alternative priorities and policies is *not*, however, misplaced. A repeated, and unanswered, question around the table during this conference was 'But what are our objectives? What are we hoping to achieve through membership of the Community?' Britain entered the Community, it was asserted, for a mixture of reasons: partly because it was reluctant to stay outside and fearful of the consequences of exclusion; partly because awareness of economic failure encouraged the hope that entry would bring economic benefits in the relatively short term. One critical review of the economic rationale for British entry, as set out in successive government statements and White Papers, concluded 'that membership of the EEC has been hawked around as the panacea for every failure in Britain's long-term economic policy' [3]. Yet since the early initiative of 1972-3 to establish the Regional Development Fund as a means of channelling Community assistance to disadvantaged industrial areas – and thus offset the budgetary emphasis on agriculture – British governments have made no major effort to place new issues on the Community agenda. The image of Britain as a recalcitrant member preoccupied with its immediate problems and unwilling to think in Community terms or to look for wider trade-offs, presented increasingly in the press of other member countries in recent years, has not been inaccurate.

Part of Britain's failure has been the inability – or refusal – to 'play' the Community as a political game, or to use its rules and its institutions to further British interests. For the last Labour government, in particular, preoccupation with the preservation of formal sovereignty was a major inhibition – an inhibition shared, incidentally, by many senior officials and by a wide spectrum of political opinion outside government circles, and reflected also within the Conservative Party. The relative failure of the Regional Development Fund negotiations was partly due to the reluctance of British negotiators to contemplate any loss of national control over its distribution and disbursement, as well as to their misjudgement of the importance of winning over the German government to their point of view [5]. In 1978 and 1979 successive British governments stepped back from exploiting the support of the European Parliament to secure changes in the Community budget, persuaded by their own fears and by the arguments of the French government that the protection of national sovereignty and the unity of the Council of Ministers must be preferred to the immediate benefits which espousal of the Parliament's intervention would bring. Some participants in the conference expressed their bafflement, too, at the Conservative government's continued resistance to membership of the European Monetary System, seeing it as clinging to an illusory doctrine of monetary sovereignty.

The underlying ambivalence of Britain's acceptance of Community membership has been still more evident in the continuing image of the Community in terms of 'us' and 'them', of British objectives against those of the Community – rather than as a club in which the members search for mutual interests. As one of the participants put it, 'Our problem is that in this country we're accustomed to one-party government, and don't understand coalitions.' For a complex of reasons, successive British governments have failed to build the close relationships with other Community governments that might have supported a more multilateral conception of Britain's relations with its partners. The triangular relationship between Britain, France, and Germany which seemed, in 1973, to be the basis for setting the direction of the Community had by 1979 become a bilateral relationship between France and Germany, with Britain protesting at the *faits accomplis* with which it was presented.

This image of the Community as something external to Britain and characteristically opposed to British interests, rather than as an entity of which Britain was now part and which could be influenced to further British interests, has been compounded by a succession of ideological inhibitions. The preoccupation with national sovereignty – shared only by the French and the Danes, who defend their sovereign interests from an entrenched position of advantage within the current *acquis* – has already been noted. An underlying hesitation about closer co-operation within the Community, for the Labour government, derived from the widespread belief within the Labour movement that the European Community was inherently a capitalist enterprise, likely to inhibit moves towards a more planned economy and to insist on the rigours of the free market. For the Conservative government which replaced Labour in May 1979 the contradictory belief that a more positive or innovatory attitude towards Community co-operation implied the acceptance of greater *dirigisme*, more intervention in economic and industrial policies, and increased national and Community expenditure, provided similar grounds for hesitation. Both rested upon the assumption that the Community was a body outside Britain's capacity to influence, a framework of unfavourable policies and interests that could only be resisted by maintaining a minimalist view of co-operation and holding firm to the preservation of sovereignty in economic policy. That the Community *did* represent an unfavourable balance of policies and interests when Britain joined was evident, as has been noted above. But that did not necessarily imply that the framework was not open to adaptation, particularly given the initial goodwill towards Britain from within most other member states – an asset progressively diminished by their perception of Britain as an awkward and ambivalent partner in the period which followed.

Problems Facing the Community

Thus far the analysis of Britain's uncertain strategy and tactics within the Community would command the ready assent of observers in France, Germany, and other member states. They would, however, be less ready to accept that the problem of uncertain and contradictory objectives now affects the Community as a whole and is evident in the attitudes of its other leading governments. The Community, as well as Britain, was hit by the economic crises of the early 1970s. The uneven development of common policies during the 1960s had rested upon a consensus on the sectors concerned among the member states, as well as upon the expectation of mutual advantage. But even before the monetary disorders of 1971–2 and the oil embargo and price increases of 1973–4 had derailed its momentum, the attempt to complete the common market and reinforce it with new common policies, launched at The Hague summit in December 1969, had run into difficulties. All member states could accept the principle of Community intervention in the agricultural sector, partly because all had long since accepted that principle at national level. But they had not all similarly accepted the equivalent principle of intervention in economic policy, implied by the commitment to Economic and Monetary Union by 1980; nor did member governments share the same conception of economic policy.

Differences of doctrine, as well as of interest, were thus compounded by the disruptive effect of international recession. Member states fell back upon an ossified *acquis* as represented by the common policies developed in the course of the 1960s, reaffirming their agreement in principle to the development of co-operation in other sectors but unable – or unwilling – to carry principle into practice. Not until the acceptance of Community co-ordination of industrial sectors in crisis towards the end of the decade, and the initiative of 1978 which led to the creation of the European Monetary System, did the *acquis* which Britain accepted on entry in 1973 begin to evolve. The French and German governments, in particular, have seemed at times to be defending the orthodoxy of Community doctrine against what they regard as the heretical views of the British, without being willing to consider the case for a reformation. A Community which revolves round a customs union and an agricultural policy is, after all, a peculiarly unbalanced enterprise.

Preoccupied with the protection of established national interests and able to fall back upon the rhetoric of Community solidarity to justify their positions, other governments as well as Britain display confused and contradictory attitudes to further integration. The French government, for example, insists upon the automatic mechanisms of the Community budget, but resists the concomitant extension of democratic accountability for that budget through the European Parliament. The German government insists upon the principles of the common market, but resists its extension to such sectors as banking and insurance, where German competitiveness is less assured; it holds to the Community principle in agricultural transfers, but resists the wider principle of sharing financial resources between the richer and the poorer regions of the Community. Britain is thus in no sense faced with a Community the majority of whose members are committed to any clear or settled view of its future development, let alone determined to achieve a fully fledged European federation.

A crucial question for British policy (and thus a matter repeatedly considered during this conference) is, therefore, the extent to which the Community is committed to the present balance of policies. Is it open at best to marginal adjustment, or is it alternatively open to substantial changes in the balance in the next few years? *Droits acquis* translates into idiomatic English as 'vested interests'. It has sometimes seemed to British negotiators that the majority of other member states were determined to maintain all their vested interests whatever their adverse impact on Britain. But the Community is now faced with the problem of adjusting not only to Britain's demands for change – the justice of which most other member governments now privately recognize – but also to two other destabilizing developments: its prospective enlargement to include three new member states with economies far less prosperous and less developed than the Community mean, and the financial crisis that will result from rising agricultural expenditure pushing the Community budget through the one per cent VAT ceiling.

It is by no means clear that the current *acquis* will suit the three applicant states. Greece, which is set to join the Community in January 1981, has a big agricultural sector but imports large quantities of those temperate products most supported by the current CAP, beef, cereals and dairy products, and exports Mediterranean produce less favoured by the CAP. Spain, to join the Community perhaps in 1983, is in a better position to benefit from the current balance of policies; but the addition of expanding Spanish agricultural production to a Community market already in surplus in many commodities will add severely to the strains of financing the CAP. Portugal, as a very substantial net importer of food, is potentially in the same position as Britain. All three new entrants will expect the Community to adjust to the expansion of their industrial exports, which will increase pressure for the co-ordination of industrial policies at Community level and for the extension of Community support to industries and regions adversely affected. All will expect to benefit from transfers of resources for regional development and social and industrial investment, which will place additional demands on the Community budget. Any consequent changes in Community policies will not, of course, necessarily be to Britain's advantage; the outcome will depend not only upon the interests at stake and the alliances struck between different members, but also on which governments are most successful in defining the issues to be negotiated.

The incompatibility between the upward pressure of agricultural expenditure and the agreed ceiling on VAT contributions raises large questions for the future of Community policies. Both the French and German governments have so far declared their determination to maintain the ceiling, but have not so far publicly considered the implications for the CAP and for other expenditure policies of imposing a rigid limit on the size of the budget. Formally 'compulsory' expenditure (under the Treaty definition) on agriculture should squeeze 'non-compulsory' expenditure on regional and social policies out of the budget, though several member states would be extremely unhappy with such a development. The European Parliament, moreover, provides a new joker in the pack: debating and determining issues in a different context from the Council of Ministers, and rightly seeing its intervention in the budgetary process as the most effective way open to it to influence the direction of the Community.

Directions of Change
If change is possible, even likely, then in which direction would it be most advantageous to Britain? The clear conclusion of our discussions was that the whole issue of the future shape and balance of Community policies has to be placed within a framework far wider than that encompassed by the immediate dispute between Britain and its partners or by the current *acquis*. The accepted assessment of the CAP was that prospects for change are limited, and that these at best will be gradual; the principles of common pricing, of a highly protected market, and of a substantial Community contribution to agricultural support are too well established and fit too wide a spread of interests to be overthrown. There is no way that any common agricultural policy, thus defined, can be advantageous to Britain. Some marginal benefits may come from increases in British agricultural production, to which the present government is in any event committed, at the cost of contributing further to the problem of Community surpluses. Some marginal relief may come from an element of 'debudgetization' of agricultural support. But these will still leave

Britain a substantial loser from budgetary transfers in the agricultural sector, a more substantial loser in terms of overall agricultural trade. They will also leave agricultural expenditure as the dominant element in the Community budget. Britain's budgetary problem is thus, in effect, insoluble within the current framework of Community policies, except through such exceptional and temporary measures as the corrective financial mechanism which was the main achievement of the renegotiation of 1974–5, and which the present government is attempting to extend. There is, furthermore, no evidence that this could easily be designed to operate on a scale commensurate with the problem. The prospect therefore opens up of a succession of hard-fought and bitter negotiations between Britain and its Community partners to offset the financial burdens of membership – paralleling in many ways the sad experience of the military offset negotiations between Britain and Germany – unless the whole basis for bargaining is radically altered.

The search for new fields for Community co-operation that would benefit Britain and be acceptable (or, ideally, welcome) to the rest of the Community cannot and should not be limited to looking for new fields for expenditure. There was little support in this conference for bogus policy proposals designed simply to find ways of channelling Community money into British hands; and little more for pursuing industrial subsidies as an outlet for Community funds. The present British government's approach to public expenditure and to economic and industrial policy would in any case not easily permit such solutions. New spending policies would most probably require matching expenditure from national treasuries, thus increasing public expenditure in Britain; they might well also force the government to devote resources to industries and policies from which it might otherwise have stood aside. Unless developments in the reform of the CAP prove unexpectedly rapid they would also require an increase in the overall size of the Community budget, to which the British government is currently opposed. Some participants, indeed, saw the British government's determined attitudes on these issues as a major obstacle to achieving a better balance in terms of Community revenue and expenditure.

The difficulty in determining what spread of Community policies would most help Britain is that there is little confidence within Britain that we know ourselves how best to generate economic and industrial recovery. We have, furthermore, a wide range of divergent opinions about the instruments and operations of economic policy. Nevertheless, some lines of approach emerged from the conference discussions.

Our preoccupation with the reversal of relative industrial decline necessarily concentrated attention on issues of industrial policy. It was recognized that many of the changes in the industrial and economic environment which Britain needed for recovery – more consistent government policies, better management and industrial relations – were primarily a national responsibility. But the Community framework can significantly help or hinder any attempt at recovery. The first essential is to convince our Community partners that Britain's peculiar economic difficulties must be a matter for Community concern. The consequences for the Community of a continuing decline in Britain's economy and industrial competitiveness are potentially serious, particularly if the Community as such is seen to offer no positive assistance to alleviate its symptoms. The prospect of British withdrawal would inevitably arise, in circumstances that might well deny the British market to other Community members. Other less prosperous member states with demands on the Community and on the richer members might then question the utility of the Community as a framework for industrial development. The unavoidable overlap of economic issues with political and security issues, both within British domestic politics and at the European level, would adversely affect the established pattern of defence and security co-operation in Western Europe. It must be in the Community's interest therefore, as well as in Britain's, to regard the problems of Britain's economy as a matter for common concern.

Beyond this, British official and non-official opinion must persuade our partners that the vicious cycle of low growth, low profitability and productivity, and declining competitiveness, with the accompaniment of a rising resistance to change, is difficult for Britain alone to break: that the comfortable attitude held widely, for example, in Federal Germany that Britain's economic problems are entirely the result of its own failings ignores the sharp difference between the optimism and opportunities which accompany a prolonged period of fast growth and the pessimism and obstacles to change which flow from the low-growth cycle [4]. The classic recipe for escaping the constraints of low growth is protection, the policy followed by Imperial Germany in the late nineteenth century, and by several of the successful newly industrialized countries in recent years – a policy denied to Britain and to other weak member states by the principles of the Economic Community. The relatively free and open Community market, from which the fast-growth countries gain most benefit, needs therefore to be balanced by an acceptance of compensating resource transfers to disadvantaged countries and regions. The peculiarity of Britain's position in the Community, it should further be argued, derives also from its economic history: the oldest industrialized country in Western Europe, with an industrial sector still, despite great changes, too heavily biased towards industries directly threatened by technological change and by new sources of international competition, and too heavily encumbered with traditional practices and attitudes to accept change easily. The Coal and Steel Community recognized a similar problem in the coal industries of Belgium, France, and Luxembourg and actively assisted the process of adjustment within a managed market. Pressures for industrial adaptation have already hit the entrenched attitudes of workforces in the steel, shipbuilding, and textile industries of several of the other member states and have given rise to demands for Community action. It may well prove that Britain's problems are not so unusual as some commentators contend, but rather that they offer a foretaste of the economic and industrial problems the Community will have to face in the next ten years or so, as those of a country already further down the road which several other member states may find themselves taking.

Industry and energy
Four lines of development for Community industrial policy were put forward during this conference which might assist the British economy and alleviate the disadvantages which Britain faces in the Community. The first was the extension and completion of the operation of the common market – a development that would carry almost no additional budgetary costs. One of the most apparent contradictions of the European Community in its current, half-developed shape is between the insistence on competition and the removal of barriers to free trade in manufacturing industry and the continuing resistance to the removal of barriers to invisible trade. Britain has a highly competitive financial sector, which would stand to gain from freer access to financial and insurance markets in other countries. It has

competitive enterprises too in the transport sector, on road and sea and in the air, which would benefit from the implementation of the principles of Articles 74–84 of the Rome Treaty. Britain has suffered disproportionately from the maintenance (and in some cases the reimposition) of various non-tariff barriers to trade by other member states, as a country less used to administrative discretion in bending the rules of the market than some of its competitors. More effective implementation of the rules of the common market is also therefore in Britain's interest.

A second line of development would be to build on and extend the ECSC model of Community assistance for industrial adjustment to other sectors under pressure. This clearly would carry budgetary implications, the size of the costs involved depending upon the nature of the programme and the number of sectors included. The Community has already begun to act, to moderate effect, in such 'crisis sectors' as steel; but so far it has been a holding operation, designed to reduce output and monitor demand in an oversupplied market, rather than to assist the long-term process of modernization and regeneration. Community loans and grants to modernize infrastructure in declining industrial regions and to assist with retraining would not be a new departure. But they would require a massive expansion of the sectoral activities of the Coal and Steel Community and of the limited operations of the Regional Development and Social Funds. Nor would this necessarily imply any major extension of Community bureaucracy or of direct Commission intervention. The method adopted in more developed federations of providing matching grants to assist programmes in member states, the level of reimbursement varying according to agreed criteria between more and less prosperous regions, would be entirely appropriate here. It would, however, imply some adaptation of policy by the British government, in the acceptance of additional public expenditure and in a greater degree of intervention in the industrial sectors concerned.

A third line of development would be considerably to expand the operations of the European Investment Bank, in providing finance at preferential rates through national agencies, to assist individual enterprises in modernization and expansion. The advantage of this approach is that it leaves the initiative with the enterprises concerned, rather than relying on direct government intervention. It is thus more readily available to new and small enterprises, which the British economy particularly needs to encourage. Its budgetary costs would be limited in principle to any subsidization of interest rates for loans. Such an approach would not of course come to grips with the issue of assisting and underwriting the development of high-technology industry, in which capital costs are often very high and the initial market limited or speculative. Some participants supported Commissioner Davignon's proposals for developing Community-level policies for this area, recognizing the potentially high budgetary costs which would be involved and the politically difficult choices which such a selective policy would have to face, between competing firms and competing sites for new plants. Others felt that this was too ambitious and difficult a task for the Community; but recognized that it is in Britain's interest for the Community to play a policing role in the development of, for example, telecommunications, by setting common standards and concerting and (if possible) co-ordinating national policies, rather than leaving the initiative to the strongest national treasuries and industry ministries.

A fourth line of development – the most ambitious – would be to revive the debate of 1972–3 on regional policy and to press for very substantial transfers to disadvantaged regions. The argument was made that a commitment to adjust the costs of industrial employment in regions characterized by declining industry, falling employment, or other factors over a period of years would be of more benefit to the regeneration of British industry than national protection; encouraging the movement of enterprises to those regions, and providing the context for sustained expansion. This would, in effect, be 'managed trade on a Community basis': accepting that untrammelled free trade favours the strongest regions in any market and thus promotes divergence, and compensating for this through a developed regional policy. This would not be a parallel to the Common Agricultural Policy, an extension of unconditional subsidies for particular products along the lines of the 'Common Sewing Machine Policy' lightly outlined in Bryan Gould's contribution or of the suggested remedies of some textile interests. It would focus instead on the region and on the worker employed, through some such mechanism as a regional employment premium, rather than on the firm or the industry, and its objective would be to lessen the obstacles to modernization and change. This proposal was not explored in full detail in the conference, and clearly requires considerable further development; but in outline it met with widespread sympathy. It could not be limited to Britain alone but would have to extend to some regions of Italy and to parts of other member states. It would have large implications for the size and shape of the Community budget, which in turn would require a qualitative change in the political framework of Community undertakings and commitments.

Beyond developments in industrial policy it is evident that any wider package in which the United Kingdom may hope to redress the imbalance of the current *acquis* must include a significant energy dimension. Britain's partners would in any case expect that a government concerned to find answers to Britain's problems in European terms would also be prepared to place energy policy within a Community context. There are, furthermore, potentially significant mutual benefits from a trade-off between British assurances on supply and on preferential treatment in circumstances of crisis, and the acceptance by other member states of a pricing policy which would at the same time encourage investment in energy production and promote conservation. An import levy on energy imports, covering coal, oil, and natural gas, would for example fulfil these objectives, and would also help to redress the balance on the revenue side of the Community budget. A greater degree of self-sufficiency would also be encouraged by Community assistance for investment in new production. This proposal, again, requires far more detailed discussion than is possible here. It would require some delicate negotiations over the control of oil depletion rates, with which the British government is already concerned. It would require, too, some easing of British sensitivities about 'economic sovereignty' within the Community context – a concept raised at several points in our discussions, though challenged as peculiarly difficult to define within a relatively open international economy.

A different kind of Community budget

The future of the Community budget, and the criteria for the transfer of resources among member states, underlie many of these proposed developments. Once it is accepted that changes in the CAP and its financing can only at best be gradual and cumulative, the issues of the perverse effects of current policies on resource flows and of the future size of the budget have in any event to be faced. Carsten

Thoroe's paper argues that a deliberately progressive transfer of financial resources among member states was not implied by the Treaty of Rome: that the commitment in Article 2 'to promote throughout the Community a harmonious development of economic activities' refers to the beneficent effects for all member states of access to a wider market rather than to any commitment in principle to promote convergence through positive policies and financial transfers. Certainly, the budget as it has operated so far has not been seen as an instrument of economic policy or as a means of assisting the disadvantaged states; the patterns of expenditure and resource flows have represented simply the consequences of common policies so far agreed. If new common policies were developed, of course, the resulting pattern would be different. The reaction of other member states to proposals for new common policies indeed demonstrates that they are all in practice concerned with the question of budgetary costs and benefits, whatever their governments' arguments about the principles of Community revenue and expenditure.

It has suited the British government's case to argue that the transfer of resources from richer to poorer states and regions should be seen as an intrinsic part of the Community's objectives – though the implications of this argument for its understanding of the political compact on which the Community must rest, or for the further development of policies through which such transfers could be effected, have not been fully appreciated. The argument of the Mac-Dougall Report was that deliberate transfers were needed to compensate the weaker members for the risks involved in the commitment to Economic and Monetary Union [2]. The case was made in this conference that the most effective argument for substantial transfers is the political one: that a Community committed to closer union must include among its objectives the acceptance of a degree of common obligation in financial and fiscal matters. This would involve an increase in the Community budget well beyond what most member governments, including the British, would currently regard as practical politics. The MacDougall Report suggested that a budget of around twice its current size could achieve significant transfers from richer to poorer regions if the pattern of expenditure was specifically designed for that purpose. But the politics of public expenditure in developed federations demonstrates the impracticality of such a simple design.

The combination of new policies, of the demands of the new Mediterranean member states, and of the objective of achieving significant flows of resources to the Community's disadvantaged regions, suggests a budget approaching five per cent of Community GNP or more. That poses in the most acute form for the British government, and for its partners, the question of the Community's future direction and objectives, and the parallel question of how far national sovereignty is to be compromised in order to achieve such objectives.

Economic policy and external relations

Two broader issues, of co-operation in economic policy and in external relations, aroused less vigorous debate. There was a certain sense that in its resistance to closer co-operation in economic policy the United Kingdom was tilting at windmills, protesting at constraints which are not there and refusing to recognize the modest benefits which might be gained. Of the elements of economic strategy open to Britain to promote industrial regeneration, it was argued, both protection and aggressive devaluation are constrained by the obligations of Community membership; but neither commanded support as preferred strategies. Both incomes policy and industrial policy are constrained, not mainly by Community obligations, but by domestic political and economic obstacles and doctrinal inhibitions. The utility of co-operation in macro-economic policy is limited by the uncertainties of all member governments about its aims and instruments, and by the equally uncertain link between macro-economic policy and the micro-economic factors which are at the root of many of Britain's difficulties. But the European Community provides a useful framework for discussing and concerting national economic policies which it would be to Britain's disadvantage to lose.

The sense of tilting at windmills was apparent, too, in the discussion of Britain's association with the European Monetary System. Even a Community with a more highly developed budget and range of policies, it was argued, is likely to find itself some distance from the objective of Economic and Monetary Union which many British observers fear. What has been created is an adjustable (or even a crawling) peg system, which offers Britain the prospect of achieving a greater degree of control over fluctuations in its exchange rate, and allows for a wider margin for currencies uncertain of their appropriate level or of their resistance to speculative attack. What is in prospect in the next two or three years, if the system develops, is the evolution of a common policy towards the dollar and the yen, through the operations of the proposed European Monetary Fund. It would be difficult for Britain to remain outside such a development without accepting that some important economic decisions would in effect be taken in its absence.

In each round of the debate, before entry, about the objectives of Community membership, the importance of external relations as a means of supporting and extending Britain's international influence was underlined. In contrast, the modest but useful gains from co-operation in external relations were taken as given in this conference. External commercial policy, it was noted, is an instrument of Community industrial policy which already operates in many ways to Britain's advantage, providing a substantial level of protection in some sectors, partly at Britain's insistence, even if on a piecemeal basis. The perceived importance of the European Community as an international actor, evident for example in the attitudes of the United States, of the Soviet Union, and of Commonwealth countries, made it difficult for participants to conceive of a British foreign policy (in the widest sense) outside the Community framework: a difficulty compounded by the recognition of the close though implicit links between the economic, political, and security dimensions of foreign policy, both within Western Europe and in relations between Western Europe and third countries. Britain has benefited in a number of ways from the operations of Community external policy and of European Political Co-operation. But the overriding preoccupation with domestic economic problems has largely displaced the optimism about enhanced international political influence which characterized the pre-entry debate.

Wistful reflections were made on several occasions at the exclusion of defence from the framework of European co-operation. Defence expenditure has been an early and central component of federal budgets in all existing federations and has often served to facilitate the transfer of resources from richer to poorer states through the progressive action of the tax system and the distribution of defence establishments. Moves by the Community in this direction would raise the issue of ceding sovereignty in perhaps its most sensitive form. The path is, however, blocked for the foreseeable future not only by the French insistence on sovereignty and independence in defence matters but also by the reluctance of the British and German governments, among others, to test too far the American commitment to the defence of Europe.

Prescriptions for Policy

The implications of this analysis are awkward, for Britain and for the other member states. British policy has not been far-sighted, nor has the British case always been well presented; but there are real obstacles to the resolution of Britain's difficulties in the current *acquis*. It is fruitless to ask for a more 'European' approach from any British government, let alone a commitment to any maximalist view of the European Community, if the balance of policies remains unchanged. A more positive commitment can grow only from a change in the balance. For this to happen, other Community members must accept the case for a new *acquis*; and the British government must devote a great deal more attention to defining its objectives and to persuading both its Community partners and its domestic public of the case for its proposals. The alternative, for the Community as a whole as well as for Britain, is a continuing pattern of ill-tempered negotiations over short-term mechanisms. This would distract the Community from more constructive business and sour British attitudes towards the Community and towards European co-operation as a whole.

The elements of a British strategy towards the Community have been sketched out in the preceding section. The case for immediate and temporary relief on the budget must be set in a broader context, which should include proposals for adjustments in the cost and the operations of the CAP. British representatives should argue for a redefinition of the role of the Community budget, for its conversion into a vehicle for progressive financial transfers. They should press for the fulfilment of Treaty commitments which have not yet been implemented, and for the extension of the principles of the common market. They should work for a Community framework for energy policy which can offer a balance of advantage to both producers and consumers in the Community. They should encourage the extended development of existing Community instruments in industrial, regional, and social policy and reopen the argument for an effective and large-scale regional policy.

Above all, Britain needs a strategy towards the Community, rather than the series of reactive policies which have characterized the last seven years. No government has ever publicly defined its objectives for European co-operation in any detail since Britain joined the Community. The contradictory stances adopted on particular issues suggest that objectives and priorities have not been much clearer within the government machine. The exasperation of other member governments with Britain's tactics on the budgetary issue derives partly from their belief that this is not contained within any wider or more constructive strategy.

There are several obstacles to a coherent British strategy. Some derive from the doctrinal framework of the British approach to Community issues, some from the constraints of public opinion, some from the unavoidable problems of time-scale involved in shifting the balance of Community policies, some from the uncertain response of the other member states. The conceptual difficulties for a unitary state with a centralized government in coming to terms with the sharing of powers between different levels of authority are very considerable. Only twenty years ago the incompatibility of Community membership with the principle of parliamentary sovereignty was, after all, considered by many politicians to be an absolute bar on British accession to the Communities [1]. Yet an imaginative leap will have to be made. It will be far more difficult for a British government to persuade its partners to accept a commitment to substantial transfers unless it accepts in parallel Community policies which must to an extent escape national controls. Some reconsideration of British attitudes to the relationship between the Council and the European Parliament, the role – and reform – of the Commission, and the management and accountability of Community policies, must therefore form part of any coherent strategy.

In most member states there is a sufficient degree of consensus across political parties on economic and industrial policy issues to ensure, by and large, broad continuity of policy as governments change. Britain is exceptional in this respect within the Community. Deep divisions persist between (and within) its major parties on the principles and priorities of economic policy. The resulting discontinuities in policy as governments change raise major problems for commitments made within the Community framework and for domestic dispute about Community obligations and priorities. Community policies evolve from the coalition politics of compromises worked out among member governments. It may be necessary for the British political process to bend a little in that direction, if each new government is not to give its partners the impression of carrying the mentality of opposition on to the Community stage.

How strong an obstacle is presented by domestic opinion is a matter for politicians to assess. It was argued by some at this conference that the British public is not so much opposed to the European Community as confused and sceptical. In the period before British entry opinion poll evidence reflected the fluctuating guidance of political opinion-leaders, wavering up and down in the wake of the changing policies of the Labour leadership. Public scepticism and lack of a sense of European identity are major obstacles to changes in British policy. But public attitudes, deeply conscious of Britain's weakness, may be more open to political persuasion on this issue than any government has attempted to discover since 1973.

There are important and difficult problems of time-scale. The immediate budgetary imbalance clearly requires a short-term response. Other member states recognize this and will probably go some way at least towards removing the financial burden. The crucial question is how far the British government can or should simultaneously be emphasizing related issues: radical reform of the CAP, changes in the structure and balance of the budget, proposals for new Community policies. All these require the careful balancing of both short- and long-term interests that has so far been strikingly absent from British policy. A package of new policies on these lines will inevitably take several years to produce direct and indirect benefits to Britain.

Much depends, of course, on the response of other member states. They also have doctrinal inhibitions and contradictory objectives in their approaches to the Community. The strongest argument for Britain to place its approach to the Community within a wider framework is that, by doing so, it may push its partners into reconsidering their own framework of policies towards the Community, so moving the argument about the Community's future direction on to a new basis. This might provide the political foundation for a new *acquis* more appropriate to the problems of a Community of Twelve facing the problems of industrial adjustment and economic recession. There can be no guarantee that the British government will be able to generate the response it hopes for. Politics necessarily includes large elements of uncertainty. But it will certainly not meet with an understanding response from the rest of the Community unless it makes the effort to present its case within a framework of policies which can offer benefits to the Community as a whole.

It is easy at first glance to dismiss such a conclusion as beyond the bounds of practical politics, either in domestic or in European terms. But the implications of the alternatives open to Britain are not particularly 'practical' either. There was no support within this conference for British withdrawal from the Community, except in the circumstances of a failure to achieve any substantial changes over a period of years in the current *acquis*. Continuation of the present situation, with British dissatisfaction and continental exasperation leading cumulatively to a deterioration in relations – and so potentially towards a break – is hardly more attractive. The Community already faces a number of pressures for change, from further enlargement, from the approaching budgetary ceiling, from the demands of threatened industries throughout the Community, from external monetary and economic instabilities, and from the developing ambitions of the European Parliament. It is open to Britain to push for changes in a direction that favours British interests, or to sit by protesting while others define priorities and shape policies.

References

[1] Camps, Miriam, *Britain and the European Community, 1955–1963*, London, Oxford University Press, 1964.

[2] Commission of the European Communities, *Report of the Study Group on the Role of Public Finance in European Integration*, Brussels, 1977, 2 vols. (Chairman of the study group, Sir Donald MacDougall).

[3] Morgan, A. D., 'Commercial policy' in F. T. Blackaby *et al.*, *British Economic Policy 1960–1974*, London, Cambridge University Press for NIESR, 1978.

[4] Stout, D. K., 'De-industrialisation and industrial policy' in Frank Blackaby, ed., *De-industrialisation*, London, Heinemann for NIESR, 1978.

[5] Wallace, Helen, 'The establishment of the Regional Development Fund: common policy or pork barrel?' in Helen Wallace *et al.*, eds., *Policy-Making in the European Communities*, Chichester, Sussex, John Wiley, 1977.

2 Maximalism or Minimalism? Britain's European Options

by David Marquand

Two variables must be taken into account in any discussion of the future of the Community: the area over which the Community is competent to make policy, and the extent to which its policies are made by a supranational process rather than by intergovernmental agreement. The founding fathers thought the Community would develop in two stages in both these respects. The Treaty committed its signatories to sweeping measures of what has been called 'negative' integration: to the elimination of tariffs and quantitative restrictions on trade between member states, to the establishment of a common external tariff, and to the abolition of obstacles to the free movement of persons, services, and capital. It also looked forward to certain measures of 'positive' integration – in other words, to the development of co-ordinated Community policies, which would in certain fields replace national policies. But the only form of positive integration about which it was at all specific was the commitment to a common agricultural policy. Although it mentioned a common transport policy and the 'co-ordination' of national economic policies the provisions on these were much less binding.

Much the same was true of its provisions on decision making. The Economic Community was modelled on the Coal and Steel Community, but initially its decision making was to be much less 'supranational'. In the Coal and Steel Community, the High Authority was the decision-making body; in the new Economic Community, the Council was to take the decisions. On the other hand, the Council was to take decisions on proposals submitted by the Commission; and the Commission was modelled on the old High Authority. After a transitional period, moreover, most Council decisions were to be taken by majority vote. Provision was also made for the direct election of the European Parliament, the only body by which the Commission could be removed from office.

Both as regards scope and as regards decision making, in other words, the Treaty envisaged a *dynamic* process. The Community would begin with the comparatively easy task of negative integration, and move on to the more difficult task of positive integration later. The supranational element in its decision-making process would gradually increase by way of majority voting in the Council and the direct election of the European Parliament.

As everyone knows, these hopes have been belied by events. Though negative integration has gone a long way, positive integration has been almost confined to agriculture. The expected move from intergovernmental decision making to supranational decision making has not occurred; if anything, the movement has been in the opposite direction. But although the Community has not developed as the founding fathers expected, it has shown remarkable vitality in other ways. It may not have moved significantly towards positive integration in the way that the Treaty envisaged, but it *has* moved into areas which were not envisaged in the Treaty at all – for example, into the area of foreign policy co-ordination. Partly because of this and partly because its economic weight has turned out to be even greater than the founding fathers thought it would be, it has become a significant factor in world affairs. Last, but by no means least, two important new developments – one envisaged in the Treaty, but the other not – occurred during 1979. The first is the belated implementation of the Treaty commitment to direct elections to the European Parliament; the second is the establishment of the European Monetary System.

The implications of this pattern are more complicated than is sometimes appreciated. Clearly, there are powerful centrifugal forces at work in the Community; and the founding fathers undoubtedly underestimated their strength and persistence. But powerful centripetal forces are at work too; and no discussion of the Community's future will get very far unless due attention is paid to them. It is in the light of that general conclusion that the terms maximalist and minimalist should be defined. A maximalist Community would be one in which the centripetal forces had been strong enough significantly to widen the scope of Community policies and significantly to strengthen the supranational element in Community decision making. A minimalist Community would be one in which the centrifugal forces had significantly narrowed the scope of Community policy and/or significantly weakened the supranational element in decision making.

A maximalist path would probably look something like this. The Community would build on the establishment of the European Monetary System, and move further towards full-scale monetary union, as envisaged in the 1972 Paris summit. Eventually it would probably move into yet another new area, not envisaged in the Treaty – namely defence. Meanwhile its decision making would become more supranational, partly because the extension of the Community budget which monetary union would make necessary would automatically increase the powers of the directly elected European Parliament, and partly because the member states would agree to move much further along the road to majority voting on the lines laid down in the Treaty.

If the Community followed a minimalist path, its policies would narrow in scope and its decision making would become even less supranational and more intergovernmental. This might happen in a number of ways. The Common Agricultural Policy might collapse. Enlargement of the Community might clog up an already slow-moving decision-making system. Protectionist pressures within the member states might erode the unity of the market. The supranational element in decision making might be weakened by a slide back towards unanimity in the Council of Ministers; by a further weakening of the Commission's status and authority; and by a refusal on the part of member governments to give the directly elected Parliament a more significant voice in Community affairs, which might lead to damaging conflicts between the Parliament on the one hand and the Council and Commission on the other.

Which Way is the Community Going?
There is no way of telling which path the Community will take. What is clear is that it cannot stay where it is. Other things being equal, enlargement will strengthen the centrifugal forces at work in it. It is bound to be more difficult for twelve governments to reach agreement than for nine governments to do so; and when the interests

of the twelve diverge more than did those of the nine, the difficulties will be multiplied. Meanwhile, a crisis is approaching in the Common Agricultural Policy. Agricultural spending is now pressing against the limits of Community revenue and is likely to break through them in the near future. The collapse of the CAP, however welcome it might be in anti-European circles in this country, would mean that the most important single positive Community achievement had had to be abandoned, and that the powerful farming interest would no longer be locked into the Community structure. It is unlikely that it will be allowed to collapse altogether. But the search for a solution is bound to be acrimonious and divisive. The current world recession poses a third danger. So far, the Community has managed to maintain the unity of the market, but this state of affairs is more precarious than it looks. Covert restrictions on intra-Community trade are already more frequent than is generally appreciated, and it would not be difficult for the member states to extend them. Widespread resort to such restrictions would destroy the unity of the market and the procedures by which it is maintained; and these are the foundations on which the whole Community structure is based.

There are political dangers too. The American nuclear guarantee to Western Europe is slowly losing credibility. At the same time, the Soviet arms build-up continues in Eastern Europe. As European perceptions of the weakening of the American guarantee become stronger Rapallo-ism might rise from the grave in West Germany; the neutralist tendencies which can still be detected in France and Britain might gain new strength and respectability; and a process of 'finlandization' might be set off. Finally, last summer's elections to the European Parliament may have the perverse effect of strengthening the centrifugal forces instead of the centripetal forces. Unless Parliament is given more power, it may turn in frustration against the other Institutions of the Community; since the only Institution it can effectively embarrass is the Commission, the Commission could become its chief target. But, with all its weaknesses, the Commission is the only motor of integration the Community has, or can have; if the directly elected Parliament engages in a series of jurisdictional struggles with it, the process of integration – and the supranational element in Community decision making – can only suffer.

These problems exist; if they are not solved, or if they are solved in the wrong way, the Community will move rapidly along the minimalist path. But it is not inevitable that they should be left unsolved or solved wrongly. Each of them could be solved in a maximalist fashion. The undoubted danger that enlargement might lead to intolerable delays in Community decision making could be avoided by agreeing to implement the Treaty provisions on majority voting; if that were done, the net result would be to make the Community more cohesive, not less. Though the coming crisis of the Common Agricultural Policy will not be settled without fierce battles, a solution that combined lower prices with income support for poor farmers, and less protection for 'northern' products with more protection for 'southern' ones, would leave the Community stronger than it is now. The member states are not obliged to lurch back into protectionism; if they had the will, they could knit their economies closer together by building on the foundation provided by the EMS, co-ordinating their economic policies more closely, and taking further steps towards full-scale monetary union. That would require big increases in the size and redistributive power of the Community budget; such increases would speed up the pace of integration still further. The weakening of the American nuclear guarantee to Western Europe might lead the Community's member states to co-operate more closely in the defence field. The danger of futile squabbles between the directly elected European Parliament and the other Institutions could be avoided by giving the Parliament more power; that, too, would push the Community in a maximalist direction.

All we know, in short, is that the Community has reached a watershed from which it can either make further advances or slip back. We do not know, and cannot know, how it will behave now it has got there. The most that can be done at this stage is to try to gauge the strength of the opposing forces.

Chief among the forces making for a less cohesive Community is the financial cost of the policies needed to make it more cohesive. Full-scale monetary union could not be sustained by the weaker member states without very large transfers of resources from the stronger. In their report to the Commission in 1977 the MacDougall Group of economists showed that this could be achieved with a Community budget accounting for only five per cent of Community GDP. But the MacDougall Group's proposed budget was deliberately tailored to redistribute resources from the rich to the poor areas of the Community. Given the inevitable resistance of the electorates in the richer areas, such transfers will be hard to make. Moreover, maximalism must entail further transfers of power from the national to the Community level. Since the middle Sixties, at any rate, the member states have clung tenaciously to all the power remaining to them; it is reasonable to suppose that they will want to do the same now. Thirdly, it is clear that the economic divergences between the richer and poorer member states of the Community are becoming wider, and clear also that this makes it objectively more difficult to move towards monetary union.

Yet it does not follow that the minimalist forces will prevail. Despite all the political difficulties discussed above, the richer member states have an overwhelming interest in keeping the common market in being, for it is the common market which has made them rich. Given a choice between the collapse of the common market and a big, redistributive Community budget on MacDougall lines, they would be cutting their own economic throats if they chose collapse. It is worth remembering that Helmut Schmidt – not a committed 'European', and at first a sceptic about the whole notion of monetary union – played the central part in the establishment of the EMS. He did this because he came to the conclusion that continued monetary instability in Europe was a threat to Germany's economic interests; once he had been convinced, he was prepared to overcome strong opposition from the Bundesbank and to pledge much more German financial support to the venture than any German government had pledged to similar ventures in the past. Of course, this does not prove that a future German or French government, confronted with a choice between a MacDougall budget and the destruction of the common market, would behave in the same way. But if enlightened self-interest can prevail over unenlightened self-interest once, it can do so again.

At a different level, direct elections to the European Parliament have made it possible, for the first time in the Community's history, to transfer power from the national to the Community level without transferring it from democratically accountable bodies to unaccountable ones. If the transfers were accompanied by corresponding increases in Parliament's powers, a maximalist Community might be more, not less, democratic than the present one. Direct elections can also be expected to strengthen the maximalist forces in the

Community in a more straightforward way. In seven out of the nine member states, the Community is popular, and the proposition that it should become more supranational is popular also. Support for that proposition will now be articulated by the one institution in the Community with a direct mandate from the people; since there is a strong integrationist majority in the new Parliament it is likely to articulate its support with some vigour. The overwhelming rejection of the budget in December 1979 provides a foretaste.

If the Community could mark time, allowing its members to retain the advantages they derive from belonging to a strong negotiating *bloc* and from the trade liberalization of the last twenty years, without transferring power from the national to the Community level, that is what it would probably do. But the central premise of this paper is that that option is no longer available. The Community's centrifugal forces have often been strong enough to stop it from moving forward, but hitherto they have never been able to move it backwards. It is unlikely that they will prove strong enough to do so now. The Community's movement along the maximalist path will no doubt be slow and halting. It can be expected to move all the same.

What are Britain's European Interests?

Britain's European interests should be assessed against this background. They can best be considered under three headings. As everyone knows, certain British interests conflict with strong interests in other member states. Secondly, however, some important British interests are common to the rest of the Community as well. Finally, Britain has important interests which, though not in conflict with the interests of other member states, are not common to them either.

Two familiar British interests come into the first category. To begin with, the British undoubtedly have a strong interest in correcting the present imbalance in the Community budget, as a result of which British taxpayers could make a net contribution to the Community of more than £1,000 million in 1980. It is, by any standards, inequitable that one of the poorer member states should make a net contribution to more prosperous ones, but it is not the inequity of the present state of affairs which matters most in the present context. It is the fact that, by definition, Britain's interest in correcting the budgetary imbalance runs counter to the interests of the other member states in maintaining it. The same applies to Britain's well-known interest in lower food prices – the second British interest which falls under this heading. It is a British interest because high food prices are largely responsible for the budgetary imbalance, and because the British are paying higher prices for their food as Community members than they would pay if they were not in the Community. But, as with the net budgetary contribution, the British interest in smaller agricultural expenditures and lower food prices runs counter to the interests of a number of continental member states. Like the first, this conflict is a fact of Community life.

But Britain also shares important interests with the rest of the Community. The reasons which led successive British governments to seek entry in the first place, and which led the 1974 Labour government to recommend continued membership to the electorate in the 1975 referendum, are still valid. Chief among these was the discovery that Britain, outside the Community, had little influence on world affairs. That discovery still holds good. So does the more particular discovery that, in a cold world in which the balance of economic power is shifting from the industrialized countries to the primary producers, and in which the older industrial countries face increasingly severe competition from the newly industrialized countries, Britain benefits from belonging to a more or less cohesive block of states which can work together in international negotiations on trade and development. Like the other member states of the Community, Britain also has a vital interest in the military security of Western Europe. In the past, that interest has been pursued largely through the Atlantic Alliance. If the American nuclear guarantee to Western Europe is now losing credibility, Britain has as strong an interest as her partners in seeing the Community acquire a defence dimension. Finally, Britain shares the common Community interest in maximizing intra-Community trade.

Far overshadowing all these, however, is the central, over-riding British interest of the present and the foreseeable future: that of halting, and if possible reversing, the decline in relative prosperity and economic efficiency which has afflicted her at least since the early part of the twentieth century. There is room for argument about the causes of this decline, and even more room for argument about the remedies. There is no doubt about the fact. Not only is Britain's rate of economic growth pathetically low in comparison with that of her competitors; her capacity to stand up to competition, particularly as measured by the crucially important index of investment in research and development, is falling.

This suggests a different, and more alarming, perspective than that of the simple budgetary imbalance discussed above. Britain is not alone in being poorer than Germany, the Benelux countries, France, or Denmark. She is alone in being less competitive, relatively poorer, and relatively less efficient than she was twenty years ago. The other poor countries have enjoyed rapid rates of growth since the Community was established; though Italy has been no better than Britain at coping with inflation the Italian economy has continued to grow more rapidly than the British – as, of course, have the Greek and the Spanish. The other eight member states of the Community (and, after enlargement, ten of the other eleven) can be likened to a convoy moving forward at different speeds. Britain is moving backwards. The chief priority for any responsible British government in the foreseeable future must be to change this state of affairs; and it is in the light of this priority that her European policy should be framed.

Which Kind of Community is Better for Britain?

The best way to decide whether Britain would benefit more from a maximalist or from a minimalist Community is to work out how the three sets of interests described above can be pursued in practice. It is convenient to begin with the linked questions of agricultural prices and the net budgetary contribution. The most important point here is that the conflict between Britain's interest in cheap food and the interests of the member states with large farming populations in keeping up farm incomes will continue to exist, no matter what happens to the Common Agricultural Policy or to the Community. Reform of the CAP is desirable for its own sake; but no conceivable reform could do more than mitigate Britain's budgetary burden.

The problem of the net budgetary contribution is more complicated. In pure logic Britain's interest in correcting the present imbalance, and in reducing, or if possible eliminating, her net budgetary contribution could be satisfied in either form of Community. The reason why Britain makes a large net contribution to the Community budget is less that her gross contribution is excessive than that her receipts from Community expenditure are too small in relation to her gross contribution. The position could be put right in a number of ways. One way would be to reduce Britain's gross contribution while keeping her receipts at the present level. Another way would be to build on the precedent of the so-called 'corrective mechanism' for the *gross* contribution, negotiated by the Labour government in 1975, and devise a 'receipts mechanism' for the *net* contribution through which Britain would receive a repayment whenever her net contribution exceeded an agreed figure. A third way would be to increase spending on other Community programmes which would benefit Britain more. That would make no difference to the gross contribution, but it would make a big difference to the net contribution if the benefits were significant. The first two methods of rectifying the imbalance could be achieved as well in a minimalist Community as in a maximalist one. The third would require a maximalist one.

At first sight the second possible way of remedying the imbalance seems the most promising. No one can pretend that it is reasonable for Britain to make a net contribution to the Community budget equivalent to 10 per cent of the total budget. Indeed it is hard to see why she should make a net contribution at all. The simplest way to put the problem right is to devise a receipts mechanism. Why, then, hesitate over devising one?

Unfortunately this line of argument ignores the huge backlog of suspicion and resentment which successive British governments have built up over the last twenty years. The British see themselves as reasonable people, with a manifest grievance which other reasonable people will be prepared to put right. That is not how they are seen in other Community capitals. On the continent they are seen, rather, as eternal grousers, for ever complaining about the rules of the club which they have joined, and for ever making new demands of the other members. Much more important, the assumptions underlying the current British negotiating position are contradictory – not in logic, perhaps, but certainly in emotion, in attitude, and in style. The British are saying, in effect: 'We do not want the Community to become more supranational or to transfer more power from the national to the Community level. We want it to remain what it is now, an association of sovereign states, with only a small supranational element. However, it is unjust that we, a relatively poor member state, should make a large net contribution to the budget. We therefore insist that you, the other members of this association of sovereign states, should agree to pay us back the excess which we currently pay in.' This is a message to which the other member states are unlikely to listen. If the argument is conducted in terms of national interests, they are as entitled to safeguard their interests as Britain is to safeguard hers; and it is in their interests that Britain should continue to bear a disproportionately heavy budgetary burden. If the argument is confined to the plane of interest, therefore, Britain can achieve a satisfactory settlement only in one of two ways. We can threaten the other member states with disagreeable consequences if our budgetary demands are not met; or we can offer concessions to the other member states if our demands *are* met.

In practice, however, no realistic threat is available to us. Britain could, no doubt, threaten to leave the Community altogether; if the threat were carried out, the British subsidy to the other member states would automatically end. But it is not clear that they would regard a British withdrawal as a disaster to be avoided at all costs. If the choice lay between continued British membership and no British budgetary contribution on the one hand and British withdrawal and no British budgetary contribution on the other, they might prefer the latter. Since Britain would have to pay a very heavy non-economic price for withdrawal, her last state might be worse than her first. A less drastic course would be to impose a veto on all increases in agricultural prices. But even if agricultural prices were not increased, agricultural spending would still continue to rise. What Britain needs is lower agricultural prices, and these cannot be obtained unless the other member states agree. Apart from secession or vetoing price increases in agriculture, Britain could also make life unpleasant for her partners by withholding part of her budget contribution. The alternative is to offer concessions; and this is what will have to be done if a receipts mechanism is to be negotiated. The only other way of dealing with the problem is to approach it on the plane of equity, rather than on the plane of interest – which, of course, is why Britain has dilated on the injustice of the present situation. But an appeal to equity presupposes a Community that goes beyond national interest, a Community in which the partners recognize an obligation to the common interest, transcending their particular interests – in short, a Community which, if not maximalist already, is moving in a maximalist direction.

Complete satisfaction of Britain's budgetary demands would have other unfortunate consequences for the rest of the Community as well. We were insisting in 1979 that we should make no net contribution to the Community budget at all: that we should be given a guarantee that, no matter what happens to the Community in future, our contributions should never exceed our receipts. This demand strikes at the heart of an important Community principle. If each member state were to insist that its receipts and contributions should balance exactly every year, and that no new proposal should be adopted unless they continued to balance, moves towards positive integration would be virtually inconceivable and the purpose of the Treaty would be nullified. If the British are given a guarantee that their net position shall always balance in future, a precedent will have been created for all the other member states to make the same demand.

Would a maximalist approach be any more successful? The object of such an approach would be to reduce, or if possible to eliminate, Britain's net contribution by working with the grain of Community logic rather than against it: by increasing the total size of the Community budget in such a way that Britain gained enough from new Community spending to wipe out the losses she incurs from the present mix of policies. Such an approach would entail taking the MacDougall Group's proposed budget as a goal, and arguing for new Community policies and new Community expenditures to finance them, on lines beneficial to Britain. Of course, this would not be credible – or perhaps even desirable – unless it were accompanied by a commitment to the ultimate goal of monetary union. An indispensable first step, therefore, would be for Britain to join the European Monetary System. Since monetary union would be incompatible with the fundamental principles of liberal democracy unless the authorities managing it were made accountable to the elected representatives of the people, this in turn would entail strengthening the powers of the European Parliament.

It would be wrong to suggest that this strategy is bound to yield big dividends in the short run. The other member states are not likely to move rapidly towards monetary union until they recognize that their economies cannot recover without it; it may take them some time to do this. But steps towards a MacDougall-style budget could be taken before the final goal of monetary union is reached;

and if Britain committed herself wholeheartedly and unmistakably to that final goal, and made it clear that from now on she intended to be in the van of a movement towards supranationalism rather than in the rear, she would be well placed to argue for more Community spending on programmes of benefit to her. At the worst, such a strategy is no less likely to produce a satisfactory settlement of our current budgetary demands than is our present minimalist strategy. The overwhelming probability is that it is more likely to do so.

The position with regard to the interests which Britain shares with the rest of the Community is more straightforward. As we have seen, the Community now faces a choice between moving forward in a maximalist direction and moving backwards in a minimalist one. Thus the member states cannot retain the advantages they derive from belonging to a strong bargaining bloc and from maximizing trade between themselves unless they are prepared to transfer more power from the national to the Community level. It follows that those British interests which are common to the rest of the Community would be better served by maximalism than by minimalism, since in respect of these interests, what is sauce for the Community goose is sauce for the United Kingdom gander.

But, as we have seen, Britain's overriding interest is to halt, and if possible to reverse, the economic decline of the last hundred years or so; and that interest is unique to her. At first sight, it may appear to have nothing to do with Community membership one way or the other. Britain's decline began long before she joined the Community and can be halted only by her own efforts. On closer inspection, however, it is becoming clear that economic decline and Community membership are linked after all – though in a more complicated way than the opponents of Community membership sometimes suppose. The fundamental problem is that Britain's industrial structure is inappropriate to the world in which she has to earn her living; and that it is becoming more and more inappropriate as time goes on. Too many resources are locked into 'down-market' industries, where the comparative advantage now lies clearly with the newly industrializing countries of the Third World. Too few have been shifted into 'up-market' activities, where the older industrialized world still retains the comparative advantage. As a result, Britain faces increasingly severe competition from the NICs and is not able to compete with the older industrialized countries either. The problem can be solved only by a massive restructuring of the whole economy, through which resources at present locked up in industries which are bound to continue to decline in the face of competition from the NICs are switched into industries where Britain could, in principle, remain competitive. The question, however, is how that restructuring can take place. Simple reliance on market forces is clearly inadequate. Public intervention is needed as well. The question is, what form should it take?

The answer given by the Cambridge School of economists is well known. Britain's industrial decline has gone so far that the classic 'infant-industry' argument for protection now applies to her. She can no more restructure her industries while sticking to free trade than Germany or the United States could have industrialized in the first place if they had stuck to free trade. Import controls would provide her with the breathing space she needs; since devaluation has ceased to be effective, no other way of obtaining a breathing space is in sight. It is a powerful argument; and, within limits, a persuasive one. But there are two major weaknesses in it. Import controls would clearly be incompatible with Community membership, for on the Cambridge School's logic controls would have to be imposed not only on imports from the outside world but on imports from the rest of the Community as well. The controls would have to be both long-lasting and certain in effect; a mere import deposit scheme, as used by Italy (without resignation from the Community), would not suffice. But, as we have seen, withdrawal from the Community would run counter to a large number of Britain's non-economic interests and even to some of her economic interests as well. Quite apart from their implications for Community membership, moreover, import controls also have well-known economic disadvantages. The infant-industry argument for protection presupposes that the industries to be protected are, in fact, infants. The trouble afflicting Britain's industries is senility, not immaturity. Instead of providing a breathing space for the development of the high-technology, high-skill industries which she needs if she is to survive as an advanced industrial society, import controls might merely provide a crutch for her down-market, low-skill industries, thus inhibiting the very restructuring that is needed.

The question, therefore, is whether it is possible to devise another form of public intervention not attended by these disadvantages. This is where the Community comes into the argument. The obvious alternative to import controls and withdrawal is a strong and positive Community industrial policy, combined with a strong and positive Community labour-market policy, tailored to Britain's needs and also to the needs of senescent industrial areas elsewhere in the Community. Such policies would, of course, entail maximalist developments in other areas. They would entail a bigger Community budget; and, as we have seen, a bigger Community budget automatically increases the powers of the European Parliament. They would also entail direct transfers of competence from national capitals to Brussels, for it would be in Brussels that the new policies would have to be decided and by Brussels that they would have to be administered.

The clear conclusion is that a maximalist Community would suit Britain better than a minimalist one. Minimalism offers her, at best, a grudging and partial satisfaction of her budgetary demands. It runs counter to the non-economic interests she shares with the rest of the Community. It offers no solution to her overriding problem of industrial decline. In a maximalist Community, on the other hand, she would stand a good chance of becoming a net beneficiary of the Community budget. The non-economic interests she shares with the rest of the Community would be safeguarded. The problem of her industrial decline might be tackled by Community as well as by national authorities.

A European Strategy

'Might', however, not 'would'. There is no point in adopting a minimalist strategy. It would mean retaining the disadvantages of membership of the existing Community and giving up the possibility of benefiting from a different kind of Community. But although the potential gains from maximalism are much greater there is no guarantee that a maximalist strategy would succeed. Two questions therefore have to be answered. What kind of maximalist strategy should Britain follow? What fall-back strategy should she adopt in case her preferred strategy fails?

The answers to both these questions follow from the arguments set out above. As we have seen, there are centripetal as well as centrifugal forces at work in the Community; and, if anything, the odds are that the centripetal are slightly stronger. The central element in a maximalist strategy would be for Britain to put herself at the head of the centripetal forces – while, of course, continuing to argue her own national causes when real, as opposed to imaginary, British interests were at stake. In practice, this would mean joining the European Monetary System; pressing for a more powerful European Parliament and for majority voting in the Council of Ministers; urging reforms of the Common Agricultural Policy that would benefit poor farmers in southern Europe as well as British consumers; accepting the need for a Community energy policy, and recognizing that exclusive national control over North Sea Oil was incompatible with that; fighting for a bigger Community budget on the lines set out in the MacDougall Report; and demanding new Community industrial and labour-market policies on the lines discussed above.

There is no way of telling whether such a strategy would succeed. It would have a much better chance of doing so than the present minimalist strategy, but that is not saying much. In its favour are the facts that Italy, Ireland, and the Benelux countries are all in favour of a more supranational Community and suspicious of the Franco-German axis around which Community politics now revolve; that European public opinion is, on the whole, in favour of supra-nationalism too; that the newly elected European Parliament will certainly be in favour of supranationalism; and that the Germans have always claimed to be in favour of supranationalism in the past. Against it are the Gaullist legacy in France and the fact that it would, by definition, entail substantial transfers of resources from the richer member states to the poorer.

A fall-back strategy is therefore needed as well. As we have seen, minimalism leads nowhere. It follows that the only sensible alternative to maximalism is withdrawal. The worst of all worlds is to plod doggedly on along the present path. A maximalist Community would be in Britain's interests and in the interests of the Community as a whole. We should do all we can to achieve it. If we fail, if our partners are not prepared to honour the commitments they made when the Treaty was signed and to bear the modest costs of doing so, then we would be better off outside.

Comment
by Hugh Corbet

If the European Community is to be revitalized an effort has to be made to develop a concept of European integration that can be shared by all member countries – at the time of writing nine, but soon to be more – from one general election to the next. Since the countries of Western Europe were first at sixes and sevens on the concept, back in the 1950s, there has been a curious reluctance to clarify, for the purposes of public discussion and policy formation, what the phrase 'European integration' means. At least three interpretations are discernible. Tracing them may help to distinguish what is attainable from what might be seen as desirable.[1]

Three Approaches to European Integration
Customs union theory was formulated some time before either the European Community or the European Free Trade Association was formed.[2] Various economists have since shown that under a free trade scheme the need for policy harmonization over and above what is required of countries already extensively engaged in international trade is relatively slight.[3] Further harmonization (beyond the elimination of obstacles to the free movement of goods and services) is more a matter of choosing to augment the benefits of free trade than a matter of having to harmonize as a result of free trade. Little of importance is lost through not harmonizing other policies. Such harmonization issues as do arise can be handled, as EFTA has shown, by the consultative and negotiating procedures with which governments are thoroughly familiar. They do not require elaborate agreements.

From an economic point of view, then, the harmonization of economic policies, in so far as it is necessary to overcome distortions of competition, requires a co-ordinating authority. But it is enough that the co-ordinating authority is effective. It does not have to be supranational in character. In an economist's scenario of events, political unification is therefore deemed almost incidental, as it were, to the real and primary goal of economic integration.

The whole argument has been turned upside down by those who envisage political unification as the real and primary goal. They have argued that the determination to integrate economic policies (even if the economic benefits are marginal) will compel the formation of a supranational economic government which in time will assume responsibility for foreign policy and military security. Theirs has been what used to be called the doctrine of functional inevitability (a doctrine which, with the passage of time, began to lose credibility and was discarded in favour of the notion of positive integration). Economic integration, from a politician's point of view, seems to be just a pretext for political union; it is a means to an end, not an end in itself. It does not matter how small, or how large, are the economic gains from policy harmonization. What is important is the will to go ahead regardless.

In any consideration of policies for the development of the European Community it thus seems vital to draw a distinction between the objectives of economic integration on the one hand and the objectives of political unification on the other, if only to ensure that the appropriate instruments are used for achieving whichever is deemed attainable in the prevailing circumstances. None of this is to deny the inter-relationships between economic and politico-strategic affairs. But in the 1960s the European Community made a habit of using instruments of economic policy in order, ostensibly, to achieve politico-strategic objectives, the consequences of which were predictable: the Common Agricultural Policy and the attempt to promote monetary union are cases in point.

The resultant chaos has seen the development of a *realpolitik* approach which seeks national advantage, additional powers for member governments, and the further expansion of bureaucracy. The notion is that governments associate in order to control collectively what escapes the control of any one of them.[4] It amounts to forming a cartel of states which do not want to compete among themselves, but to co-operate to regain that control; and it manifests itself, it might be added, in the approach of many of the European Community's bureaucrats to the problems of those industries which are currently having difficulty in coping with international competition.

The *realpolitik* concept of European integration, what might be characterized as a bureaucrat's approach, pays little regard, however, to the limits of the discretionary authority of governments, by which is meant the limitations on the ability of governments to achieve desired social and economic changes. If governments do indeed cherish their discretionary authority, the *realpolitik* approach to European integration is inherently self-contradictory, for it presupposes a harmonization of policies which governments administer in a discretionary fashion on the basis of a blanket authority, but the harmonization of policies in such a way is no longer discretionary.

Thus, since it lacks intellectual coherence, the *realpolitik* approach would not appear to be a course by which to revitalize the European Community, certainly not if it values its position as a bastion of democracy by representative government. For David Marquand's proposals for a maximalist strategy to be viable, the prospects for political unification among the nine – soon to be twelve – member countries would have to be promising, but they would appear to be bleak. It would appear that in the circumstances of our time the most realistic approach to European integration is one based on economic considerations: the liberalization of controls on the exchange of goods and services within the European Community. After all, it is through the static and dynamic effects of trade liberalization – on consumption, production, and exchange – that the benefits of economic integration are largely achieved.

Changes in the World Economy

Over the last decade or so the European Community has been increasingly weakened by circumstances of its own making. The Community's last enduring achievement was the completion of the customs union in 1968. Since then the edifice founded on the customs union has been shaken by a number of external shocks: trotting inflation, exchange-rate changes, fluctuating grain prices, shortages of other commodities, creeping protectionism, and the energy crisis.[5] The first impact of these shocks has been on member governments. Now governments differ in their understanding of the different situations in which they find themselves. They therefore differ in the speed with which they adjust their policies. There is consequently a widening divergence in the economic performance of member countries of the Community and in the capacity of member governments to act. It is this divergence which is shaking the common edifice.

It is in that sense, indeed, that the European Community is in a state of crisis. But should anybody be surprised? I think not. Fundamental changes have taken place in international relations since the Community's formation. In short, the Community is, I am inclined to think, being overtaken by external events, but these are not taken into account in the somewhat Eurocentric view of the world that is exhibited in Professor Marquand's paper.

What factors should be taken into account when we examine the development of the European Community? First, Europe is no longer the centre of world power; since World War II the peace of the world has been determined by a global balance of power. Second, the integration of the world economy and the resultant interdependence between national economies having increased considerably since the 1950s, these factors now exert a much more powerful influence on intergovernmental relations than in the early days of the Community. Third, two significant groups of countries, the agricultural exporting countries and the newly industrializing countries of the Third World, are expecting more from the international system of trade and payments. Fourth, being suppliers of primary commodities, countries of the Third World are playing a larger part in international discussions. Fifth, with all these developments, and as the direct Soviet threat to Western Europe has receded, there has been a profound change in the American attitude towards the Community. Sixth, in the industrialized countries, never mind anywhere else, there has been a marked increase in state intervention in the market process. The result is that, with the growing interdependence of national economies, governments are finding external obligations increasingly in conflict with internal ones – and that makes it hard, if not impossible, to concert responses to world-wide economic problems.[6] The list could be extended.

It is in the light of such changes that the political leaders of the present generation of peoples in the European Community have to reconcile the Community's internal objectives with the responsibilities they bear, by virtue of the Community's size and capacity to block decisions, in the maintenance of the international economic order.

Member governments of the European Community have seemed reluctant to face up to what that means. It is as if political thought in the Community has not kept pace with the rapid integration of the world economy. Most of the problem has been psychological in that the Community's common external tariff, its commercial agreements with outside countries, and its Common Agricultural Policy have come to be regarded as symbols of European unity, proof to the world of the new Europe's virility. But these policies are based on discrimination against other countries which is tantamount, in an age of increasing interdependence, to provoking economic conflict with the rest of the world.

Some might find it strange that such a Bismarckian approach to unity is countenanced in the European Community, given that it was formed, among other reasons, in order to prevent a repetition of Franco-German discord. But, as Sigmund Freud once wrote, 'it is always possible to bind together a considerable number of people , in love, so long as there are other people left over to receive the manifestations of their aggressiveness.' The Community must find a more constructive approach to unity. Its economic integration must be pursued in harmony with the integration of the world economy as a whole.

Even from a Eurocentric standpoint this course would appear to be advisable, for if the Community's economic integration is not pursued in harmony with the integration of the world economy as a whole, the Community will be continually disrupted by one external shock after another. Because of the economic differences between them, the member countries of the Community are affected differently by global problems, which means that their governments are bound to react in different ways.

By the same token, it is not good enough for the European Community to wait for initiatives from others, because that only invites internal dissent. Given the economic differences between them, member countries are bound to react differently to external initiatives – which is why, before discussions begin at Community level on anything of major importance, individual governments are prone to assert national positions. This partly explains why the Community has difficulty in formulating a response to proposals from others and why, in the end, the response is at the level of the lowest common denominator.

In view of all the problems facing the world economy, the European Community would therefore do itself, and the rest of the world, a considerable service if it was to develop, on an intergovernmental basis, proposals for the repair of the international economic order. Such a course would also help the Community find the distinct identity it has been seeking between the United States and the Soviet Union. The reluctance of governments to work out external initiatives only impedes economic integration and makes the search for identity more difficult.

By way of summary I suggest that the European Community is most likely to develop if its member countries consciously formulate economic policies, with respect to internal affairs and external relations, that are non-discriminatory as between member and non-member countries and promote the integration of the world economy as a whole through the removal of obstacles to the free movement of goods and services. Whatever that approach is called, maximalist or minimalist, it would involve no mean effort.

Notes

[1] This comment draws on my article 'European integration and the integration of the world economy', *British Journal of International Studies*, April 1977, which itself drew on my paper 'Political and economic perspectives on trade between developed countries' in *A Foreign Economic Policy for the 1970s*, Hearings before the Joint Economic Committee, Congress of the United States (Washington, USGPO, 1970), pp. 173–90.

[2] Customs union theory was pioneered in Jacob Viner, *The Customs Union Issue* (New York, Free Press, 1950); in James E. Meade, *The Theory of Customs Unions* (Amsterdam, North Holland, 1955); and in Richard G. Lipsey, 'The theory of customs unions: trade diversion and welfare', *Economica*, XXIV, 1957.

[3] Harry G. Johnson, 'Implications of free or freer trade for the harmonisation of other policies' in Johnson *et al.*, *Harmonisation of National Policies under Free Trade* (Toronto, University of Toronto Press, 1969). Also see Victoria Curzon, *The Essentials of Economic Integration: Lessons of EFTA Experience* (London, Macmillan for the Trade Policy Research Centre, 1974), esp. ch. 10.

[4] Andrew Shonfield, *Europe: Journey to an Unknown Destination* (London, Pelican Books, 1974), ch. 1.

[5] The ensuing argument is spelt out in Sir Alec Cairncross *et al.*, *Economic Policy for the European Community: the Way Forward* (London, Macmillan for Institut für Weltwirtschaft an der Universität Kiel, 1974).

[6] It is relevant here to recall the debate of the 1930s over how to reconcile socialism and capitalism, and, in particular, the work by Lionel Robbins, *Economic Planning and International Order* (London, Macmillan, 1973), which argued that national economic planning and direction by democratically elected governments would embroil them in cumulative and ultimately explosive international friction.

Comment
by Bryan Gould

David Marquand is right to argue that the European Community has now reached a watershed. As he says, we must now proceed either to a fully supranational European union (his maximalist solution) or to a looser arrangement of nation states, perhaps covering a wider part of Western Europe (his minimalist solution).

Reference to the Treaty of Rome unfortunately produces very little help in the choice we have to make. While it is undoubtedly true that the founding fathers had in mind a fully fledged European union as the ultimate objective, the Treaty falls far short of a blueprint for such an ambitious arrangement. Indeed the present constitutional arrangements, based on the Treaty and on state practice, provide a distinctly minimalist framework. Major decisions are still taken by the Council of Ministers, and the Commission's position *vis-à-vis* the member states has been further weakened by the establishment of the European Council.

Until recently, this did not seem to matter very much. It was thought that there was a kind of historical momentum which would carry us forward, however slowly and haltingly, towards European union; there are indeed nuances of this view in David Marquand's paper. Recent developments have, however, confounded this easy optimism. We have discovered that the Common Agricultural Policy, the one positive step towards integration achieved by the Community, is an irrational, expensive, and wasteful foundation on which to try to erect a superstructure of supranational institutions. We have also discovered that the inherent tendency of a large free-trade area to encourage economic divergence rather than convergence has been exacerbated by a regressive redistribution of wealth brought about by the CAP. These discoveries have meant that progress towards European union can no longer be safely left to the forces of history; it must be given a powerful helping hand if the growing scepticism about its desirability is to be overcome.

Nowhere is this scepticism more keenly felt than in Britain, and for a very good reason. All ascription of 'fault' excluded, it is a matter of fact that the Community so far has represented a compromise of national interests which is very much to the advantage of other members but very much to the disadvantage of Britain. This is because, in its simplest terms, we are net importers and consumers of food, whereas others are not, and we are relatively inefficient producers of manufactured goods. What we need is free trade in agricultural products on the one hand, and protectionism and intervention in manufacturing industry on the other; what we get from the EEC is the precise reverse. A Common Sewing Machine Policy, which guaranteed our inefficient producers a price for their sewing machines twice as high as the world price and which required Community taxpayers to store and eventually dispose of the unsaleable sewing machines which our industry produced, would suit us very well and is no more objectionable in principle than the Common Agricultural Policy. This is not, however, what the Community offers us.

For Britain, even more than for the Community as a whole, a choice between the maximalist and minimalist courses is crucial, since for us the course chosen must offer an escape from an increasingly less tolerable predicament. We must either break out of an arrangement which is so disadvantageous to us or we must accept the inevitability of economic divergence within that arrangement and seek some other way of mitigating its effects.

David Marquand recommends the second option. He believes that Britain can avoid the penalties of economic failure and obtain a fairer deal from the Community only by accepting, as the price of a huge transfer of resources to us from our richer partners, a greatly enlarged supranational element in Community affairs.

But it is here that the dilemma arises. A growing economic divergence between one part of an economy and another may be just about tolerable within a secure and widely accepted political structure such as that provided by a national state. Even then, if we take the United Kingdom as an example, the strains between the regions are enormous and centrifugal forces very nearly triumphed with the upsurge of Scottish nationalism. Nor are these divergences easily redressed, even within a nation state; all our experience shows that, however great the resources devoted to regional policy, they will be ineffective in offsetting the overwhelming power of those market forces which concentrate manufacturing production in the most efficient parts of the economy.

If regional policy is relatively ineffective at the national level it will be so much less effective at the supranational level. Not only will the divergences be more difficult to deal with in economic terms, but, more important, the political conditions which make them more or less tolerable will be absent. The community of interest which holds people together in one political structure, even when economic forces compel one group to accept a status as social security claimants in respect of another, will simply be missing from a supranational Europe, particularly when, as in the case of Britain, the economic divergence is perceived to be partly exacerbated by the very process which is offered as a solution.

In other words, Professor Marquand's maximalist solution for the problems caused by economic divergence and the distortions brought about by the CAP depends crucially on a pre-existing commitment to a European union which is not only not present in Britain but is actually made much less likely by the present nature of the Community.

Nor can the point be met by relying on a directly elected European Parliament to manufacture the missing element of democratic support for European union. Elections alone are a necessary but not a sufficient pre-condition for democracy. Democracy is after all a form of government in which people agree to be governed by those whom they elect for the purpose. Electing representatives to an institution does not make that institution democratic if there is no such community of view with others represented there as to make acceptable the possibility of being outvoted by those others on matters of vital interest.

The dilemma, therefore, for those seeking a maximalist solution is that they must now work counter to the forces of popular opinion from which they have hitherto sought support. They are, in effect, arguing that the political leaders of Europe should themselves take the responsibility for a major step towards European union, even though demonstrable popular support for it is lacking, in the hope that once taken it will be seen by less enlightened people to have been in their interests all along. Stated in another way, the process of unification and the submergence of national interests should proceed at a faster pace than can be made acceptable to the national governments, parliaments, and electorates of the member states. If this were not the case, it would hardly be necessary to argue for majority voting and other devices to ensure that the objections of a particular member state could not frustrate the will of the majority.

It is this absence of democratic underpinning, in Britain at least, which is the fatal flaw in David Marquand's suggested solution. For Britain, it means that we must look elsewhere for an answer.

It would not be surprising if we sought to achieve a minimalist Europe as a protection against an irreversible involvement in a profoundly disadvantageous arrangement. This might enable us to escape the quite unfair and increasingly intolerable burden of the Common Agricultural Policy; we should simply claim the freedom to pursue our own agricultural policy and allow our European partners to pursue theirs. It would also open up for us other options in the matter of sustaining our industrial base. Instead of having to pin our hopes on competitive deflation within the Community (which serves only to weaken us further), or on regional aid handouts, we could look at policies which are at present contrary to the Treaty of Rome or to its spirit, such as changes in exchange rates, the management of imports, and an interventionist industrial policy. These are after all, as David Marquand points out, measures which the European Economic Community is ready to contemplate as a protection against Japanese competition; how much more appropriate they would be for Britain whose deficit with the EEC is proportionately so much greater than the EEC's deficit with Japan.

None of this should obscure the very real potential for co-operative achievement by a minimalist Europe, which, because it was more acceptable to Britain and perhaps other prospective members, might provide a more secure foundation for developing the European Community itself. It would enable Britain, and other members actual as well as prospective, to recognize the increasing community of interest which exists in fields such as foreign affairs and defence, and the increasing interdependence of European economies in both macro- and micro-economic terms. This would be underpinned by the familiar cultural, historical, and geographical ties and Europe could proceed on the basis of an institutionalized form of continuing co-operation which would go much further than any co-operative arrangement had hitherto reached. The essence of the arrangement would be that the Council of Ministers would meet regularly with a continuing agenda but would proceed no further than could be made acceptable to the national governments and parliaments of each member state. This would have the advantage of moving with rather than against the popular will, would direct co-operative effort into the areas where it would be most fruitful, and would permit the enlargement of the Community to embrace other European states which recognized a similar community of interest. It seems to me virtually inevitable that the enlargement of the Community will impel us towards this type of arrangement.

No consideration of the Community's future, from the British viewpoint, possibly could or should ignore the option of British withdrawal as a means of achieving a minimalist Europe. A powerful argument could be raised to support the view that it would not only be in Britain's interest to withdraw but that British withdrawal would also be in the Community's interests. Britain and her European friends could continue to achieve all that might be wished of European co-operation without Britain's having to shoulder the completely unfair and irrational burden of the Common Agricultural Policy. Military, economic, industrial, and trading co-operation do not depend on Britain's membership of the EEC; these objectives can all be secured within a wider West European framework. A Britain freed from an unfair burden and constituting a more dynamic and successful economic partner outside the Community would be of more value to Europe than a carping and impoverished Britain within the Community. One thing is certain, an unwise and premature attempt to press forward to a maximalist position would be the surest recipe not only for British withdrawal but also for the collapse of the Community as a whole.

Comment
by Laurens Brinkhorst

The central premise in David Marquand's paper is that the European Community no longer has the option of marking time. The key question for the Community is how it can be made more relevant to the needs of the member states. It is a most difficult question to answer as these needs vary from country to country. Yet one thing is clear. The present mechanisms of the EEC are ill-suited and inadequate to overcome the economic problems of inflation and unemployment; to reduce the divergence between the richer and the poorer regions of the existing Community of Nine, let alone of a Community of Twelve; to maintain and promote further the role of the Community as a stabilizing factor in world affairs. Rather than looking for maximalist or minimalist solutions it is important to find a new balance of interests within the EC – a package – that will commend itself to all member states as worth striving for.

Since the very beginning a basic ambiguity has existed in the objectives and structure of the EEC: the Treaty itself is already a compromise between those who aimed at an intrinsic dynamism and those who felt that enough reservations on national sovereignty had to be incorporated to prevent an automatic spill-over into new fields of action and to keep in check the development towards a supra-national community. It is indicative that no real powers in the macro-economic or monetary field have since been transferred under the Treaty to the Institutions, whereas the operation of the 'Common Market' is largely in the hands of the European Commission. This state of affairs is reflected in the present European Monetary System, which still lacks a solid Treaty foundation: it is essentially an *ad hoc* arrangement between the central banks. The real crunch will come in 1980, when a permanent institutional basis has to be found. This will raise such awkward questions as the powers to be transferred to the European Monetary Fund (will it be an institution more like the World Bank or the IMF?), the relationship between the central banks and the ministers of finance, and the management role of the European Commission. Whether the EMS will be able to transform the EEC into a 'zone of monetary stability' depends on the resolution of questions such as these.

The paper rightly states that the European Community has moved into areas not originally foreseen by the Treaty, such as foreign policy co-ordination. Although the importance of European Political Co-operation cannot be denied, its goals are purely intergovernmental, for it is aiming not at integration but at intergovernmental co-ordination. The record so far has been mixed: even though this form of co-operation has been effective in some cases, basically it has been more verbal than concrete, less an action originating within the

Community than a reaction to outside events, and it has often left a wide margin of independent action to member states. Moreover, one may question the dynamism of EPC developments, if separated from a healthy European Community. To the extent that the EC fails to provide more integration in the future, the functioning of EPC may be affected as well. The concrete instruments with which EPC action can be backed up are intricately interwoven with mechanisms of the EC (trade and co-operation agreements and transfer of financial resources or of technology). If the EC can be compared to the body of a bird of which EPC constitutes the wings, one may question the extent to which the wings can be stretched without a comparable growth of the body. This consideration applies *a fortiori* to the question of the extent to which defence co-operation can at this stage be made a vehicle for further integration. Certainly one cannot omit defence from the agenda of the 1980s, even though it is not formally a Community matter. But until more progress is achieved in the foreign policy field it is doubtful whether much progress will be made on defence and security matters, as these presuppose a common vision of our future relationship with the United States and the rest of Europe.

The ambivalent attitude of Britain towards the Community is of course closely linked with the remarks I have made concerning the general state of affairs in the EC. But one cannot fully understand this ambivalence without examining the specific elements involved in British membership. First of all there is the UK's original motivation in seeking membership. To put it somewhat polemically, British accession appears to have been motivated by negative rather than positive factors. Successive British governments put greater stress on the need to avoid isolation from the continent than on the need to find a new role for a Britain that had lost an empire. Moreover, in so far as positive factors were involved, the European Community was 'sold' to the public as a way out of Britain's economic predicament rather than presented as a developing political structure that could be instrumental in shaping the country's future. Certainly there always have been and there are those who emphasize the political dimension of the choice for membership, but to an outside observer they are a minority. For a long time the popular name of the European Community has been the Common Market! During the 1960s there might have been good reason for this approach, as could be demonstrated by the increasing disparity between the economic growth figures of the UK and those of the EC member states. But, ironically, by the time UK membership became a reality, the EC as a whole was already faced with increasing economic instability: inflation, monetary turbulence, and growing differences between the poorer and the richer regions. Apart from the CAP it had neglected to build any positive integration instruments. Nevertheless, for most member states the Community has provided a shelter against world recession in the 1970s. And, despite the growing pressures of protectionism both outside and inside the EC, there is still reason to believe that it can stimulate the restructuring processes required by large parts of European industry, provided that more and better instruments are put at its disposal. In short, it is accepted that one is in the Community for better and for worse, and not for any short-term gains. Membership has become part of a life style, disagreeable as this life may often be! It is this basic understanding that is largely absent in Britain. Until there is a change in British perceptions of the Community I fear that the basic choice between a maximalist and a minimalist strategy cannot even be made. In the final analysis it will be a question of whether the UK believes that its need to reverse the decline in relative prosperity and economic efficiency is likely to be served better inside or outside the European Community. Difficult enough already, that choice is attended by a further complication. The British position is unique in that no other member states have comparable problems over the structure of imports, industrial regeneration, or contributions to the budget: the possibility of making more or less durable alliances based on common interest within the Community is therefore closed.

I offer no words of wisdom and shall limit myself to discussion of the Dutch attitude to UK membership and the change that it has undergone. From the Dutch point of view UK membership has always been welcome, above all since Britain could constitute a balancing factor in a larger European framework. Progress towards European union was halted in the 1960s because the Dutch and others did not want an inward-looking bloc, along French lines. They wished to build an outward-looking European Community with strong overseas ties both in the Atlantic framework and among developing countries, especially those in parts of the world other than Africa with which the European Community was already associated. Some also expected a contribution to the strengthening of the process of democratization inside the Community.

Seven years of UK membership have altered the Dutch attitude considerably. Although there is still a great wish for continued UK membership various factors are appreciated differently. Active support for British membership at all costs has been replaced by a growing indifference, engendered by the failure of the UK to make a significant contribution towards further integration. Of course our eyes are not closed to the fact that other member states – France and Germany in particular – play a more dominant role in the Community of the Nine than they did in that of the Six, and that the tendency in the Community as a whole is more to intergovernmentalism than to supranationalism. Such considerations notwithstanding, the readiness to pay a higher price for continued UK membership is less than at any time in the past. The essential message is, therefore, that the UK has to make up its own mind concerning continued membership and cannot hope that the course of others would be basically altered by its departure.

That said, it is clear that I share the view that Britain cannot hope to gain from a Community which is moving in a 'minimalist' direction. A new approach is of course preconditioned by the solution of the UK budgetary problems. In this respect I want to support strongly Professor Marquand's remark that no solutions for individual countries are possible on the basis of a *juste retour* within each policy area. In the case of Britain this implies that, whatever changes are made in the CAP, Britain will always be a net contributor. Although meetings of the European Council in 1979 have not found a concrete solution to the British budgetary problems, an indication of a wider orientation was given. In the first place even a complete lifting of the restrictions on the 1975 corrective mechanism may reduce the estimated UK deficit by only one-third (520 million Units of Account). Therefore other elements must be added as well, as was hinted at in the Council communiqués. One should not be overly optimistic about the possible savings on the CAP. They would amount to a net reduction of the UK contribution of some 100 to 150 million Units of Account. A third and more promising step for a future British budgetary equilibrium would be to look for expenditure in other policy areas (structural reform of agriculture, the Regional Fund, energy research, etc.). This implies a readiness to increase the one per cent VAT ceiling and would require the co-operation of all member states.

It is essential for Britain to understand that such solutions cannot be achieved within a period of less than two to three years and that they presuppose British willingness to co-operate fully in the decision-making process. No concessions can be extracted by following an empty-chair policy. And it is necessary to keep priorities in mind: illogical action such as British voting behaviour in the Budget Council of November 1979, where the UK refused to back the European Parliament's proposal to cut farm spending (*in casu* the cost of the milk-powder mountain), should be avoided.

In the short run another option for Britain may be to work towards a broader package, including elements of the above as well as energy, fisheries, and the EMS. Gradually this would lead to a transformation of attitudes and enable a more maximalist approach. Criticism of the British attitude in the EC should not hide the fact that very few other member states, if any, are at this stage ready to commit themselves to such an approach.

But one thing should be said in conclusion: experience has shown that the Community can be influenced only from within. Outside negotiating partners are often frustrated: once a compromise is found between the Nine themselves, change is very difficult. Even the United States has experienced this on a number of occasions. The United Kingdom outside the Community would experience it even more strongly and could not expect co-operation *à la carte* – unless the EC itself was further diluted. Even though the short-term prospects of the Community are not very bright, the longer-term pressures for closer unity are likely to prevail. One hopes it will be a Community with Britain playing its full part.

The Balance of Payments and British Membership of the European Community

by Ann D. Morgan

Introduction and a Reminder: Pre-entry Estimates of the Effects of Membership

When Britain applied for membership of the European Community it was generally accepted that the impact effects of entry would involve a substantial balance of payments cost in the form of contributions to the Community budget, higher food import costs arising from the excess of producer prices under the Common Agricultural Policy over world prices, and, possibly, a deterioration in the balance of trade in manufactures. The official estimate in the 1970 White Paper *Britain and the European Communities: an Economic Assessment* (Cmnd 4289) was that there would be such a deterioration, since increased exports to the Community after the abolition of tariffs would be outweighed by additional imports from the Community and by the loss of export markets in the Commonwealth and EFTA as preferences for British goods were abolished or shared with Community suppliers. However, some outside estimates, made by Resnick and Truman [3] and by Kreinin [1], suggested that there would be a small net increase in the surplus on trade in manufactures. Further, both in the White Paper itself and in several independent estimates summarized by Miller [2] it was suggested that the food import bill might actually be reduced despite higher prices, since they would promote domestic output and reduce consumption, thus curtailing the volume of imports. But even the most sanguine forecasters did not suggest that the possible improvement in the trade balance would outweigh the certain budgetary costs. The estimated net cost ranged from the equivalent of about 0.5 to 1 per cent of the Gross National Product.

There was no such agreement on the dynamic effects of membership. The official view in the White Paper was that there would be substantial (unquantified) benefits if British industry exploited the opportunities that would arise for securing economies of scale and increasing specialization, and so for achieving faster growth. Membership would make Britain a more attractive location for foreign, especially American, investment. Additional benefits might follow from an increase in invisible earnings, though removing capital controls might entail a net capital outflow. Those who supported entry put a favourable gloss on the possibilities, those who did not argued that financing the impact costs of entry would impose so heavy a burden on the economy that growth would be retarded and the dynamic gains would remain unexploited.

Since the pre-entry estimates of the effects of membership were largely made in terms of balance of payments 'gains' and 'losses' it is convenient to follow a similar approach in looking at the record since 1972. The first section below reviews broad developments in the balance of payments with the world as a whole and is followed by an examination of the balance with the rest of the Community. The development of agricultural trade and budgetary transfers are described in those sections for the sake of completeness, despite the risk of overlapping with other papers.

Such evidence as there is on capital movements suggests that some American investment in overseas manufacturing facilities may have been switched from the Six to Britain. There are also indications of changes in the pattern of direct investment flows between Britain and the Community, with a lower proportion of funds being devoted to manufacturing and a higher to other (non-oil) industries. There is, however, no evidence that large changes in the volume of capital flows have been induced by membership; the predominant influence on the capital account since Britain joined the Community has been North Sea oil.

Trade in manufactures is analysed in the final section. It appears that UK exports have benefited significantly from Community membership and that, although there has also been an increase in imports as a result of tariff reductions, there has been a small net gain to the balance of payments in this sector. It has clearly been insufficient to offset the costs of the budgetary contribution and the Common Agricultural Policy.

The Balance of Payments 1972–8

The estimates of the effect of Community membership referred to above were made about 1970 and 1971, at a time when it was reasonable to expect that world output and trade would continue to grow both steadily and rapidly, when exchange rates were (relatively) fixed, when the rate of inflation though high by historical standards was still well below double figures, and when above all the UK balance of payments on current account was comfortably in surplus. Moreover, in 1971, for the first time since the early 1950s, Britain's share in exports of manufactures from the world's major industrial countries had actually increased – if only by 0.1 per cent. In the first few years after Britain joined the Community, all this was radically changed. During 1972 and 1973 the balance of payments deteriorated sharply under the combined influence of rising consumption expenditure, accelerating inflation, and higher commodity import prices. The Bretton Woods system finally collapsed and the floating pound began the decline that was not to end till 1977. Britain's share in world markets began to fall again. In 1973–4 came the oil price rise and the world economy plunged into the worst recession since World War II. The only gleam of light on the horizon came from the promise of North Sea oil.

Table 3.1 shows the development of the balance of payments on current account during this period and the subsequent years of recovery, distinguishing the balance on crude oil, on transactions likely to be significantly affected by Community membership, and on all other transactions. The principal items included in the final column are the surplus on private invisible trade and the deficits on trade in basic materials and on government services and property income. The two columns printed in italic show the immediate impact, excluding second-round effects, of the oil price rise and the growth of domestic oil output. The additional costs of imports and of dividend payments associated with the development of North Sea oil are included in the two final columns.

The deterioration in the balance on current account in 1973 and 1974, excluding oil, was £842 million. None the less, even in 1974 there was a sizeable recovery in terms of transactions measured at

Table 3.1   UK balance of payments on current account 1972–8 (£ million)

	Total	Crude oil			Other	
		Actual	Oil price*a*	North Sea oil*b*	Affected by EEC entry	Other
1972	+ 208	− 646	—	...	+ 421	+ 433
1973	− 875	− 918	− 211	+ 2	− 712	+ 755
1974	− 3307	− 3319	− 2616	+ 3	− 684	+ 696
1975	− 1621	− 3039	− 2490	+ 58	+ 750	+ 668
1976	− 842	− 3911	− 3397	+ 644	+ 1365	+ 1704
1977	+ 293	− 2770	− 2429	+ 2222	+ 1743	+ 1320
1978	+ 1032	− 2045	− 1771	+ 2795	+ 688	+ 2389

*a*Difference between actual value of net imports and value at 1972 prices.
*b*Gross value of sales at transaction prices or landed c.i.f. value as reported in source.
Sources: *United Kingdom Balance of Payments*, 1979; *Energy Digest*, 1979; NIESR estimates.

constant prices, reflecting principally an improvement in the volume of exports, though it was masked by the continued deterioration of the terms of trade. During 1975 the non-oil terms of trade recovered sharply, and, helped by the low level of domestic activity, the volume of exports fell less than the volume of imports. In 1976 the volume of exports of goods and services rose both absolutely and relative to the volume of imports, while the big fall in the exchange rate helped to maintain British price competitiveness. During these two years the swing in the non-oil balance of payments was more than £3,000 million. In 1977 and 1978 the non-oil terms of trade recovered still further, almost back to the level of 1972, partly because of a slower rise in foreign prices but more because of the sharp rise in British export prices. Sterling depreciation no longer offset Britain's above-average rate of inflation and in 1978 the exchange rate began to rise. Thus competitiveness was eroded and there was an ominous slowing down in the rate of increase in the volume of exports while the rise in import volumes quickened. The surplus on current account, excluding oil, was largely unchanged in these two years.

These developments influenced both the 'affected' and the 'other' balances shown in the two final columns of Table 3.1, but the former more than the latter because of the higher proportion of trade involved. The balance on 'other' transactions was more directly influenced by changes in the exchange rate (especially in 1976), in interest rates and international borrowing, in domestic and foreign profit levels, and by the erratic timing of oil company receipts and payments. There is no reason to suppose that Community membership had any significant direct effect on these transactions whatsoever.

The balance on transactions that have been particularly affected by membership is shown in Table 3.2. The figures in the upper part of the table show the actual balance on trade in food, drink, and

Table 3.2 Elements in the balance of payments particularly affected by Community membership (£ million)

	Food, drink, tobacco	Manufactures	of which: finished	Government transfers
Actual balance				
1972	−1501	+2132	+1634	−210
1975	−2705	+3822	+3158	−367
1976	−2959	+5108	+3813	−784
1977	−3302	+6156	+4102	−1111
1978	−2798	+5186	+3526	−1700
Difference between actual balance and balance at 1972 ratio to GDP				
1975	−174	+227	+403	−13
1976	+26	+869	+564	−366
1977	+77	+1356	+423	−638
1978	+1043	−270	−656	−1163

Sources: as Table 3.1.

tobacco, on manufactures, and on government transfers as recorded in the 1979 edition of the *United Kingdom Balance of Payments* – the Pink Book. The lower part of the table shows the difference between the recorded balance and what the balance would have been had its ratio to the Gross Domestic Product been the same as in 1972. These calculations are merely intended to provide a measure of whether things have gone better or worse than might have been expected had the relationship of receipts and payments to GDP at current prices been unaffected by the events of recent years and had nominal GDP developed as it actually did. The difference between actual balances and balances at the 1972 ratio to GDP reflects differences between the rate of increase of the volume of trade, both imports and exports, and of domestic output, and between prices in the UK market and in international trade. They are not in any way an indicator of the effects of Community membership.

By 1978 the deficit on trade in food, drink, and tobacco was much smaller than might have been expected. This improvement was wholly due to changes in the volume of trade. Import volumes remained fairly stable – as they had done during the preceding decade – until 1977 and then fell slightly. The fall might have occurred sooner but for the disastrous weather conditions of 1975 and 1976, which seriously depressed farm output, and but for the British consumer's increasing taste for wine. Meanwhile the volume of exports has grown rapidly and at an accelerating pace. Until 1976 import prices were rising faster than export prices whereas in the following two years the position was reversed, but even so UK export prices rose less between 1972 and 1978 than did import prices. The rise in import prices was partly a reflection of the world-wide rise in agricultural prices over the period, but it also reflected the influence of the CAP and so part of the cost of Community membership to Britain. Against this, movements in the volume of trade and more particularly in exports also owed something to membership, offsetting the price effect at least in part.

In the late 1960s the long-run tendency for the volume of imports of manufactures to grow faster than exports was briefly reversed, but in the years immediately preceding entry it re-emerged more strongly than ever. Already in 1972 there had been a sharp fall in the surplus on trade in manufactures, both relative to GDP and in absolute terms, and in 1973 there was a further large fall. But once recovered from the effect of the 1973 boom, the balance on manufactures was better than might have been expected, by 1977 very substantially better. During these years the growth of the volume of exports relative to GDP was slightly faster than it had been in the pre-entry period, and, helped by a bigger rise in export than in home prices, the ratio of exports to GDP at current prices rose from the 14.5 per cent of 1972 to 21 per cent in 1977. At the same time the volume of manufactured imports was growing very much more slowly than before 1973. Even so, both the volume and value of imports of manufactures continued to grow more rapidly than exports, mainly because of the continued disparity in the real rates of growth of imports and exports of finished goods. In 1978 the volume of exports barely rose and the surplus on manufactures fell as imports continued to rise. What happened then is unhappily similar to the events of 1967 and 1972 – sharply rising consumption and stagnant production following on a period of deteriorating price competitiveness, depressed exports, and boosted imports. And, even in 1977, the surplus on trade in manufactures relative to GDP had not recovered to the level of 1969–71.

Furthermore, the UK share in exports of manufactures from the industrial countries has still not regained the 1972 level of 10 per cent. It reached a low of 8.8 per cent in 1974, recovered the next year, and fell back to the 1974 level in 1976. Thereafter it rose to 9.4 per cent in 1977 and to 9.5 per cent in 1978, but had UK export prices not risen relatively to those of its competitors the UK share would have fallen once more in 1978. The decline since 1976 in UK competitiveness as measured by relative export prices has been very sharp, the index (1975 = 100) moving from 97.9 to 108.1 in 1978. Though this almost certainly exaggerates the loss of price competitiveness (other indicators show a much smaller deterioration), it does show a trend.

The final column in Table 3.2 can be directly related to Community membership, since this is the balance of payments heading under which payments to and receipts from the Community budget and various Community agencies are recorded. The growth of transfer payments over and above those implied by the 1972 ratio of net payments to GDP is close to the figure of net transfers to the Community as recorded in the balance of payments. They were £233 million in 1976, £458 million in 1977, and £913 million in 1978.

The Balance of Payments with the Community and the Direction of Trade

Since 1973 the Central Statistical Office has with some (justifiable) reluctance published estimates of the balance of payments with the rest of the Community. They show a massive deterioration of the balance on current account, from a deficit of £914 million in 1973 to one of £2,952 million in 1978. These estimates are misleading and biased, because of the British practice of recording trade on a consignment rather than an origin/destination basis. Trade overland to and from the rest of Europe and the Middle East and goods shipped via continental ports are thus attributed to the Community. In addition, under the general system of recording trade used in Britain, goods temporarily exported and imported and re-exports are included in the totals. The result is that exports to and imports from the Community are seriously overstated, but the latter more than the former. Moreover, invisible transactions with the Community include some exceptional items which increase the bias. Most of the large UK deficit on government services – over £700 million in 1978 – represents the cost of maintaining British forces in Germany, which has more than doubled since 1973.

The official statisticians have themselves pointed out the very great difficulties involved in allocating many transactions on a geographical basis; the resulting errors are included in their estimates under the heading covering the balancing item and multilateral settlements. This item is almost always very substantially positive in the balance of payments with the Community, partly because of genuine multi-lateral settlements where the UK is in surplus but partly also because of errors and omissions in the current account. Since 1976 the surplus on this heading has greatly exceeded the official estimate of the deficit on current account, which hardly inspires confidence.

Therefore in Table 3.3, which shows the development of the UK's current balance with the rest of the Community and of the balancing item, an alternative estimate of the current balance is included. This

Table 3.3   UK balance of payments with the rest of the Community 1973–8
(£ million)

	Current account balance		Alternative estimate of balance with EEC 8[a]	Balancing item	
	Total	EEC 8		Total	EEC 8[b]
1973	−875	−914	−321	+15	−180
1974	−3307	−1791	−997	+130	+1716
1975	−1621	−2487	−1334	+30	+963
1976	−842	−2208	−529	+229	+3220
1977	+293	−2160	−516	+2662	+4062
1978	+1032	−2952	−1380	+773	+7605

[a]Derived from EEC trade data and official UK estimates of private invisible transactions and of government transactions with the EEC authorities.
[b]Including multilateral settlements.
Sources: as Table 3.1 and *OECD Foreign Trade Statistics*.

is derived from other member countries' statistics of trade with the UK, which more nearly approximate to trade on an origin/destination basis and exclude re-exports and temporary trade. The difference between the c.i.f. (cost, insurance, freight) and f.o.b. (free on board) valuation of the trade flows covered is in most cases trivial, very much smaller than the difference between consignment and origin/destination figures. Private invisibles are taken from the Pink Book, as are government services and transfers with the Community authorities; other government transactions are excluded. The result is still a very large deficit, but it is half or less than that of the official figure.

Estimates of changes in the direction of trade since the UK joined the Community are also affected by classification according to consignment rather than origin/destination; while use of the general system of trade, which covers all goods crossing the geographical frontier (thus including goods exempt from customs duties), rather than the special system covering only goods crossing the tariff frontier, makes UK data peculiarly unsuited to measuring the effect of tariff changes. In Table 3.4, therefore, showing the shift towards the

Table 3.4   EEC-6 share in UK trade[a]

	Food, drink, and tobacco			Manufactures		
	UK exports	UK imports	Balance (£mn)	UK exports	UK imports	Balance (£mn)
	(% of total UK trade)			(% of total UK trade)		
1968	14.1	9.7	− 123	19.1	24.4	+ 111
1972	20.5	11.7	− 140	21.3	32.5	− 221
1973	25.2	17.3	− 313	22.3	32.8	− 501
1974	20.5	22.7	− 634	23.5	34.9	− 942
1975	29.9	27.0	− 743	22.5	35.1	− 785
1976	31.2	25.3	− 731	26.7	37.4	− 611
1977	29.1	23.8	− 771	26.9	38.2	− 939
1978	35.4	22.1	− 325	27.0	39.2	− 2121

[a] Calculated from EEC-6 data for exports to and imports from the UK and UK data for total trade.

Sources: *OECD Foreign Trade Statistics; UK Overseas Trade Statistics.*

Community in trade in food, drink, and tobacco and in manufactures, UK exports to and imports from the Six, and the development of the trade balance, have again been measured by partner country statistics. In this table trade with Ireland and Denmark has been omitted since both countries were in preferential relations with the UK before 1973.

Clearly there has been considerable diversion of trade in food, drink, and tobacco to the Six on both sides of the account, as evidenced by the jump in shares in 1973 and the large increases thereafter. So far as imports are concerned, it is probable that the shift represents pure trade diversion at the expense of all other major suppliers of temperate foodstuffs to the UK market, especially Australia and New Zealand. The remarkable increase in the share of UK exports going to the Six and the fall in the deficit in 1978 do, however, suggest that trade may have been created, providing further evidence of the gain to UK exports from Community membership that has, in part, offset the higher cost of food imports.

The change in the direction of trade in manufactures has been nothing like so drastic. UK exporters appear to have reacted slowly to tariff reductions and it was not until 1976 that there was a decisive shift towards the Community. Even so, the share of the Six in UK exports rose not much faster between 1972 and 1976 than it had done from 1968 to 1972 and in 1977 and 1978 the rate of increase declined sharply. It appears also that the share of imports from the Six has throughout risen less rapidly than in the pre-entry years. The change in the direction of trade has been partially obscured by the behaviour of certain large and erratic items – diamonds for example – and by the growth of imports from the new industrial countries. If the figures are adjusted to exclude the erratic items, trade with the Six rises faster after entry than before on both sides of the account, though the increase in the Community's share of imports is not very pronounced. If the data are further adjusted so that imports from the Six are compared with imports from other major industrial exporters, and the new industrial countries are excluded, then the post-entry rise in the Community's share of UK imports is faster again.

Yet whatever allowance is made for special factors, it is plain that Community entry has not involved so drastic a reorientation of UK trade in manufactures as was the case for the original members when the EEC was first established; and part of the shift towards the Community probably represents not so much diversion as reversion of trade previously diverted by the formation of the European Free Trade Area and the original Community. To a considerable extent, also, the increase in the deficit on manufactures with the Six is simply the result of a geographical shift and is associated with a larger surplus with the rest of the world than would otherwise have been the case. Since the Six have a larger share in UK imports of manufactures than in UK exports, and since total imports have increased more rapidly than total exports, the deficit was bound to widen in any case and the horrifying £2 billion deficit of 1978 is not a simple consequence of Community membership.

The Effect of Membership on Trade in Manufactures

Changes in the direction of trade give a very imprecise indication of the effect of tariff reductions; so the development of UK exports of manufactures was examined in the context of a constant market share analysis of the exports of fifteen countries: the Nine, the USA, Canada and Japan, and the four industrialized EFTA countries. The results suggest that by 1977 UK exports were perhaps as much as five per cent larger than they would have been had Britain not joined the Community.

The analysis was conducted in the framework of sales to six market areas: the EEC-6; Ireland and Denmark; industrialized EFTA; the USA; Canada, Australia and New Zealand; and the rest of the world. Erratic items were deducted from all trade flows and some other adjustments were made; UK exports, however, still include re-exports and goods temporarily exported. The results are expressed in Table 3.5 in the form of the ratio of the actual increase in the value of UK exports in successive periods to what the increase would have been had UK goods maintained a constant share in exports to each market distinguished between the initial and terminal year of the period. A ratio less than unity indicates that the UK share of the market fell during the period in question and *vice versa*.

From 1964 to 1968 and from 1968 to 1972 the ratios are uniformly less than unity. UK exports lost ground particularly badly in the major preferential markets in the Commonwealth – Canada, Australia, and New Zealand. They also did exceptionally badly in

*Table 3.5   Ratio of actual growth of UK exports of manufactures to exports
at constant market shares[a]*

	1964–8	1968–72	1972–6	1976–7
Exports to:				
EEC 6	0.19	0.76	1.34	2.16
Ireland and Denmark	0.80	1.00	0.73	2.09
EFTA[b]	0.67	0.86	0.60	1.40
USA	0.70	0.69	0.87	0.63
Canada, Australia, and New Zealand	0.03	0.50	0.36	1.33
All other	0.27	0.83	0.59	1.48
World	0.32	0.73	0.76	1.49

[a]The potential (constant market share) growth of exports has been calculated on
the assumption that the UK maintained its share in exports by the fifteen industrial
countries to each market unchanged between the initial and terminal year of each
period. Trade in diamonds, silver, ships, aircraft, aero engines, and works of art
is excluded.
[b]Austria, Norway, Sweden, and Switzerland only.
Source: NIESR calculations based on *OECD Foreign Trade Statistics*.

the EEC from 1964 to 1968, when the Community was establishing
its customs union. During 1972 to 1976 the ratio for exports to the
Six exceeded unity. Although they continued to lose ground elsewhere,
UK exporters were able to increase their share of the EEC market
after entry. The figures suggest that there was some offsetting loss
in sales to Ireland and Denmark and to EFTA, and some part of
the loss in Canada, Australia, and New Zealand may have been due
to the actual or prospective loss of tariff preferences there. However,
in absolute terms, by far the biggest losses during this period occurred
in the rest of the world, especially in the oil-exporting countries where
British exporters, starting with a disproportionately large share of
the market, put up an abysmal performance. Although there may
have been some diversion of UK exports from other markets to the
Community it seems unlikely that this had much effect on trade with
the OPEC countries, or indeed on trade in general.

Had Britain not joined the Community it is reasonable to suppose
that exports would have done less well in Community markets from
1972 to 1976, but better in EFTA and Commonwealth markets and
in the Irish Republic. The ratios would have looked like those

calculated for 1968–72 in Table 3.5, rather than the ratios actually achieved. Assuming that total import demand in these areas (and hence UK potential exports at constant market shares) was not affected by Community enlargement, the value of UK exports in 1976 under pre-entry tariff régimes can be roughly estimated by applying the 1968–72 ratios to potential UK exports. The result gives a figure for total UK exports in 1976 some £575 million less than that actually recorded. In view of the poor performance in most neutral markets during 1972–6, which suggests a further deterioration in UK competitiveness, this figure may be an underestimate. During 1977 the difference between the ratios in Community markets and elsewhere suggests a further export 'gain'. The general recovery in UK export performance was responsible for a good deal of the improvement in the ratios for other member states, as for others. But if performance had been only as good in the Community as in the EFTA countries or the rest of the world (and assuming that improved competitiveness owed nothing to Community membership), then exports would have been some £500 million to £550 million less than they were. Thus the total export 'gain' was at a conservative estimate some £1075 million to £1125 million between 1972 and 1977.

A parallel calculation for exports of manufactures from the Six to the UK shows a slight loss of market share from 1964 to 1968, possibly because of trade diversion associated with the creation of EFTA. Thereafter the ratio was successively 1.33, 1.35, and 1.28, considerably higher than the ratio for Community exports to the world which was 1.15 for the period 1968 to 1972, 0.97 from 1972 to 1976, and 1.07 for 1977. The Six clearly secured an exceptional increase in their share of UK imports in the years immediately following UK entry to the Community.

In calculation of the export effect for the UK it was implicitly assumed that the value of world and Community imports was unaffected by UK entry, and that trade was not created. Since the reduction in the EEC's average tariff on imports of manufactures after enlargement was very small – some three-quarters of its imports of manufactures from the industrial countries came from member countries and were traded free of duty in 1972 – this assumption is unlikely to have affected the result. The tariff cuts were relatively much more important for Britain's import trade; additional imports may have been created; and so another method of calculating the Community effect on Britain's imports must be adopted.

The reduction in UK tariffs on finished manufactures, including duties on imports from third countries, averaged 4.8 percentage points between 1972 and the end of 1977. This was actually a smaller fall than occurred in the course of the Kennedy Round. Measured by the incidence of duty charged, the fall was smaller still, something over 3 percentage points. If we take changes in import duties on finished manufactures over the whole series of major tariff cuts since 1959, it is clear that joining the Community was responsible for between one-quarter and one-third of the reduction. To estimate the effect of these tariff reductions, an equation was used which related annual changes in the volume of imports to changes in domestic expenditure at constant prices and in relative prices during 1959–1977. The expenditure variable covered spending on non-food consumer goods and investment in plant, machinery, and vehicles; the price variable measured the change in import prices adjusted for tariff changes (and for the temporary import surcharge) relative to domestic wholesale prices; the impact effect of each set of tariff cuts was picked up by a dummy. Thus the effect of EFTA and Kennedy Round cuts was explicitly allowed for. All coefficients were significant and had the expected sign, but the results were not wholly satisfactory since there were indications of large, unexplained changes in the coefficients during the 1970s. The calculations yielded an expenditure elasticity of 2 to 2.5 and a price elasticity of − 1.1, indicating that only some 10 per cent of the increase in imports of finished manufactures from 1972 to 1977 (£500 million or so at current prices) was due to Community membership.

For semi-manufactures the fall in tariffs was only 1.6 percentage points between 1972 and 1977 though the incidence of duty charged fell by a full 2 points. This was between one-fifth and one-quarter of the fall over the whole period since 1959. An equation similar to that for finished goods imports, but using industrial production rather than expenditure as the demand variable, yielded a price elasticity of − 1.7 when calculated over data from 1959 to 1972. It was not possible to re-estimate this equation for 1959 to 1977 because of data problems; and a direct estimate using the pre-entry price elasticity is complicated by the apparent substitution of imports of semi-manufactures for raw materials over recent years. When allowance is made for this, it appears that the increase in imports of semi-manufactures between 1972 and 1977 due to tariff changes was of the order of £250 million to (at the outside) £350 million measured at current prices, bringing the total for all manufactures to between £750 million and £850 million.

On these estimates and the earlier estimate of £1,075 million to £1,125 million for exports, there was a net improvement of between £225 million and £375 million in Britain's balance of trade in manufactures between 1972 and 1977. (This is rather larger than the Treasury estimate of £80 million reported by *The Economist*, but how this latter figure was calculated is unknown.) At best the gain falls far short of the known costs of membership, and, though useful, it is fairly trivial in the context of Britain's total trade in manufactures. As to the dynamic gains, if they exist, it is in the highest degree unlikely that they would offset the excess costs. They are not detectable but that is hardly surprising, in view of developments in the world economy and in Britain since 1972 that have nothing to do with membership of the Community.

References
[1] Kreinin, M. E., *Trade Relations of the EEC*, New York, Praeger, 1974.
[2] Miller, Marcus H., 'Estimates of static balance-of-payments and welfare costs compared' in John Pinder, ed., *The Economics of Europe*, London, Charles Knight for Federal Trust for Education and Research, 1971.
[3] Resnick, S. A. and Truman, E. M., 'An empirical examination of bilateral trade in Western Europe' in B. Balassa, ed., *European Economic Integration*, Amsterdam, North Holland, 1975.

4 The United Kingdom and the Community Budget

by Wynne Godley*

Mechanics and Magnitudes

Payments into the budget

Gross contributions to the Community budget are based on a principle known as 'own resources', which, in this context, means the *Community's* independent revenue: member countries under this convention are paying over to the Community what in some sense already belongs to it. Thus proceeds from common external tariffs and levies on agricultural imports from non-member countries, since their structure is determined by the Community in its supposed common interest, are considered to belong to the Community. In addition, the Community may precept up to the yield of one per cent of member countries' VAT, formally part of own resources though actually derived from national taxes.

It is important to note that the yield of VAT up to one per cent is part of the Community's own resources, as defined by the Council Decision of 21 April 1970 (on the basis of Article 201 of the Treaty of Rome). Anything beyond one per cent requires further legislation, which would have to be approved and ratified by all the member states.

As levies are chargeable on imports of food from non-member countries the gross contribution of food importers such as the UK is (other things being equal) a larger proportion of their GDP than for

* I am extremely grateful to Richard Bacon of the University of Cambridge Department of Land Economy for very extensive help in the preparation of this paper.

countries that are self-sufficient or are net exporters. In addition, non-agricultural imports by the UK from external sources are above average and generate a relatively large yield from customs duties. For these reasons the UK will – under existing arrangements – be contributing in 1980 about 20 per cent of total budget receipts while its GDP will be about only 16 per cent of the Community's total GDP.

Table 4.1 shows the estimated gross contributions of all Community members in 1980, the share of each contribution in the total, and the share of each country in the total GDP of the Community.

Table 4.1   National contributions to the Community budget

	Gross contribution in 1980		% share of each member in Community GDP in 1977	
	£mn^a	% share	at current exchange rates	at current purchasing power parities
Belgium–Luxembourg	617	6.1	5.1	4.3
Denmark	244	2.4	2.9	2.3
France	2016	20.0	24.1	23.2
Germany	3039	30.1	32.7	28.1
Ireland	91	0.9	0.6	0.8
Italy	1162	11.5	12.4	15.7
Netherlands	843	8.4	6.7	5.8
United Kingdom	2067	20.5	15.5	19.8

^a Figures have been calculated from Commission figures at an exchange rate of 1 EUA = £0.664.
Sources: For contributions, Commission of the European Communities' 'Reference Paper on Budgetary Questions', COM (79) 462 Final, 12 Sept. 1979; for GDP shares, Eurostat, *National Accounts ESA*.

The revenue of the Community budget comes 14 per cent from agricultural levies, 32 per cent from industrial tariffs, and 54 per cent from VAT. Table 4.2 shows for 1980 the proportion of each of the three sources of revenue provided by each country.

Receipts from the budget
About three-quarters of the expenditure of the Community budget

Table 4.2 National contributions by sources of revenue 1980 (percentage)

	Agricultural levies	Industrial tariffs	VAT
Belgium–Luxembourg	11	7	5
Denmark	2	2	3
France	13	15	24
Germany	20	30	31
Ireland	0.5	1	1
Italy	20.5	9	14
Netherlands	15	9	6
United Kingdom	19	27	16
Total	100	100	100

Sources: as Table 4.1

is accounted for by agriculture, predominantly to support farm prices; the rest goes mainly to social and regional fund projects and to administration.

It is important to note that under Article 203 of the Treaty of Rome, as modified in April 1970 by the Treaty Amending Certain Budgetary Provisions, expenditure on agriculture is regarded as compulsory but expenditure from the social and regional funds is not. If the budget came up against a revenue ceiling, agricultural spending might under present arrangements necessitate a reduction in other areas.

Expenditure on agriculture being preponderant, receipts by member countries depend largely on the extent to which their agricultural production exceeds what can be sold at home or to other Community countries.

Estimated gross receipts by each member country in 1980 are shown in Table 4.3.

Receipts by Belgium in this table are swollen by the fact that the EEC administration is mainly situated in Brussels. This means that the foreign exchange gain to Belgium should be considered to be slightly abated by remittances home from non-Belgian employees, while the direct gain in income to Belgian nationals is overstated by all the income received by non-Belgian employees. Similar considerations of course apply to Luxembourg as well.

Table 4.3   Gross national receipts estimated for 1980

	Gross receipts[a] (£mn)	% of total
Belgium–Luxembourg	1169	11.9
Denmark	432	4.4
France	1968	20.0
Germany	2315	23.5
Ireland	380	3.8
Italy	1653	16.8
Netherlands	1036	10.5
United Kingdom	864	8.7

[a] Monetary Compensatory Amounts paid to exporters.
Sources: as Table 4.1.

Net budgetary contributions and excess food costs
The concept of a net budgetary contribution is less clear than is sometimes supposed. Considered as a net financial contribution by a *member state*, the concept is clear enough. But whether it is appropriate to treat the net contribution as being what its *government* pays is highly questionable. In the case of Britain, payments *out of* the Community budget are not in any direct sense payments to the British government: they are payments to British farmers, warehousemen, and so on, over which the government has only limited control. The fact that these payments pass through the UK government accounts does not mean they should be netted off in the presentation of its public expenditure estimates, because there have to be counterpart entries in (positive) public expenditure on agriculture and on regional and social programmes. In other words, the total public expenditure cost of the EEC is the gross contribution, not the net contribution as the White Papers on public expenditure would have us believe. This must be emphasized, for it is not at all clear that, if the UK were not a member of the Community, there would be a public expenditure cost for the support of agriculture on the scale at present undertaken by the EEC.

Now, contributions less receipts must sum to nil across all countries; therefore some countries receive more than they pay, others pay more than they receive. (The statement that contributions less receipts must sum to nil across all countries is not strictly accurate because there has been a small but significant increase in cash balances held by the Community which exercises a small disinflationary effect on the system as a whole.) The estimated net budgetary contributions or receipts of all member countries for 1980, derived directly from the first column of Tables 4.1 and 4.3, are shown in the first column of Table 4.4.

Table 4.4   Net national receipts estimated for 1980 (£ million)

	(1) Net budgetary receipt	(2) Excess food gain	(3) Total net cash receipt (1) + (2)
Belgium–Luxembourg	+ 557	– 60	+ 497
Denmark	+ 188	+ 244	+ 432
France	– 48	+ 528	+ 480
Germany	– 724	– 358	– 1082
Ireland	+ 289	+ 173	+ 462
Italy	+ 491	– 515	– 24
Netherlands	+ 193	+ 694	+ 887
United Kingdom	– 1203	– 127	– 1330

Sources: Col. (1), see text immediately above. The figures in col. (2) are taken from J. M. C. Rollo and K. S. Warwick, *The CAP and Resource Flows among EEC Member States*, London, MAFF, 1979; they are for 1978 trade volumes and are a 'central' estimate from the 'net effect on the trade account' presented in their Table VII.

The net contributions shown in column (1) of Table 4.4 relate solely to sums of money paid into and out of the Community budget. Although these accurately represent the results of the Community system of budgetary transfers they are seriously misleading if taken as a representation of the whole transfer system between member countries, which arises from the CAP and the budget combined. This is because, when trade takes place between member countries, the exporting country's farmer receives his EEC price directly from the consumer in the importing country, not from intervention purchasing (or subsidization of exports to non-member countries) paid for ultimately out of the Community budget. I am assuming for the time being that the green currencies of each country have the same relationship to 'par'. For a brief explanation of the green currency system the reader is directed to Appendix 1 at the end of this paper.

One way to bring this point home is to imagine two member countries which are identical to each other except that one exports its butter surplus to the USSR, the other to a member of the Community. The position of each exporting country in respect of internal prices, total foreign exchange receipts, and farmers' incomes is the same – but only the exporter to the USSR receives cash from the Community budget for this trade. That member gets EEC prices less disposal prices in the form of an export restitution, whereas the exporter to another Community member receives the whole price directly from the importing member. Another way of illustrating this point is to consider how much would be lost by the rest of the Community if the UK ceased to be a member. Clearly our net budgetary contribution of £1, 203 million odd would be lost, but even if it could be assumed that the volume of our food imports from the Community continued the same, export restitutions would have to be made to Community farmers to bring the 'world price' we would then be paying up to the Community price – the level at which we now pay. Thus while (what we have called) 'excess food costs' are at present non-budgetary transfers, *they must be included in any estimate of the additional net charge that would fall on the budget if we were not members.*

There are serious difficulties in estimating the precise scale of excess food costs. In particular it is difficult to know what is the appropriate 'world price' that should be compared with the EEC price.

Fortunately some official estimates of excess food costs have recently been published by Rollo and Warwick. On the one hand they are based on the actual rates of levy which importers had to pay when importing from non-member countries, on the other hand on the actual rates of export restitution which exporters received when exporting. The results of this calculation (taking an average of the two estimates) are shown in column (2) of Table 4.4 above. (A suggestion was made at the conference that transfer payments arising on trade in industrial products should also be taken into account. For a note on this topic see Appendix 2 at the end of this paper.)

Each country's total net cash transfer (the sum of budgetary contributions and excess food costs) is shown in column (3) of Table 4.4. Now, the figures in column (3) can indicate how much each country gains or loses through the transfer system only if we assume that, if the Community did not exist, each country paid for the support of its own agriculture at the same level and used essentially the same method as the Community does (and that implies the same level of food prices and, therefore, of domestic production and consumption); second it must be assumed that the scale and pattern of trade in food would be as at present. The first of these assumptions seems quite appropriate; for instance we are showing, for France, how much extra (£480 million) the French taxpayer would have to find if French farmers continued to be supported at existing levels. The second assumption is more questionable. Importing countries (notably Britain) would almost certainly obtain a higher proportion of their supplies from sources outside the Community. This would not, taken by itself (assuming an external levy at the present rate), make Britain better off, but it would damage the Community's exporting countries by reducing their exports and therefore give rise to more intervention buying.

Here I would like to emphasize two points in relation to the figures in Table 4.4, bearing particularly in mind the confused public discussion in Britain of all these issues.

The first point is that it is absolutely essential to count *both* the net budgetary transfers *and* the excess food costs. This drastically alters not only the scale but also the ranking of the inter-country transfers. For instance, the transfer cost to Britain is not going to be £1,200 million in 1980 as the public generally supposes, but (according to present estimates) about £1,300 million. Italy, which appears a substantial net beneficiary if the budget alone is considered, roughly breaks even when both figures are taken into account. France's net contribution is about nil, but when trade gains are included she becomes the second largest beneficiary of the whole system.

The second point is to recall that we are showing, in column (3) of the table, net payments which must sum to nil across countries. As the figures show, there are only two net payers of any magnitude, Britain and Germany; all other countries (except Italy) are substantial net recipients.

Assessment

Consider first how a budget works within a unitary state or an established federation. On the one hand services (for example, education and defence) are generally provided to a common standard and to the benefit of all component areas; on the other hand taxes are raised according to the component areas' ability to pay. Such a budget achieves objectives common to all areas through public expenditure but at the same time there exists a redistributive cash transfer system from the relatively rich to the relatively poor areas.

In sharp contrast, outlays from the Community budget do not in any real sense achieve common standards of any service throughout the Community and the contributions are incoherently related to members' ability to pay.

The beneficiaries are mainly the agricultural industries of major producer countries which are protected *vis-à-vis* world markets and indeed are being supported on a scale that is excessive, judged by the criterion that stockpiling and dumping or destruction of produce are occurring. And the cost of all this is spread through the Community according to no principles of equity. The arbitrary and often perverse nature of the pattern of EEC transfers may be demonstrated by expressing the total net cash receipt or payment of each member country on a *per capita* basis and setting the result alongside figures indicating relative levels of national income per head.

Table 4.5   Per capita net receipts compared with per capita income

	Estimated receipts per capita 1980 (£ per annum)	National income per capita (% un-weighted mean at market exchange rates 1977)	National income per capita (% of un-weighted mean at purchasing power parities 1977)
Belgium–Luxembourg	+49	129	109
Denmark	+86	136	119
France	+9	113	113.5
Germany	−18	130	118.5
Ireland	+154	48	62
Italy	−1	55	72
Netherlands	+63	120	108
United Kingdom	−24	69	92

Sources: as Table 4.1

Table 4.5 shows once again only two net contributors apart from Germany, of which the larger is the UK, while Ireland and Denmark are by a very long way the largest *per capita* beneficiaries. The UK and Italy, among the three member countries that came off worst from the EEC transfer system, are among the three with the lowest national income per head. A notably anomalous gainer is Denmark, which receives over £86 a year per head (equal to about two per cent of its GNP), although Denmark's income per head is the highest in Europe – just over double that of the UK. The one 'good' aspect of the system is that Ireland, still by far the poorest member of the Community, also receives the largest *per capita* benefit; Ireland has been gaining rapidly in prosperity, both absolutely and relative to other member countries.

Although this transfer system is arbitrary, perverse, and wholly disadvantageous to Britain, no Briton should be surprised at it or *newly* indignant about it. The White Paper *Britain and the European Communities*, Cmnd 4289, which was published in 1970 and formed the official prospectus for UK entry, states in paragraph 44 that 'the trade effects and the financial charges' consequent on adopting the Common Agricultural Policy would be likely to lie in a range exceeding £175–£250 million. As prices have risen more than threefold since 1970, the forecast then made appears to be in the correct parish.

Future Prospects under Existing Policies

I believe it to be the case that if existing or similar policies are continued, that is, if farm prices on average through the Community rise a few percentage points each year, the cost of the CAP will still rise much faster than the growth rates of nominal GNP. By implication the pattern of net transfers will remain the same as at present but all the magnitudes will grow both absolutely and relative to GNP. What can check or reverse the process?

If the growth of expenditure is unchecked the whole tax potential of the 'own resources' system (that is, the total of levies and customs duties and the yield of one per cent from VAT) will quite soon be exhausted. The Community will be incapable of financing further increases in expenditure without further increases in VAT, which the net payers (Britain in particular) could impregnably refuse to pay. If there were a ceiling on revenue there would presumably first be a cut in expenditure from the social and regional funds, implying a further increase in Britain's net contribution. But before long, because the commitment to maintain farm prices is open ended, the CAP would surely collapse.

Short of this outcome a severe limitation in the growth of, or a freeze in, farm prices (in nominal terms) could be imposed. But it is very doubtful whether any feasible farm-price policy would actually prevent budget expenditure from continuing to rise.

Even if total expenditure *were* checked or reduced that would not alter the pattern of net contributors and recipients. The UK would still be a net contributor even if not on quite the present scale.

But there is another reason why a stringent policy towards farm prices may not be a satisfactory, let alone sufficient, policy for Britain. As long as sterling was weak it was possible for the UK government successfully to oppose a general increase in farm prices within the Community and simultaneously to obtain an increase in prices for British farmers by devaluing the green pound. And this is indeed what happened in the first half of 1979. The general increase in farm prices throughout the Community between April and September 1979 averaged about five per cent but because of green pound devaluations British farm prices, both to producers and consumers, rose about 12 per cent in this period.

However, strong sterling would make it impossible for the UK to have it both ways. Green currencies may only be devalued or revalued towards par, never away from it. Sterling recently reached a level which brought our green pound to within one or two per cent of par, and therefore no significant further devaluation of the green pound would then have been possible under the existing rules of the CAP. In other words, British farm prices could then rise only at about the same rate as European prices in general, except to the extent that sterling depreciated.

The foreign exchange market is so volatile that any prediction must be conditional. Should sterling remain strong a deep conflict will emerge. If EEC farm prices are raised significantly, net transfers from the UK to the Community will rise even faster than is at present foreseen and the mountains will grow. If EEC prices are not raised, British farmers will have their real income substantially and progressively squeezed between the stability of the prices they will receive and the increase in the cost of labour, fuel, and other materials, which looks like being about 15 per cent during this financial year alone.

On a longer time scale, unless spot sterling is devalued almost to the full extent of the UK inflation rate (its absolute rate, *not* its rate relative to that of other countries) a progressive squeeze of British farm incomes is the inevitable consequence of preventing any significant growth of prices throughout the Community. Britain would then be in the astonishing position of having to pay out vast sums of foreign exchange every year mainly to support the incomes of Community farmers, while simultaneously being deprived of the power to protect the incomes of her own farmers.

More radical possibilities

Consideration of more radical possibilities for reform of the budget and CAP mechanisms cannot sensibly be considered in isolation from the major alternative ways in which the Community might now develop, many of which have been ably summarized by William Wallace in his introductory chapter. I mention three such possibilities below.

The simplest and least disruptive way in which the transfer system could be reformed would be explicitly to separate the CAP (defined as a particular level of support and protection for agriculture) from the way in which it is financed. It is very commonly supposed that reform of the transfer system necessarily requires reform of the CAP itself. In my opinion that is an incorrect judgement, just as it would be incorrect to suppose that the structure and incidence of taxation within a country could not be reformed without altering the structure and scale of public expenditure on defence, health, or education.

The CAP is indeed in need of reform, if only because of the enormous waste of resources that is daily being incurred. However, if the Community, for political or other reasons, wishes to preserve the CAP in its present form, there is nothing to stop it from doing so and at the same time radically altering the pattern of net transfers. The way in which that was done should of course reflect the objectives of the Community. It is sometimes pointed out (see, for example, Carsten Thoroe's contribution) that redistributive policies are not part of the Treaty of Rome. *But redistribution of resources is precisely what the Treaty of Rome is generating!* If it is no part of Community policy to redistribute resources, the financial reform is in principle simple to devise: let all net recipients shown in my Table 4.4 pay out of their own exchequers, to the Community, the sums of money shown in column (3) and let these be paid back to the net payers. It is easy to see possible ways of varying this theme. For instance, if it was considered inappropriate that Ireland, still the poorest Community member, should receive less than at present, Ireland alone could be spared the requirement to refund her net positive transfers.

Any or all such solutions to the manifest inequity of the existing transfer system may well encounter insuperable objections of a political nature from those countries which stand to lose. My sole concern here is to point out that there is no reason in logistics why a pattern of transfers acceptable to Britain should not be implemented without delay. Above all it is not necessary to wait for a major and probably painful restructuring of the CAP, which would certainly take many years.

Another possibility is that the scope of the Community budget could be greatly enlarged so as to make it something like a genuinely federal budget. Such budgets normally have equalizing properties since they aim to provide a uniform standard of service, say education, health or roads, in every region of the whole area.

However, to change the ranking of net payers and recipients in such a way as to make it correspond in any degree with the ranking of GDP per head would require a very large increase in total expenditure and a correspondingly large increase in total gross contributions.

On the one hand the contributions, both gross and net, of the richer countries would have to be very much increased, which they might find unacceptable. But in addition individual governments would have to hand over to Brussels very substantial powers to spend money on a new range of services. The political institutions to which such important powers would be delegated do not at present exist. It would thus be a risky, cumbersome, and expensive way of achieving an equitable transfer system. It would certainly take several years.

A third possibility, which the conference discussed at some length, is that substantially larger sums might be paid out to assist the development of poorer, or declining, regions or even whole countries. Such expenditure would have a fundamentally different character from the refund mechanisms adumbrated in the first of the three suggestions discussed in this section. Instead of consisting of un-hypothecated transfers of foreign exchange, such regional or quasi-regional expenditure might, for instance, generate investment that would otherwise not be undertaken; it could even directly subsidize employment in the less successful and competitive areas, following the pattern of the Regional Employment Premium which was operated in Britain with some limited success during the 1960s.

Appendix 1: The Green Currency System

The original intention to institute uniform food prices throughout the Community was abandoned because of major changes in the exchange rates between the currencies of member countries, which greatly exceeded the differences in their inflation rates. These exchange rate changes have been governed by factors – notably performance in world markets for manufactured products and the conduct of monetary and fiscal policy – which have little to do with trade in agriculture. Had agricultural trade continued to take place at common prices calculated at actual exchange rates, the farmers in those member countries which have been most successful in world markets – particularly Germany – would have suffered a disastrous fall in their incomes; consumers in the relatively unsuccessful manufacturing countries would have had to face extremely sharp increases in food prices, and their farmers would have made extremely large profits. It was principally for these reasons that, when exchange rate parities flew apart, the 'green currency' system was invented. In form this system introduces a new *numéraire* in terms of which agricultural prices are denominated. But the simple way to think of it is as a device whereby agricultural prices in individual countries are partly or wholly insulated from the process of exchange rate adjustment; in other words, internal prices do not necessarily change at all when currencies are adjusted. In consequence, prices differ from country to country when measured at actual exchange rates, and when trade takes place between countries this difference has to be made up by a cash levy or subsidy. If Germany exports butter to be sold in the UK at a price in sterling which is only 60 per cent of the price received by the German farmer (and 60 per cent of that paid by the German consumer), the difference is made up by a 'monetary compensatory amount' (MCA) paid out of the Community budget.

Now MCAs are sometimes paid out of the budget directly to the exporting country, in which case the importing country is paying a price equal to the Community price expressed at par *minus* the MCA; but sometimes the importing country pays the full Community price and itself receives the MCA. The difference between these two ways of arranging things is one solely of administrative convenience; the position of neither importing nor exporting country is in any significant way altered by the method chosen.

In 1976 the arrangements for the UK were changed. Until then MCAs were paid to the UK as an offset to the high prices being paid to exporters; since 1976 MCAs have been paid direct to the exporter and the UK has paid a correspondingly lower price. Again, no significant difference was made to anything important but the UK's net contribution to the budget was increased to be precisely offset by a reduction in the amount paid as 'excess food costs'.

This example underlines the importance of always including both excess food costs and net budgetary contributions when measuring the total scale and pattern of the transfer system; so long as both kinds of transfer are included no difference is made to the presentation (in accordance with the realities), regardless of whether MCAs are credited to exporters or importers.

Unfortunately this matter has given rise to much misunderstanding, largely because budget figures are habitually presented on their own. And confusion has been positively invited by the double presentation of net contributions, with MCAs credited on the one hand to exporters and on the other to importers.

Appendix 2: Transfers Arising from Trade in Industrial Products

Trade in industrial products between member countries gives rise to transfers between them which are in principle the same as the transfers arising from trade in food (see Appendix 1 above). The existence of a common external tariff implies that, as in the case of food, there is a world price for competitive industrial products which (ex tax) is lower than the price at which trade takes place inside the Community.

The scale of these transfers cannot, however, be very large. Not all imports from outside countries are subject to the common external tariff, and the 'world price' (an even more difficult concept for manufactures than for food) is probably lower than the Community price by something less than the tariff. Suppose the world price to be on average six or seven per cent lower than the Community price, the net transfer could be estimated by applying this percentage to the deficit or surplus in the balance of trade in manufactures of any member country with the rest of the Community. As the UK is now in heavy deficit in its manufacturing trade with the rest of the Community its total net transfers would be somewhat increased (conceivably by £100–£200 million) compared with the figures shown in Table 4.4. Net transfers by Germany, on the same principle, would be somewhat reduced.

Comment
by Stephen Milligan

I fully share the general thesis advanced by Godley – that Britain's share of budget costs added to the cost of trade transfers is absurdly high. I also agree that reform of the system is going to be extremely difficult, but I am not quite as pessimistic as he is about possible solutions.

At the beginning of his paper he refers briefly to the concept of own resources, the Community's independent revenue. The Community's own resources are, by formal agreement among member states, the property of the Community and therefore escape the control of national parliaments. When the Community instituted the principle of own resources in the early 1970s the Dutch insisted that, as a counterpart, the European Parliament should be given some control of the budget. The French reluctantly accepted this extension of the Parliament's role, because they believed that the introduction of own resources would prevent national parliaments from interfering each year with the budget for agriculture. Thus VAT is in this sense very much an 'own resource', derived from a harmonized base of assessment, even though VAT rates and coverage are not fully harmonized throughout the Community.

The system agreed has two important consequences for the present debate. First, the European Parliament has the right to alter the Community's annual budget. In 1979, for the first time, the newly elected

Parliament attempted to cut the amount of cash devoted to the CAP (the Dankert amendment) and then rejected the budget altogether, with the aim of obliging member governments to accept its proposals. The notion that the Parliament has no power over farm spending is wrong: it can significantly alter the CAP budget – although it needs the support in the Council of a blocking minority of governments to achieve success, for example Britain and Italy.

Second, the present ceiling on own resources will be hit by 1982. At that point the Community will run short of cash – and no more will be available until *all* nine national parliaments agree to a new *tranche*. Thus each country will have a veto over additional resources (Britain, Germany, and France have already said that they are opposed to increasing revenue). Germany and France may well change their minds when they come to terms with the threat that the ceiling represents to the CAP. Britain is left with an irresistible bargaining counter in the right to withhold agreement on new own resources until the CAP and/or its budget contribution is reformed. The Parliament is unlikely to change the shape of the Community budget radically from one year to the next, but it could have an important impact over a period. The fact that the Parliament more accurately represents the urban citizens of Europe than does the pro-farmer Council of Ministers will be a continuing force for a better balanced budget.

Godley argues that, if a ceiling was imposed on EEC spending, agriculture might simply swallow up more and more cash at the expense of, for example, the regional fund. Theoretically, he is quite right. But in practice, I do not think that would happen. The combination of a majority in the European Parliament and the votes of Britain and Italy in the Council would be enough to stop it (even if, for example, the Dutch and the Irish agreed to support 'swallowing up' – which I doubt). 'Compulsory' expenditure means that it is obligatory for the EEC to provide price support for, say, milk – but the level of support, which is the crucial question, is not specified. I therefore believe that the crisis presented by the exhaustion of own resources will offer a most promising way to reshape the EEC's spending. And such a crisis might also help the reformers within the German and French governments (including Helmut Schmidt), who have long sought a means to tackle the excesses of their own farm ministers.

On the question of what reform should be introduced there are various options. The immediate problem of Britain's excess budget bill can be tackled by a reform of the corrective mechanism established during the renegotiation of 1974–5. This mechanism has so far proved useless, partly because it is linked only to Britain's gross contribution, and partly because it is hedged about with conditions – for example, that Britain can claim a refund only when running a trade deficit. If the mechanism was linked to net contributions and the hedging conditions removed, most of Britain's 'excess' bill could be eliminated. If Britain's problem was resolved the Community budget overall would not be quite as regressive as Godley suggests. This is because his figures are partly based on 1978, which was an erratically bad year for Italy. The Commission's projections for 1980 (Table 4.6) show that Italy will become the biggest beneficiary from the EEC. A variety of new EEC policies, for example interest-rate relief grants for EMS membership, the Mediterranean aid programme, and the increase in the regional fund, have all helped.

The apparent high benefits for rich Belgium and Luxembourg are based on the assumption that *all* cash paid for the EEC institutions in those countries is a transfer to those countries. This is obviously an exaggeration. (British Eurocrats, for instance, transfer some of their

Table 4.6 Forecast net transfers 1980 (£ million)

United Kingdom	– 1161
Germany	– 671
France	– 12
Luxembourg	+ 187
Denmark	+ 237
Netherlands	+ 271
Ireland	+ 328
Belgium	+ 352
Italy	+ 470

Note: Monetary Compensatory Amounts are attributed as a subsidy to exporting countries. The orders of magnitude are not greatly changed if they are attributed to importers, because MCAs in 1980 are likely to be much smaller than in recent years.

Source: based on Commission of the European Communities paper COM (79) 620, 31 October 1979.

salaries back to Britain – and much of the cash they spend in Belgium is in exchange for resources supplied by Belgium and is thus not simple profit for Belgium.)

Godley's Table 4.5 also exaggerates the spread of income within the Community by comparing countries at market exchange rates. Table 4.7 shows that the dispersion at purchasing power parities is considerably less and slightly alters the ranking. However, it should be pointed out that budget payments are of course made at market exchange rates not at purchasing power parities.

In the long run two reforms are needed to make the budget system fairer. First, as and when an agreement is reached on new own resources, revenue should be raised on a progressive basis. The Commission has already proposed that the next *tranche* should be raised from a further one per cent on VAT – but at a variable rate linked to relative GNP. (In any case, the higher the fraction of Community revenue raised from VAT – as opposed to tariffs and levies – the fairer the system will be. Part of Britain's unfair gross contribution stems from the fact that it pays an unfair share of tariffs because of its high share of non-Community trade.) A progressive key could even be extended to cover all VAT payments – including the existing one per cent *tranche* paid to the Community.

Second, part of the financial cost of the CAP must be transferred to national governments, as Godley suggests, and the level of price support must be cut. The problem for Ireland would indeed be

Table 4.7 Estimated dispersion of GDP at purchasing power parities 1979 (EEC = 100)

Germany	118
Denmark	116
France	112
Luxembourg	111
Belgium	108
Netherlands	105
United Kingdom	91
Italy	77
Ireland	61

Source: Commission of the European Communities, *Annual Economic Review*, November 1979.

serious – but Ireland would remain a net beneficiary under any hypothesis and it would be easy to adjust other spending policies to compensate.

I disagree with Godley's argument that a low farm price policy would not suit Britain. It is true that once British farm prices are aligned on Community prices, there is no scope for giving British farmers 'real' price increases while at the same time freezing Community prices. But why should Britain want to give its farmers real price rises? Britain's farm prices, like those in the rest of the Community, are now well above world prices – with a corresponding burden on consumers. Traditionally, real farm prices have fallen by some one per cent a year to reflect rising productivity. An illusory argument is that rising British real farm prices would benefit the British trade balance. This ignores the welfare cost of transferring resources towards farming from other sectors of the economy.

Surely there is a confusion here. British farmers are worried that, without the possibility of regular green-pound devaluations, they will not even be able to obtain nominal price rises. But either British inflation will be low – in which case farmers will not need large nominal price rises – or British inflation will be high, in which case the real pound will fall again and there will once more be scope for nominal price rises via devaluation of the green pound. The only risk for British farmers is if the real pound is valued at an exaggerated level.

5 British Interests and the Common Agricultural Policy

by Christopher Ritson

Introduction

When we joined the European Community it was generally accepted that the adoption of the Common Agricultural Policy would involve the most difficult adjustments for the UK economy. Assessing just what would be the impact of the CAP on the UK economy, however, seemed a relatively straightforward task. A desire to protect the living standards of the Community's millions of small farmers had led its policy makers to set farm product prices at levels well above those at which farm produce could be bought and sold on world markets. Common Agricultural Policy prices were also generally much higher than the prices guaranteed to British farmers during this period. Adoption of the CAP was therefore going to mean higher prices for British farmers and an era of rising agricultural prosperity was expected. (A detailed account of the issues thought to be involved in British adoption of the CAP will be found in chapter 5 of Marsh and Ritson [18].)

Britain supported domestic farming mainly by deficiency payments to producers, financed by government subsidies, thus keeping consumer prices down. The CAP operated by raising market prices to ensure that they provided a decent return to farmers. British food consumers were therefore going to have to pay higher prices, first because of the change in the system of support, and second because farm product prices were, in any case, to be supported at much higher levels. The latter was in fact the more significant of the two because of the UK's fairly modest level of guaranteed prices for farm products before accession to the Community.

As far as the economy in general was concerned, Britain was going to have to pay higher prices for imported food, either because we would now be buying high-priced European food or because imports from outside the Community would be taxed and the levy revenue transferred to the Community budget. This was sometimes called the 'balance of payments cost' of entry, but, as explained later, it is more correctly described as a welfare loss – much the same effect as when an individual suddenly finds that something he regularly buys jumps up in price while his income remains static. In fact, it was hoped that the UK's 'income' would rise as a consequence of joining the EEC. The main economic prize of membership was thought to be a stimulus to a higher rate of economic growth in the UK.

A number of publications went further and made specific forecasts of the impact of the CAP on the UK. In particular there were two White Papers [8, 9], one from a Labour government in 1970 and one from a Conservative government in 1971, and a report from the Confederation of British Industry [7]. Forecasts related to four main effects: the balance of payments cost; the impact on food prices; and the effects on farm output and on farm incomes.

The most authoritative balance of payments estimate came from the Confederation of British Industry, which predicted an annual net loss of £300 million or about one per cent of national income at that time. The first White Paper predicted a rise in food prices of between 18 and 26 per cent as a consequence of adopting the CAP, but in 1971 the second one moderated this to a rise of 2.5 per cent per annum, or about 16 per cent by 1978. On farm output, the 1970 White Paper suggested that agricultural output would increase by between three and 10 per cent; and, more confidently, that of 1971 stated: 'The Government expects additional expansion of some eight per cent overall on this account [i.e. higher product prices] by 1977.' This was followed by: 'With these prospects, the industry can plan ahead and invest with confidence.'

The forecasters were more reticent concerning the impact on farm incomes, the 1970 White Paper indicating only that: 'Farmers' net income would nevertheless [i.e. if we joined] be higher than it would otherwise have been, although its distribution, and so the gains and losses, would differ greatly between commodities, types of farm and areas of the country.' The 1971 version was: 'In the enlarged Community, British farmers generally can expect better overall returns for their product despite higher feed costs.'

The CAP and the UK Economy

The general consensus at the time of accession over the likely impact of the CAP on the UK leads one to wonder why there has been so much commotion over recent estimates of the net cost of the policy to the UK. Calculations by the Cambridge Economic Policy Group [3, 4, 5] seem to confirm that, by the end of the five-year transitional period to full integration with the CAP, the income transfer from the UK to other EC member states was about one per cent of national income. Similarly, consumer food prices were considerably higher than they would have been if the UK had continued to operate the previous deficiency payments system. In 1979 the *Annual Review of Agriculture* [11] indicated that the net product of the sector, valued at constant prices, was some 16 per cent higher in 1978 than the average for the five years immediately prior to membership. Reliable information on farm incomes is hard to come by, but the evidence suggests that, although farming has not experienced the bonanza many expected, nevertheless farm incomes have risen in real terms compared with their level immediately before entry (Ritson [23]).

Party politics in the UK excluded, there are three reasons why the impact of the CAP in the UK has re-emerged – but apparently as a fresh issue – in the late 1970s. First, during much of the transitional period climatic factors both in Britain and elsewhere produced effects that made the predicted results of adopting the CAP look wildly inaccurate. No sooner had the first transitional step towards higher food prices been made than a sharp rise in world wheat prices signalled the onset of the period that has become known as the 'world food crisis'. This caused a surge in prosperity for arable producers and a rapid rise in consumer food prices. Neither had anything to do with the CAP; nevertheless, in the first year of transition, market conditions in the UK were similar to those predicted as a consequence of full adoption of the policy (due to take place in 1978). Therefore, by the time of the 1975 referendum, the CAP no longer looked like the expensive price of British membership; rather it appeared to many to provide a secure supply of food in an uncertain world. Indeed, one study (Ashby *et al.* [2]) showed that in the first two years of membership prices to British food consumers were slightly lower as a consequence of the CAP than they would have been if Britain had retained its previous farm policy.

The government's response to the world food crisis was set out in the White Paper *Food From Our Own Resources* [10], which contained projections of the growth in output of the major farm products. As the White Paper was published before the referendum the assumption behind these projections – that UK farmers would receive full CAP prices by the end of the decade – could not be made explicit.

However, the weather intervened. Farm output fell by 12 per cent in 1975 and a further 9 per cent the following year. Net farm income, in real terms, fell back a little, and in 1976 the rapid depreciation of sterling was not carried through into rising farm product prices because under the system of Monetary Compensatory Amounts the green pound was kept at an artificial level; the UK did not, after all, seem to be closing the gap between the prices received by British and continental farmers. So the view developed in farming circles that, in terms of both output and incomes, the CAP was not having its predicted effects.

It was 1977 before the UK intervention price for wheat (rising) met the world wheat price (falling) and the CAP became really effective in supporting farm product prices in the UK. The food import bill was therefore now inflated because of taxes on imports from third countries and the higher cost of Community supplies rather than because of high world prices. In fact, the levies on third country food imports were then still credited to the UK Treasury, rather than transferred to Brussels, so the British economy received some benefit from the fall in world food prices, to the extent that it continued to import from third countries. It is also arguable that consumer food prices would not have been any lower in recent years in the absence of Community membership. The government would have been tempted to impose its own import levy system as world food prices declined (rather than allow the Exchequer cost of deficiency payments to rise), since it is much easier to take a policy action which prevents consumer food prices from declining than to take action which raises them.

The fall in world food prices also had its effect on the rest of the Community. The cost of surplus disposal has risen alarmingly over the past few years; and, as discussed in Wynne Godley's paper, so consequently has Britain's net contribution to the Community budget. (See also Whitby [28].) In short then, one reason for the sudden re-emergence of concern over the impact of the CAP on the

UK is that the predicted consequences took rather longer than expected to emerge, and for a time many believed the predictions to be inaccurate.

A second reason has probably been growing doubts over the economic and political benefits of membership. The considerations for the debate on agriculture are, presumably, as follows. If one per cent of national income as a contribution to the CAP is regarded as an annual membership fee (and the fee remains at one per cent) then it represents good value for money if Britain achieves a better economic performance because of membership. After all, it is only necessary for the UK growth rate to be one per cent higher in *one* year to cover the annual fee in succeeding years. But if the economic benefits fail to materialize, the fee comes into prominence again and probably gives rise to concern lest, in itself, it is contributing to the nation's economic problems via various secondary effects. (This at least was the contention of the second Cambridge Economic Policy Group article [4], in which an estimated direct cost to the UK balance of payments due to EEC membership of £1,000 million per annum is converted into a UK national income loss of £3,000 million via the multiplier process, under the assumption of a balance of payments constraint on the level of activity in the economy.)

The third and possibly most important reason for the present debate on Britain and the CAP has been the development of Europe's green money system. At the time of accession it was assumed that the UK would be able to influence farm product prices only as one voice among the other eight on decisions over common prices and in discussions over (hoped for) reform of the policy. The latter would be a lengthy process and in the medium term there seemed very little that could be done about the cost of the policy to the UK, a net food importer. The only thing seemed to be, therefore, to accept the inevitable and try to think about something else. However, the green money system has in fact given countries considerable freedom over the choice of their domestic farm product price levels, and, perhaps more significantly, the price (in foreign exchange) which they receive for exports and pay for imports. As a consequence, the impact of the CAP on the UK is influenced both by the British government's green pound policy, and also by the attitude taken by other member states to their own national price levels. (For example since a decision by – say – the Irish government to devalue its green rate and raise Irish prices increases the cost of disposal of surplus dairy products, part of which must be financed by the UK.) Since the present conference is specifically concerned with the British interest in the European Community, and in particular with the various strategic choices available to British policy makers, in the context of agriculture, some discussion of the country's green pound policy seems inevitable.

The green pound

Virtually all governments now regard it as necessary to control agricultural prices. For the economically advanced countries this has typically meant ensuring that domestic farmers receive prices in excess of those at which produce is traded internationally. In the UK this was previously achieved via the system of guaranteed prices and deficiency payments, with prices to consumers determined mainly by international prices. Under the CAP, prices are controlled by a mixture of minimum import prices supported by import taxes, and intervention prices supported by intervention buying and export subsidies. The CAP therefore, in effect 'guarantees' the intervention price in the case of surplus products, and anything up to the minimum import price for products in which the Community is a net importer.

When the CAP is examined from a national perspective, however, and particularly from a farmer's viewpoint, what is peculiar about it as an agricultural policy is that the price guarantee is given in foreign currency. With fixed exchange rates, this is of no consequence; but with fluctuating rates, support prices should, in theory, always move in response to variations in the country's exchange rate. Since one of the main objectives of government intervention in agricultural markets is to stabilize prices, it is not surprising that member states have refused to accept the implications for domestic agricultural markets of currency instability, and that administered prices under the CAP have continued to be converted from units of account into national currencies at historic market exchange rates, called representative or 'green' rates. This has resulted in a divergence of agricultural price levels between member states, and a complicated system of border taxes and subsidies – called Monetary Compensatory Amounts (MCAs) – has been required to sustain the differences in prices. (The relationship between the green pound and the UK interest is discussed in detail in two Centre for Agricultural Strategy papers [18, 25] and analysed more formally in two articles in the *Journal of Agricultural Economics* [20, 22].)

If it had been simply a matter of fluctuating exchange rates, however, Europe's green money system would never have become such a controversial topic. The problems stem from the fact that member states' exchange rates have tended to diverge (mainly because of differences in rates of inflation). Two issues have developed from this.

First, green rates have been used, not so much to stabilize prices as to delay and ease adjustments to new levels of farm product prices. Looking at this from the point of view of the UK without the green pound, we see that the rapid appreciation of sterling would have involved much more rapid rises in farm product (and food) prices than is implied in other sectors. The green pound was, therefore, a justified – indeed necessary – policy instrument during periods of sterling depreciation. Equally, however, if the green pound is used to hold farm product prices constant in the UK indefinitely, domestic farming suffers relative to other sectors, since costs will be rising. Few, therefore, are likely to argue seriously that, during a sustained period of sterling depreciation, no devaluations of the green pound are justified. But inevitably there has been much disagreement about when and by how much the green pound should be devalued and much confusion over the rights and wrongs of MCAs paid on farm product exports from other member states to the UK.

Second, and following from that, the green money system has given member states (at least in the medium term) the opportunity to control their domestic farm product prices at different levels, simply by delaying green rate changes (and refusing to agree to the Commission's proposal for automatic phasing-out of MCAs). It is argued elsewhere (Heidhues *et al.* [12], Ritson and Tangermann [24]) that, in as much as governments control farm product prices in order to maintain farm prosperity, one would expect different member states to experience different pressures over the degree to which farm product prices should be supported.

In particular, the lower the average size of farm and the higher the incomes of the non-farming population, the greater the pressure on governments to raise farm prices. On this basis one might expect the UK to aim for a rather lower level of farm product prices (given the resulting benefit to consumers) than other member states, because of its good farm structure and relatively low non-farm incomes. It is probably for this reason that the debate over government green pound policy has been as much about the national interest as about farm incomes and farm output. As such, it is really no more than the latest chapter in a continuing debate over the role of agriculture in the national economy, and it has embraced wholeheartedly the traditional confusion between the impact of a change in agricultural policy on the balance of payments and its impact on the country's real national income.

'If over a period of time a country spends more than it earns then at some other period it must earn more than it spends in order to correct the situation' (Josling [13]). Thus any method of reducing a balance of payments deficit, that is, anything which 'contributes to the balance of payments' bears a cost in the form of exported products or reduced imports which could otherwise have been consumed; or in the case of UK agricultural expansion imports are replaced, but extra resources are used in domestic agriculture which could otherwise have produced something else.

However, correcting a balance of payments deficit may have secondary effects in restraining growth in national income. In these circumstances a country can be said to have a 'balance of payments constraint' on expansion to attain full employment. If it is then possible to take a policy action which aids the balance of payments, but does not have undesirable effects on the level of general activity in the economy, then that action might be said to increase national income as it allows expansion of the economy, which would not otherwise be possible. (Similarly, something which bears a balance of payments cost may be said to depress national income.) If there has ever been a case for agricultural expansion to aid the balance of payments then these are its grounds: that expansion of agriculture, saving imports, is free from the depressing effect on investment and employment associated with general deflationary policies, and from the problem of imported inflation associated with currency depreciation. Just why agricultural expansion as a mechanism for contributing to the balance of payments should be so problem-free has never been made clear by its exponents.

It was always accepted that British adoption of the Common Agricultural Policy, by raising prices to British farmers, would be likely to generate agricultural expansion and reduce imports. But in addition to the resource cost of expansion there was an additional cost to the UK. If a country chooses to increase domestic farm product prices by taxing imports, it retains the tax revenue. Under the CAP, UK farm product prices are raised, but many of our food imports are now bought at higher prices from other member states. Imports from third countries are taxed, but the levy revenue is paid into the Community budget. Furthermore, the UK has to contribute to subsidies paid on exports by other member states. It is this higher cost of food imports, together with the net contribution to the Community budget, that has come to be referred to as the 'balance of payments cost' of the CAP – estimated at between £300 and £400 million annually before accession and now thought to be about £1,000 million – much the same as predicted once inflation has been taken into account.

This cost can, however, be varied by changes in the green pound. A devaluation of the green pound raises prices in UK markets, but it also raises the price we pay for imports from the Community and it raises the tax on third country supplies. Conversely, if the green pound is held constant while the pound sterling depreciates, the gap between world food prices and the price at which Britain imports under the CAP declines. So the discussion over UK green pound policy involves precisely the same considerations as did the calculations over the cost to the economy of adopting the CAP.

Where, then, does this leave agriculture and the balance of payments? Clearly, it is vital to distinguish between balance of payments cost and balance of payments effect. Once the distinction is made, a number of conclusions follow. First, either adopting the CAP or devaluing the green pound looks like a poor method of trying to help the balance of payments, because of the balance of payments cost. If a country taxes imports, that will almost certainly help the balance of payments. But if those taxes are not retained, the response of domestic production to higher prices must be sufficient to offset this loss before a positive contribution to the balance of payments is made. In addition, this method of contributing to the balance of payments involves the extra cost associated with the income transfer to other member states of the Community.

Nevertheless, raising farm product prices may make a positive contribution to the balance of payments. This was indeed the prediction made by Josling [14] in 1971 when he estimated that the response of British agriculture to higher CAP prices would more than offset the impact of higher priced imports from EEC countries and the transfer of levy revenue to the Community budget. A year earlier he had estimated the net cost of the policy to the UK to be £365 million [13]. In other words, there is a balance of payments cost, but a positive balance of payments effect of adopting the CAP.

Similarly I have myself argued [22] that, although a devaluation of the green pound imposes a welfare loss on the economy (that is, increases the balance of payments cost) it is likely to make a positive contribution to the balance of payments. A recent National Farmers' Union study [19] concludes that a 12.5 per cent green pound devaluation would involve a total gain to the balance of payments of £354 million.

Previous research on UK agricultural expansion and the balance of payments would have left it at the point of estimating the balance of payments contribution, and sometimes the cost involved in attaining that contribution. However, the NFU study takes a second, controversial step; that is to convert the balance of payments contribution into a gain in real UK national income, via the multiplier process (of £420 million). There is a more complicated, but essentially similar MAFF study [29] which follows the same procedure. The rationale is that, during a period of less than full employment, UK agriculture can expand at no cost to the nation; similarly, induced secondary expansion can also be at no cost. Thus, because green pound devaluation increases the amount of money spent on domestically produced products, there is an increase in UK national income.

The weakness of this approach is that, if it is so easy to suck unemployed resources into productive use by a policy which increases domestic expenditure, why choose green pound devaluation as that policy, when this particular option involves increasing the income transfer from the UK to other member states (increase being occasioned by the higher cost of food imports and contribution to the Community budget)?

However, the paradox of one group of economists [4] arguing that the import price level imposed on the UK by the CAP depresses national income and others [19, 29] that it increases national income (which seems extravagant, even for economists) is now resolved. The Cambridge Economic Policy Group approach is to compare the position of the UK under the CAP with an alternative in which imports are obtained at lower world prices (and in which there is, of course, no UK contribution to the Community budget), but in which domestic farm product prices are supported by deficiency payments at their prevailing levels. UK farm output, and thus food imports, are the same under both alternatives and the balance of payments effect is the same as the balance of payments cost. The resulting negative balance of payments effect is then converted, via a multiplier process, into a larger national income loss.

The economists of the NFU and the Ministry of Agriculture, on the other hand, *are* concerned with the domestic farm product and food price changes which follow a green pound devaluation. In their analysis, therefore, imports contract by a sufficient amount for there to be a positive balance of payments effect, even though the rise in import prices involves a balance of payments cost. The positive balance of payments effect is then converted, via a multiplier process, into a larger UK national income gain.

Prospects for reform
From a UK perspective, there are really two kinds of reform of the Common Agricultural Policy: amendment of the policy so that it came closer to meeting the objectives set for it in the Treaty of Rome; and changes in the policy which would have the effect of reducing the cost to the UK attributable to the CAP. The distinction has not always been clear-cut in the UK because, generally speaking, the kind of amendment of the CAP which has typically been proposed would also tend to benefit the UK in the narrower sense.

There have been numerous plans for reform (see, for example [1, 6, 12, 15, 16, 17, 18, 21, 26, 27]) and most have involved, to a greater or less extent, a reduction in price support levels, together with compensation for small farmers by some form of direct income supplementation scheme. The major prizes would be relieving the Community of its high-cost marginal output; an end to the political embarrassment of surplus disposal; and better relations with agricultural exporting countries. There would be the subsidiary advantage that the transfer to agriculture could be distributed within the farming sector in a way more consistent with overall income distribution objectives (rather than most of the benefit going to the prosperous larger farmers).

The problem with this approach, which might be termed a

'traditional' economic analysis of the CAP, is that it assumes an unrealistic degree of economic and political union. The excessive level of price support, and the failure to implement desirable reform proposals, have been attributed to the strength of the farm vote and the tendency for decisions over CAP prices to be taken by agriculture ministers cast adrift from their national ministerial colleagues. However, I am increasingly coming round to the view that the CAP cannot be analysed in the same way as any other agricultural policy – that is, in terms of the use of alternative policy mechanisms to attain objectives of farm income support, improved farm productivity, and so on – because, from the point of view of each member state, one of the most significant impacts of the CAP is that it induces transfers of income between member states.

This has always been recognized in the UK – it is the balance of payments cost mentioned in the previous section – but it has assumed a Community-wide significance with the development of the MCA system, which gives member states considerable freedom over their national price levels; and a change in a country's price level alters the cost or benefit to it of the CAP. In essence, the net exporting country is able to sell its export surplus at the same price level it obtains for its domestic market; commonly financed subsidies, either in the form of MCAs or restitutions on exports to third countries, ensure that this happens. Conversely, the net importing country must pay for its imports whatever price applies to its domestic market.

Table 5.1   Percentage of EAGGF expenditure taken by different commodity sectors in 1978

Cereals (including rice)	12.4
Milk and other dairy products	44.6
Oils and fats	3.6
Sugar	9.8
Beef and veal	7.1
Fruit and vegetables	1.1
Tobacco	2.4
Other products	5.1
MCAs	10.1
Guidance section	3.6

Source: Based on J. M. C. Rollo and K. S. Warwick, *The CAP and Resource Flows among EEC Member States*, London, MAFF, 1979, Table I.

If countries were able to ignore the internal consequences of variations in farm product and food prices the best strategy for the net exporting country would be to eliminate any negative MCAs (and keep any positive ones). Its approach to increases in common prices would depend on whether, as an exporter, it was weighty enough for its own gain from a rise in prices to outweigh its increased budgetary contribution. Conversely, the net importing country would attempt to prevent price increases in other member states and would also try to reduce its national price level, by allowing negative MCAs to accumulate.

Can the Cost of the CAP be Reduced?

Against this background, then, what are the prospects for reducing the cost of UK membership by changes in the CAP, either as an alternative to, or in parallel with, direct action on the budget?

In 1978 about three-quarters of Community expenditure was taken by the CAP. Nearly half of that went on dairy products (Table 5.1). The dairy sector, with cereals and sugar following, was the most expensive mainly because of the surplus over domestic consumption in these products (Table 5.2) and the extent to which CAP support prices exceeded disposal values on world markets (Table 5.3). The main reason for Britain's net budget deficit is that very little of

Table 5.2   Self-sufficiency in certain agricultural products (EEC-9) 1976/7 (percentage)

Wheat	105
Sugar	123
Fresh vegetables	92
Fresh Fruit	78
Wine	102
Butter	107
Cheese	104
Milk powder	114
Eggs	100
Beef and veal	96
Pork	100
Poultry meat	105

Source: *Yearbook of Agricultural Statistics*, Eurostat, 1978

*Table 5.3 Prices of certain agricultural products in the
EEC as a percentage of world market prices 1977/8*

Wheat	216
Barley	206
Sugar	255
Beef	196
Pork	137
Butter	388
Milk powder	494
Oilseeds	153

Source: as Table 5.2.

expenditure on surplus products occurs in the UK. Reducing Community expenditure on dairy surpluses is therefore fundamental to reducing the adverse impact of the CAP on the UK.

Various possible ways of tackling the dairy problem are under discussion. From the UK's point of view the following questions need to be asked about them: Is the scheme administratively feasible? Will it significantly reduce the cost of the policy? If it will, does it involve adverse implications either for the economy of the UK or for its agriculture? Is there any prospect of other member states' agreeing to the scheme?

The most radical suggestion, involving not a reform of the policy mechanisms but a transfer of costs to national budgets (known as '*debudgetization*'), has come from France. This would certainly benefit the UK but has little else to commend it, and is therefore unlikely to attract wider support. It would be manifestly unfair, apportioning the blame for the cost of dairy support according to where produce happened to go into intervention (or from where it was exported), rather than according to where milk or butter was produced. And it would probably be unworkable, since member states would use every means open to them to pass the responsibility for dairy intervention to other countries. In any case, there really is no logic in singling out the dairy sector for abandoning the principle of Common Financial Responsibility.

The attraction of debudgetization for France derives from the realization that some reform of the dairy policy may soon be inevitable and this method would be preferable, as far as France is concerned, to a price cut. That is because much of France's export surplus in dairy products finds a market (or goes into intervention) in *other* member states. This, incidentally, again emphasizes the necessity, when considering member states' costs and benefits associated with the CAP, to include the inflated value of intra-community trade in agricultural products as well as budgetary flows. For example, another suggestion from France has been that Britain could reduce its contribution to the budget by importing less food from third countries (thus reducing import levies) and more from other member states. That is true, but the gain on the budget would be offset by a rise in Britain's food import bill.

Concerning reform of the CAP dairy policy itself, one suggestion which sometimes appears in UK literature – a 'return' to *deficiency payments* – should also be dismissed. Most milk produced in the Community finds an (unsubsidised) domestic market. Another way of looking at this is to say that by far the major part of support for the dairy sector is paid by Community consumers, and the budget only tops this up. Unfortunate though it may be, it is as well to recognize that any reform of the dairy policy must retain high consumer prices. If they were allowed to fall towards world market levels, either millions of small dairy farmers would be put out of business or a much greater amount of public finance than currently spent would be required.

This leads to the *co-responsibility levy*, which has the attraction of cutting producer prices but not consumer prices, thus retaining the support for the dairy sector which comes from consumers. From the UK's viewpoint a major difficulty with the co-responsibility levy is that it seems logical to apply it in a discriminatory manner, exempting small farmers but cutting prices for larger farmers – who would be more likely to respond by using less feeding stuffs and producing less milk. This would also mean discriminating against UK farmers, and a weakness of the approach of successive UK governments to the problem of dairy surpluses has been the view that UK milk production should continue to expand.

However, the main problem with the co-responsibility levy is that many believe it would be used, not to cut producer prices (and thus reduce the cost of surplus disposal), but as a new source of Community finance; that is, the levy would be offset by a rise in CAP support prices. Producers' prices would not fall (and nor would the cost of surplus disposal) but there would be a new source of finance that would in effect be a consumer dairy product tax.

A variant on the co-responsibility levy, suggested by myself, is for a much more substantial tax than hitherto proposed, together with a freeze on dairy product support prices. Producer prices would be cut by a sufficient amount to reduce significantly the cost of surplus disposal. However, the tax would yield considerable revenue which could be used to compensate farmers for the price cut. The revenue could be distributed in a variety of ways, preferably in lump sums per farmer, but in any case, in a way not related to current output (though it could be related to historic output) to maintain the disincentive to production of the price cut.

Production quotas for the milk sector have found little favour in the past. First, the administration of a system to limit milk production on the farm has generally been regarded as, at best, very costly and, at worst, impossible. Second, the freezing of production patterns that would result is regarded as the greatest possible departure from the concept of a common market. For both reasons, quotas have not to date received serious attention in the Commission. However, the apparent intractability of the dairy problem is causing some commentators to conclude that quotas may be the only possible answer to the problem of surpluses.

The first problem raised by a quota scheme would be how to negotiate a *low enough* quota. It really would be pointless for the Community to embark on a costly and complicated quota scheme if all it did was to restrict output to existing levels. What is required is to limit each dairy farmer to something like 80–85 per cent of previous deliveries to dairies. But it would be unrealistic to expect dairy farmers immediately to reduce milk production. If dairies were obliged to refuse milk in excess of quotas, the result would be a mixture of embarrassing scenes – as farmers poured milk down drains in front of TV cameras – and an erosion of consumer prices as 'illegal' milk found a domestic market. Under the scheme, therefore, dairies would have to accept milk in excess of individual quotas, but pay a (very much) lower price for it, related to its international disposal value. However, it may be useful to point out that the experience with sugar has not been encouraging, with full support given to output well in excess of domestic requirements. And in the case of sugar a quota system is much easier to operate, since the number of farmers who must contract with a processing factory in the locality is considerably smaller.

The introduction of a milk quota system should perhaps no longer be dismissed out of hand. But it is important to ensure that any system introduced does eliminate the milk surplus. The danger is that the Community might accept all the disadvantages associated with quotas and not gain the benefit of cutting the cost of surplus disposal.

There remains what is variously known as a 'prudent price policy', a 'rigorous price policy', and a '*price freeze*'. This approach has recently lost some of its popularity in the UK. There is doubt over the length of time that would be needed for a freeze to cut output, and whether in fact it could be expected to do any more than restrict the growth of output. This is partly based on the fact that recent increases in 'common' prices have been very modest – yet milk production has continued to expand. Two points should be made in this context. First, there is a tendency to see the problem of surpluses in quantity terms. In fact, it is the *cost* of surplus disposal that matters, not the existence of surpluses in themselves, and any development which narrows the gap between CAP intervention prices and disposal prices does reduce the cost of surpluses, whether or not it reduces the size of the surplus. Second, during the period in which the Agricultural Unit of Account was tied to the appreciating Deutsche Mark, restricting increases in common prices was not successful, since prices were fixed in an appreciating unit. This caused the automatic accumulation of negative MCAs in most member states, giving them freedom to raise national price levels independently by green rate devaluations. But there is a strong probability that the European Currency Unit will not appreciate in the same way. In 1980 a decision to increase unit of account prices by 1.5 per cent probably would not again mean an average increase in member state prices nearer to 10 per cent. It would still mean something more than 1.5 per cent, since there would still be some green rate devaluations. But it may not be long before we have a common price level at the bottom (rather than nearer the top) of the range of member state price levels, with few negative MCAs but more and larger positive ones.

What seems to emerge from this discussion of cutting the cost of UK membership by CAP reform is that no proposal will be acceptable. None is likely to cut the cost of the CAP without involving unacceptable consequences for UK agriculture; and none is likely to be considered seriously by other member states (precisely of course because it does benefit the UK without hurting British agriculture). What it is necessary to look for is a reform that does not depend on agreement. Herein lies the strength of the price freeze strategy. With high inflation rates a major *de facto* reform of the policy could occur by a prudent price policy. (No major reform of the CAP has ever been negotiated, but there has nevertheless been one major reform. This is the development of Europe's green money system, which occurred via a mixture of the Council's not appreciating what was being agreed, and simply not agreeing.) The point is that no country is likely to agree to a policy change which reduces the transfer benefits (or increased the transfer costs) it experiences under the CAP. But it is still necessary for nominal common price increases to require ministerial agreement, and, as mentioned above, the introduction of the EMS will very probably make a price freeze much more effective. This has already become apparent in the UK, where there is concern that a price freeze might also involve some restriction on UK prices, because of the reduced scope for the UK to give its own farmers price increases by green rate devaluations. The loss of this freedom has been ascribed to the strength of the pound, but it may very well also reflect the fact that common prices are no longer fixed in an appreciating unit.

Thus the optimum strategy is to continue to insist on a price freeze for surplus products and willingly to agree that member states should be allowed to compensate farmers for price cuts by *nationally financed* income compensation schemes. Indeed it should use this mechanism itself if the prosperity of UK agriculture is genuinely threatened, otherwise the resolve to freeze prices will be compromised by pressure from UK agriculture.

References

[1] Agostini, D. *et al.*, 'Wageningen memorandum on the reform of the European Community's Common Agricultural Policy', *European Review of Agricultural Economics*, vol. 1, no. 2, 1973.

[2] Ashby, A. *et al.*, *The CAP and the British Consumer*, London, Federal Trust for Education and Research, 1975.

[3] Cambridge Economic Policy Group, 'The cost of food and Britain's membership of the EEC', *Economic Policy Review*, no. 3, 1977.

[4] —, 'The direct costs to Britain of belonging to the EEC', *Economic Policy Review*, no. 4, 1978.

[5] —, 'Policies of the EEC', *Cambridge Economic Policy Review*, no. 5, 1979.

[6] Commission of the European Communities, 'Memorandum on the Reform of Agriculture in the European Community' (the Mansholt Plan), COM (68) 1000, Brussels, 1968.

[7] Confederation of British Industry, *Britain in Europe: a Second Industrial Appraisal*, London, CBI, 1970.

[8] Great Britain, Prime Minister, *Britain and the European Communities: an Economic Assessment*, Cmnd 4289, London, HMSO, 1970.

[9] — —, *The United Kingdom and the European Communities*, Cmnd 4715, London, HMSO, 1971.

[10] —, Ministry of Agriculture, Fisheries and Food, *Food From our Own Resources*, Cmnd 6020, London, HMSO, 1975.

[11] — —, *Annual Review of Agriculture*, Cmnd 7436, London, HMSO, 1979.

[12] Heidhues, T., Josling, T., Ritson, C. and Tangermann, S., *Common Prices and Europe's Farm Policy*, London, Trade Policy Research Centre, 1978.

[13] Josling, T., *Agriculture and Britain's Trade Policy Dilemma* London, Trade Policy Research Centre, 1970.

[14] —, 'The agricultural burden: a reappraisal' in J. Pinder, ed., *The Economics of Europe*, London, Charles Knight for Federal Trust for Education and Research, 1971.

[15] Koester, U. and Tangermann, S., 'Supplementing farm price policy by direct income payments', *European Review of Agricultural Economics*, vol. 4, no. 1, 1977.

[16] Marsh, J. (rapporteur), *A New Agricultural Policy for Europe*, London, Federal Trust for Education and Research, 1970.

[17] —, *UK Agricultural Policy within the European Community*, University of Reading, Centre for Agricultural Strategy, 1978.

[18] —, and Ritson C., *Agricultural Policy and the Common Market*, London, Chatham House/PEP, 1971.

[19] National Farmers' Union, 'The effects of a devaluation of the green pound on the gross domestic product', *NFU Insight*, no. 115, London, 1978.

[20] Peters, G. H., 'The green pound – a simplified expository analysis', *Journal of Agricultural Economics*, vol. 31, no. 1, 1980.

[21] Ritson, C., *A Proposal for the Reform of the Common Agricultural Policy*, London, European Movement, 1975.

[22] —, 'A note on the green pound and the balance of payments', *Journal of Agricultural Economics*, vol. XXIX, no. 3, 1978.

[23] —, 'Looking back to look forward' in *Farm Business Data*, University of Reading, Department of Agricultural Economics, 1979.

[24] —, and Tangermann, S., 'The economics and politics of monetary compensatory amounts', *European Review of Agricultural Economics*, vol. 6, no. 2, 1980.

[25] Swinbank, S., *The British Interest and the Green Pound*, University of Reading, Centre for Agricultural Strategy, 1978.

[26] Uri, P. (rapporteur), *A Future for European Agriculture*, Paris, The Atlantic Institute, 1970.

[27] Van Riemsdijk, J., 'A system of direct income compensation to farmers as a means of reconciling short term and long term interests', *European Review of Agricultural Economics*, vol. 1, no. 2, 1973.

[28] Whitby, M., ed., *The Net Cost and Benefit of EEC Membership*, Wye College, Kent, Centre for European Agricultural Studies, 1979.

[29] Wildgoose, J. and Dickinson, S., *A Framework for Assessing the Economic Effects of a Green Pound Devaluation*, Government Economic Service Working Paper no. 23, London, MAFF, 1979.

Comment
by Elizabeth Dakin

In any discussion of the impact of Community membership on the United Kingdom attention inevitably falls on the CAP – the Community's major common policy – and on the one aspect of British policy markedly altered by accession. Christopher Ritson is right to remind us that, at the time of accession, adoption of the CAP was expected to produce certain effects and that the outcome has been broadly as predicted, albeit delayed for a variety of reasons. The implication of his paper is that British interests can best be served on the one hand by seeking to modify the policy and on the other (as opportunity arises) by limiting its impact on British farm and food prices via manipulation of the value of the green pound.

I agree with much of his general argument. Where I differ is in looking to the future. I am perhaps a little more optimistic. My comments therefore are mainly an enlargement upon Christopher Ritson's paper and an attempt to place the CAP in perspective.

Although all member states share the same basic interests in securing adequate food supplies for their largely urban populations and maintaining acceptable living standards in their rural areas, there are several reasons why the priorities of each nation might differ and why agreement on a truly common policy is therefore difficult. Nevertheless, the reasons that originally prompted the founders of the Community to devise a common policy for this difficult area still hold good. Any attempt to abandon the CAP – an option that might appear attractive superficially to the UK – would be regarded as an extremely retrograde step and meet with strong resistance, not only from those committed to the current policy but also from many proponents of the European ideal.

If the Community is to become more than simply an industrial free-trade area then a common approach to farm policy is essential; without an agreed policy it seems almost inevitable that permanent and sometimes substantial tariff barriers against trade in certain farm produce would emerge as each member state sought to protect its own industry. The principal aim of the Community – free trade between its members – would be violated across a significant section of the Community's economy.

The contrasting historical traditions of British farm policy and the policies of most European countries inevitably meant that the adjustment to Community conditions required of the UK was substantial. The interests of Britain, a major net importer of food, had been well served in the past by supplies obtained at a relatively low cost from the world market (in many instances from Commonwealth suppliers) and use of the deficiency payments system to promote domestic agriculture. This arrangement clearly had advantages, but is it an option for the future? In respect of most agricultural products, this system does not lend itself to Community conditions, where markets are generally well supplied and the number of individual producers enormous. The basic system adopted by the Community is much more suited to the needs of the majority of its members.

It is arguable that even if the UK had remained outside the Community British agricultural policy would in fact incorporate certain – obviously not all – aspects of the CAP. Indeed, Christopher Ritson suggests that after the world commodity boom in the early 1970s governments in the UK would have been reluctant to let import prices fall back to their previous levels and that import levies would probably have been imposed in order to contain the cost to the government of farm support. I support this view. I therefore suggest that the main impact of the CAP on Britain is not really to be found in any comparison of farm and food prices in the UK and other parts of the world or in examining past and present policy mechanisms, but in the effect on the balance of payments of transferring to Brussels the revenue derived from agricultural levies together with the additional revenue required to fund the CAP.

The expansion of British agriculture can reasonably be expected to have offset the adverse balance of payments effects caused by the transfer of levy receipts to the Community budget. However, the much larger financial requirements of the CAP pose a difficult problem, dealt with elsewhere in this volume. Presumably at the time of accession to the Community it was thought that transfers of the current order were an acceptable cost of membership. It is becoming increasingly apparent that this is no longer true. Assuming therefore that a common policy for agriculture is to continue – and that seems a realistic assumption – then British interests can best be served by seeking constructively to reduce the cost of operating the policy either in total or with respect to British liabilities.

In looking to the future Christopher Ritson points to the divergence of national interests as an obstacle to change and draws particular attention to the importance of the financial transfers brought about by the CAP. But there is one important development that may substantially alter the situation. This stems from the mounting cost of the CAP and the real danger that the ceiling of available resources will be reached by 1982 and possibly sooner. Those countries currently gaining most from the CAP stand to lose most from any limit to the funds available for the policy. There is therefore a possibility that the current tendency for agricultural decisions to be relatively unaffected by Community financial considerations will end.

At present farm price support is the only area of EEC activity financed entirely from the Community budget; all other policies require an element of national financial involvement. One way of overcoming the current financial restrictions would be to introduce an element of national financing into CAP price guarantee operations. This would have obvious advantages for improving decision making, and, by reducing the demands made on the Community budget for agriculture, might also help to reduce Britain's net budgetary liabilities. In the longer term more funds would be available for other purposes, enabling the UK to benefit in a way that is very unlikely to be realized so long as farm spending dominates the Community budget.

There is therefore a real opportunity for a shift in the traditional pressures on the CAP. Prudent pricing decisions seem more likely than at any time in recent years. At a time of significant inflation throughout the Community such decisions must be expected to curtail production and avoid further inroads into consumption, and thereby contribute to an improvement in market balances. As Christopher

Ritson says, a 'major *de facto* reform' of the CAP could eventually occur. Furthermore, should attempts to stabilize European currencies succeed, then the extent to which any member state can mitigate the effects of price restraint by green currency adjustments will be greatly reduced. The impact of common pricing decisions would become more significant.

Pricing decisions are important, but price manipulation alone is unlikely to solve all the Community's farm problems. In particular it is unlikely to resolve the CAP's most pressing problem – the dairy surplus – within an acceptable time scale. Yet while this problem persists the drain on Britain's balance of payments caused by the CAP is unlikely to be moderated substantially. Additional measures will be necessary to tackle this problem; these should include efforts both to boost consumption and to encourage contraction of the dairy industry. Only by reducing the number of productive cows in Europe can a balance between supply and demand be restored.

No comment concerning Britain and the CAP would be complete without reference to the green pound. I have chosen to leave this subject until last, not because I regard it as the most important item but because I believe that it is much more appropriate to consider Britain's approach to a common farm policy in the future than to concentrate on a mechanism essentially designed to avoid a common policy. Moreover, in present circumstances the scope for 'using' this particular instrument as anything but a very temporary expedient (in fact allowing it the role it was originally intended to have) is very limited. While the strength of sterling continues to be unrelated to Britain's economic performance the inflation of farm costs in the UK relative to other parts of the Community will be such as to ensure that the agricultural case for a green pound adjustment will allow little scope for the green exchange rate to differ from the market exchange rate.

The debate on the economics of the green pound, a debate prompted by the emergence of a very large 'green pound gap', is interesting. However, in the absence of a great deal of empirical evidence, views on the dynamic and longer-term effects of a devaluation almost inevitably differ. At present, it seems that the best available evidence confirms the view that a green pound adjustment serves to improve the balance of payments and that in the longer term, while resources remain under-utilized in other sectors of the economy, it is able to promote the growth of national income. In his discussion of the green pound Christopher Ritson says that this instrument would be a poor way of improving the balance of payments. There may well be more effective ways of boosting the balance of payments, but the case for a devaluation is unlikely to be based on balance of payments considerations alone. Clearly the agricultural and so-called 'equity' reasons favouring a devaluation would provide the main justification. However, the overall case is obviously strengthened if wider benefits for Britain's economy can be identified.

6 British Industrial Regeneration: the European Dimension

by Daniel T. Jones*

Introduction

It is appropriate that the present investigation should include a consideration of industrial policy, for it was in this area, by the establishment of the European Coal and Steel Community in 1951, that the first practical steps were taken towards the creation of an institutionalized European Community. Since then, however, progress in developing industrial policies at a multinational level has been somewhat slow, not only because national governments have been unwilling to relinquish what control they have over their domestic industry but also because of the considerable uncertainty about what the aims of a Community policy should be. Greater success was achieved in the area of commercial policy, with the elimination of trade barriers in the successive GATT rounds and the creation of a tariff-free zone in the EEC. It was only after the historically unprecedented period of economic growth in the 1950s and 1960s came to an end that the issues of industrial policy assumed a higher place on the agenda of international discussions.

From Britain's point of view this is an area of critical importance. An ever-widening gap between British economic, and particularly

* This paper was written in the context of a larger research project of the Sussex European Research Centre into government intervention and structural adjustment in European industry, funded by the Volkswagen Foundation and the Anglo-German Foundation for the Study of Industrial Society. I am grateful for the useful comments on an earlier draft from colleagues at the University of Sussex, particularly Christopher Saunders, Lesley Cook, and Giovanni Dosi, and from the editor of this volume. However, the author alone is responsible for the views expressed here.

industrial, performance and that of the other members of the EEC will continue to place British membership in question. From the Community's point of view this divergent performance is making the pursuit of common policies increasingly difficult. In order to assess the strategic choices open to British policy makers in the field of industrial policy it is necessary to arrive at a diagnosis of the problems underlying Britain's poor performance. In a short contribution this can be done only in summary form. Before discussing the alternative strategies open to Britain in the industrial policy area we review the experience to date of industrial policy in Britain and the Community.

British Industrial Performance

It is increasingly being recognized, or more accurately we are again becoming aware, that the roots of Britain's poor industrial performance go back a long way in time and are deeply engrained in British attitudes and institutions. The greater awareness arises not so much from comparisons of recent performance with past British performance but from comparisons with our major industrial competitors, particularly in western Europe.

One of the most useful indicators of relative industrial efficiency is labour productivity. The accompanying chart, which refers to the whole economy and not just to the industrial sector, shows in a quite dramatic way not only the emergence of a substantial difference in levels of productivity between Britain and her European partners in recent years, but also that the slower rate of growth of productivity in Britain is not by any means a recent feature; indeed in relation to her main competitor, Germany, it has been apparent for at least

Sources: Base period estimates of relative GDP *per capita* in 1970 at purchasing power parities obtained from Irving B. Kravis *et al.*, *International Comparisons of Real Product and Purchasing Power* (Baltimore, Johns Hopkins University Press, 1978), p. 10, adjusted to GDP per person employed using *OECD Labour Force Statistics* 1965–76. Extrapolations to 1959 and 1978 using series from OECD and national sources; for years between 1913 and 1959 using the growth rates in Deborah C. Paige *et al.*, 'Economic growth: the last hundred years', *National Institute Economic Review*, no. 16 (July 1961), pp. 37 and 48–9; and from 1870 to 1913 the series in Angus Maddison, *Economic Growth in the West* (London, George Allen and Unwin, 1964), p. 231, and Kazushi Ohkawa, *The Growth Rate of the Japanese Economy since 1878* (Tokyo, Kinokuniya, 1957), p. 250.

Gross domestic product 1870–1978 (UK 1970 = 100)

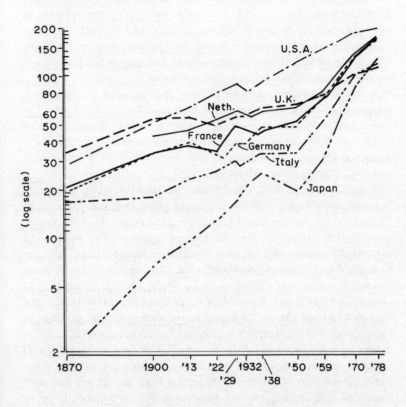

Notes: (i) The series throughout has been adjusted for territorial changes; Germany has been treated as though, after 1925, it comprised the territory of the present Federal Republic.

(ii) No unemployment statistics are available for the Netherlands before 1900; the same is true of France, Italy, and Japan before 1950 and in these cases statistics of the labour force were used instead, which means that pre-1950 cyclical variations may be somewhat understated.

(iii) The extent of the depression is indicated, subject to (ii) above, by the choice of trough years in each country; otherwise the same years were chosen, except for the USA and Germany in 1871, Japan in 1878, and Germany in 1925.

a century. In terms of productivity in manufacturing industry Germany was about to, or did, overtake the UK in 1913 and again in the mid-1930s, before decisively doing so in the early 1950s. In 1976 West Germany, France, and the Benelux countries produced over 70 per cent more per employee in industry than the UK, and Italy some 15 per cent more. On present trends Britain may even be overtaken by some of the new entrants from southern Europe, particularly Spain, in a few years' time. I have shown elsewhere (Jones [6] and [7]) that this divergence took place during a period when British output and productivity growth were both high by historical standards. The only other period of above-average output growth in Britain, between 1932 and 1938, was not accompanied by above-average productivity growth, and even then it was almost entirely accounted for by a small number of progressive industries alone.

A similar picture is obtained if one considers the relative shares of manufactured exports of the main industrial countries of western Europe, North America, and Japan. While Germany has consistently accounted for between one-fifth and one-quarter of manufactured exports throughout this century and France has recovered her pre-first world war share of one-eighth in the last decade, the UK share has fallen continuously from one-third at the turn of the century to under one-tenth now. Of course in the postwar period the most rapid change has been the rise of Japan to the second largest exporter of manufactures in the world. Not only has Britain been less successful in exporting manufactured goods but the technological sophistication of the goods she does export has been falling seriously behind that of her main competitors. Christopher Saunders [14] has shown that unit values of engineering exports were broadly comparable between France, Germany, and the UK in the early 1960s, whereas by 1975 German and French unit values were about 60 per cent and 40 per cent higher respectively. Perhaps not surprisingly these developments have given rise to a chronic and worsening visible balance of trade.

Issues Facing British Industrial Policy Makers
Although the symptoms of these particularly British problems first emerged and were widely discussed in the period leading up to the first world war they did not do so again with such force until the mid- or late 1960s, when Britain was again exposed to the full force

of international competition. In the meantime Britain and her main export markets in the empire were protected by high tariff barriers. Germany on the other hand was more severely affected by both world wars and by the interwar depression, and has throughout this century sold more than two-thirds of her exports in highly competitive markets in Europe. Britain's traditional export pattern, in which two-thirds of her exports went to mainly empire markets outside Europe, survived almost intact until well into the 1960s; indeed it was only in 1973 that for the first time more than half her exports went to western and eastern Europe. This concentration on less competitive and slower-growing export markets had the unfortunate consequence that Britain was slow to follow Germany's lead in developing new industries such as advanced chemicals, electricity generation, and advanced machinery and to move resources from declining to more advanced sectors.

While the long-term trends were fairly clear it is perhaps understandable that a certain sense of false confidence pervaded British thinking in the early 1960s. At that time the gap between British and European industrial performance in terms of productivity levels and product sophistication etc. had not yet appeared. The experience of the subsequent two decades was a harsh lesson in the realities of how far behind we have fallen. The great danger is that this relative decline may well turn into an absolute decline. A period of world recession will not only make the necessary structural adjustment more painful but will also further delay the response of British industry.

It must clearly be the objective of any set of industrial policies to halt this relative decline and begin the process of catching up with our European partners. To do so will mean tackling some of the fundamental characteristics of the British economy that have been at the root of this relative decline. Over such a long period it is difficult to assess the extent to which particular factors are a cause or are themselves the symptoms of poor performance. Nevertheless four main points seem to emerge time and time again in the numerous studies of the British disease over the last century or so: namely technical innovation; education and training; management and industrial relations; and the inter-relationships between firms and between industry, the banks, and government. Some of the most useful of these studies are Marshall [10], Hobsbawm [4], Landes [9], Barnett [2], and Allen [1].

Although Britain has always had a high reputation for the quality of its scientists it has not been renowned for its success in translating scientific and technological advances into marketable products. Despite relatively high spending on research and development much of it was not directed to the bread-and-butter industries of international trade, namely mechanical and electrical engineering and consumer durables. Christopher Freeman [3] has recently summarized a major study edited by Keith Pavitt [12] confirming the importance of the link between resources devoted to technological effort and success in export markets. Marketing has traditionally had a low priority in Britain and consequently less attention was paid to developing products to suit identified market needs.

The second characteristic of British industry is the lack of appreciation of, and hence demand for, technical and managerial education and industrial training generally. This does not apply only at the managerial level, where, on the continent, a much higher proportion of senior management has received a thorough training at a technical university, not available in this country. It also applies at the shop-floor level where in continental industry the acquisition of skills is associated with achieving a monitored standard and not simply (as in Britain) with serving time. Furthermore, the extensive provision of vocational training for 16–18 year olds, which has existed for more than a century in parts of Germany and elsewhere in Europe, again has no counterpart in this country. Though some progress has been made in recent decades attempts to adopt some of these features in Britain have had little success in the face of indifference from industry and the educational establishment.

The interaction of poor management and a hostile and fragmented trade union structure is responsible not only for chaotic industrial relations in Britain but also, even where apparent peace reigns, for a deeply entrenched inefficiency. The failure to arrive at a more cooperative system for reconciling differences not only hampers the introduction and full exploitation of new technologies but leads also to greater unpredictability in management decision making. Recent studies by Smith *et al.* [15], Jones and Prais [8], and Prais [13] have also shown that the problems are concentrated in a few industries, such as steel and motor vehicles, with the result that economies of scale are not fully exploited and that the government has been forced to intervene to try to save the situation.

The final area of inter-firm relationships and the relationships between firms, banks, and governments is complex. We have already noted that close attention to user needs is crucially important in developing the right product. This is greatly facilitated by close co-operation between the customer firm and the supplying firm. Germany and more recently Japan have had a tradition of such co-operation, greatly reinforced by the more direct involvement of the banks in Germany and by the inter-company links within Japanese industrial groupings, such as Mitsubishi, supported by the Japanese government through the Ministry of International Trade and Industry. Such direct collaboration is not characteristic in this country, where the trading mentality of buying in the cheapest market still pervades business thinking. An exception is probably the close involvement of Marks & Spencer management in the running of their supplying companies in the clothing industry in Britain. Not only do such links give more weight to non-price factors in product design and marketing; they also increase the incentive to purchase important inputs in the domestic market. French government intervention has sought to promote such links for precisely these reasons.

With the more direct involvement of German banks in the strategic decision making of German firms through their own and proxy share-holdings and by membership of the boards of most large companies and the existence of powerful industrial associations circulating in-formation and forecasts between members it is much easier to develop a consensus within an industry on the appropriate solutions to problems facing that industry. This system operates as an extremely efficient substitute for a planning process involving government. In the absence of such institutions or attitudes many of the efforts devoted to industrial policy in France and Britain since the second world war have been in trying to create a substitute for these methods of developing an industrial consensus. The early phase of French plan-ning was fairly successful in doing so. As we shall see below, British industrial policy was not.

Changes in the International Context

It now seems unlikely that we shall see a return to the historically unprecedented economic growth of the first twenty-five years after World War II. Moreover it is also likely that the 1980s will see a further shift in the focus of economic growth away from western Europe to the newly industrializing countries of southern Europe, Latin America, and southeast Asia. Because of its position at the lower end of the product sophistication spectrum, i.e. increasingly producing more mature products where price rather than non-price factors are important, Britain is likely to be one of the countries most severely affected by competition from the newly industrializing countries.

Another development with profound implications for relative competitiveness is the extent and speed of the diffusion of recent advances in electronics technology throughout the rest of industry. The most successful countries in advanced products will be those with a strong and innovative electronics industry closely linked to downstream user industries, particularly the capital goods and consumer durables industries. With strong government support Japan has invested massively in electronics technology, with the specific objective of overtaking the US, and appears to be succeeding. Japanese dynamism is such that she may well become the pace setter, closely followed by the US and Germany, in advanced technology products. Technological innovation, directly combined with close identification of (initially domestic) customer needs in the manner discussed above, will undoubtedly play a greater part in determining export success. Ensuring that sufficient resources are allocated to technological development and creating the environment where such advances can be fully exploited will be a prime task of industry and industrial policy makers.

Britain is in the awkward position of being left behind by the technological leaders in more advanced products while at the same time facing growing competition from the newly industrializing countries in more mature, price-sensitive products. These two developments will, one way or another, call for greater structural transformation of British industry than in the past. Reversing this traditional weakness of British industry will be all the more difficult in a period of slower growth, rising economic and social demands of the workforce, and continuing inflation. Up to now it can hardly be said that British industry has shown itself capable of an adequate spontaneous response.

Experience and Options in British Industrial Policy

From the above diagnosis of the problems of British industry it is clear that the focus of attention is what Svennilson [16] calls the process of transformation of the industrial structure, which is an essential accompaniment to the process of economic growth. Transformation involves the introduction of new products and new production methods that use different input combinations and human skills, a redistribution of resources from one industry to another, and the adaptation to changing trade patterns. Policies to promote transformation therefore include policies such as those to improve engineering education and industrial training which have a longer time horizon, as well as the more conventional direct measures to intervene in particular industries or enterprises in order to gain a more immediate impact. Both are essential components of a supply-side policy relating to industry.

Because of the poor industrial performance of the British economy it is not surprising that direct intervention has been mainly concerned with rescuing firms or industries in difficulties. A recent, thorough study of direct intervention in industry in Britain by Peter Mottershead [11] concluded on a very pessimistic note by suggesting that 'increased intervention has ... made little contribution to improving our economic performance' and that it had been particularly unsuccessful in rescue cases. In assessing the success of such measures one has to ask what the consequences would have been of accepting the verdict of the market and not taking any action.

Most of the rescue cases involved firms, sometimes synonymous with the domestic industry or a large part of it, in highly oligopolistic markets. The essence of competition between oligopolies producing similar products involves staying in the market. In this case markets do not provide a long enough view, and mistaken strategic decisions raise the possibility of industries' being eliminated with little chance of re-entering the market later because of the high cost of entry. This is complicated by the long gestation period in designing an aero engine or car model, for example; the consequences of wrong decisions become evident only much later, by which time the situation may have compounded itself. It is at this stage that the government has to decide whether it can save the firm and bring about an improvement by offering a breathing space in the form of subsidies, protection, etc., or whether improvement is no longer possible. This involves a massive exercise of judgement on the part of the government. This judgement is both on the ability of the management to reverse one or more wrong strategic decisions and effect the necessary improvement and also on the longer-term prospects for the firm after such an improvement.

With hindsight it seems clear that successive British governments have seriously misjudged both the long-term prospects and the managerial ability to effect changes in many British industries. The reader should refer to Mottershead's study for a detailed survey of the record in this respect. The government and industry also failed to see that other countries were moving ahead so fast. The slower growth of the British economy and the underlying structural weaknesses outlined above meant that once the government became involved in a particular sector it soon found itself in a situation where it had bitten off more than it could chew. This is perhaps best characterized by the slow and painful decline of British Leyland and more recently the rescue of Chrysler UK against the advice of its own experts. Not all the halving of British Leyland's share of the domestic car market can be laid at the door of the government, though the delay in carrying out the necessary restructuring of the company until it is almost too late must be. Other direct interventions in industries such as steel and shipbuilding or companies such as Alfred Herbert, the machine tool producer, have involved ever-increasing government intervention and eventually also nationalization.

In a number of these cases the strategy to improve the performance of a company was positively frustrated by government interference to prevent the closure of obsolescent plant. The conflict between short-term employment and longer-term efficiency objectives was usually resolved in favour of the former, placing the continued survival of the firm in greater jeopardy.

The British government, like many others, has also been concerned to promote industries with more favourable prospects. It has done so in three ways, by assisting mergers in key sectors to achieve greater economies of scale and maintain domestic ownership, by direct support for technological innovation, and through the purchasing policy of the nationalized industries and government departments. Probably the most successful case, by European standards of comparison, involving all three is that of International Computers (ICL), though even here this has involved continued government support. The most expensive failure is undoubtedly Concorde, developed at the cost of well over £2 billion, shared equally between the British and French governments. The promotion of advanced technology involves critical decisions about the risks of failure, the existence of future markets, and the capacity of the domestic industry to develop, produce, and market new products successfully. British governments have shown a predilection to support large, very technologically advanced projects, such as nuclear power plant and aerospace projects for which almost no export market materialized, a possible exception being the RB211 aero engine. Where the government attempted to promote technological innovation of a less grandiose kind in the engineering industry, such as the promotion of numerically controlled machine tools, these results were disappointing because of the weakness of the rest of the engineering industry in taking up these tools in the required volume.

The first major reason for the poor record of direct government intervention in British industry has been that, to quote the Mottershead study, industrial policies have been 'limited to a peripheral role of tidying up at the edges of the economy, rather than providing any central thrust ... to improve industry's performance and that of the economy as a whole'. There has been no coherence or common purpose behind industrial policy. Moreover there has been little continuity of approach or institutions under successive governments – a lack that has increased the mistrust and uncertainty with which private industry regarded industrial policy making. The second factor derives from the prevailing attitudes of the Civil Service towards industrial issues. The strong non-discriminatory predilection of the British Civil Service, plus the lack of an interchange of staff at all levels between ministries and industry, has meant that civil servants have proved ill-suited to judge the merits of particular rescue cases and therefore to act selectively and effectively. The third set of factors derives from the inadequate links between private industry and industrial policy makers. It is not only the degree of such contacts but the quality and context in which they take place that is important. We have already discussed above and elsewhere (Jones [7]) how the creation of an industrial consensus in Germany and the close relationships between industry and government in France and Japan greatly facilitate resolving the same issues that face policy makers in this country.

What is obviously needed in Britain is a turn-around in industrial performance and attitudes of the kind that was achieved in France after 1946, for which the planning process initiated by Jean Monnet was largely responsible. In Britain, however, prevailing attitudes do not favour further experiments in general planning. We must find other methods of achieving this objective.

The most recent experiment, the Labour government's Industrial Strategy exercise, begun in 1975, has not provided the answer. Focused around the sector working parties of NEDO, it has been primarily an attempt to obtain a greater recognition that serious problems exist in many sectors and to gain trade union backing for increased productivity and rationalization schemes. As such, it has achieved a limited degree of success, diffused over a wide range of sectors. However, it has not been an attempt to select key sectors for particular government support, i.e. picking winners, and has not involved the appropriate senior management involved in strategic decision making that would be necessary for such an exercise.

We have already argued that any reversal of British industrial performance involves tackling the deep-seated problems outlined earlier. This often engenders a great sense of pessimism among observers and practitioners of industrial policy in Britain. However, I would argue that the task is far from being impossible and all the more urgent because of its delayed impact. Moreover there are signs that the awareness of, rather than disbelief in, the seriousness of the problems facing British industry has now gained widespread acceptance by the population at large, which is an essential prerequisite for movement on these issues.

There are three ways in which the British government could try, and to an extent is trying, to influence the technological capability of industry; by promoting the development and diffusion of the current heartland technology, i.e. micro-electronics; by ensuring that sufficient electronics engineers are trained; and by promoting a greater awareness of the importance of this and other technologies throughout industry. To be effective this must lead to a change of attitudes within industry towards new technology. On improving education and training the Finniston Committee may result in improvements in the quality and status of professional engineers. Action is now required on the provision of post-school vocational training for the bulk of the work force, i.e. carrying out the one area of the 1944 Education Act that was never implemented.

At the time of writing, in November 1979, various developments suggest that the entrenched inefficiency resulting from the stalemate – or social bargain struck between weak management and intransigent trade unions – is beginning to break. A combination of increased awareness tinged with resignation, intensified competitive pressures, and a new government less prepared to underwrite massive losses is responsible for this change. Whether the aggressiveness on the part of British Leyland and British Steel in finally carrying out long-awaited restructuring is successful and leads to a re-definition of this social bargain remains to be seen.

Serious thought also needs to be devoted to how the framework of relationships between government, banks and industry, i.e. the process of reaching an industrial consensus, could be improved in the respects discussed above. For a number of reasons it is unlikely that a system for resolving mistaken strategic decisions and supporting the longer-term strategies of particular companies could be developed that functions effectively with minimal government intervention, as it has in Germany. Overcoming the reluctance of British banks, and more so the pension funds and insurance companies who own a growing proportion of shares in British industry, to involve themselves in such company decision making would be a first step in this direction. The private sector should be actively encouraged to find its own solutions. However, British governments are likely, one way or another, to be involved in discriminatory intervention of this kind and will have to come to a view on which sectors are worth fostering, etc. Measures to improve the capability of the Civil Service to make these judgements would include reform of Civil Service recruitment, training, procedures, and attitudes in the industrial area. Direct involvement of industrialists in this process is also vital to such an exercise; an involvement that is difficult to achieve with the constant changes in policy and institutions that have characterized industrial policy to date.

Success in all the areas discussed above will depend heavily on maintaining the pressure of change, both on industry and on government policy makers. Continued external competitive pressure has, for instance, forced British management drastically to rethink its strategies and has opened up the possibility of redefining the social bargain in industry. It has also led to a painful rethinking of government industrial policies, so that more weight is given to efficiency and mobility than to the short-term preservation of employment. Given a chance to avoid these difficult decisions under a system of generalized protection, British industry would in all probability go back to sleep. The cold shower approach can bring results only if it is accompanied by awareness of, and willingness to respond to, the challenge. Those who dismiss this approach as already having failed ignore the delay in achieving this widespread awareness, which has in turn delayed the responses of both government and industry. It is certainly too early to judge. It should be noted that none of these domestic changes is constrained by Community membership; indeed, in several instances such changes would bring the framework of British industry closer to that within which its continental partners operate.

Acceptance of the need for continued pressure does not, however, imply blind acceptance of market forces. Indeed it will be necessary to give temporary help to certain industries, whether for traditional infant-industry reasons or to provide a breathing space for firms in trouble. Success in either of these will depend on the quality of government judgements on the merits of the case and on the ability of governments to resist pressures to allow such help to degenerate into feather bedding. In addition there will also be a need for selective protection against distortions of the free trading system arising from government intervention elsewhere, for instance from strong political lobbies in the USA, or to allow an orderly adjustment process to take place in an industry, thereby minimizing the disruptive social consequences. Membership of the Community places important constraints on government activities in this area, but it also has certain positive advantages. It is to these that we now turn.

EEC Industrial Policy and Britain

The evolution of an industrial policy within the EEC has suffered frequent setbacks and progress has been far more limited than in either the competition or commercial policy areas. As such, industrial policy is not specifically mentioned in the Treaty of Rome. The only relevant Articles of the Treaty concern the free movement of goods, competition policy, rules governing state aids to industry, and the establishment of a common commercial policy. A separate Directorate-General for industrial affairs was created only in 1967 when the High Authority of the ECSC was merged with the Commissions of Euratom and the European Economic Community. Initial attempts to define a comprehensive programme for industrial policy in the Colonna Memorandum of 1970 and the Spinelli Report of 1973 were unsuccessful. Michael Hodges [5] has provided a detailed study of the evolution of industrial policy making in the EEC.

There have been varying degrees of success with different lines of industrial policy originally pursued by the Community. Steady, if unspectacular, progress has been made in harmonizing national regulations and eliminating technical barriers to trade. This is an ongoing task with new technical barriers arising with increasing frequency in recent years. Almost no progress has been made in opening up public procurement markets to companies from other member states. After the initial enthusiasm for promoting transnational mergers and the European companies had died down, attention was limited to harmonizing company law.

Although the powers of the Commission are often discussed it has few powers to intervene in particular sectors. Apart from the coal and steel industries, for which greater powers existed under the ECSC Treaty, support for restructuring exercises in declining industries has been limited to certain funds channelled through the Social Fund, the Regional Development Fund, and the European Investment Bank. More recently, some progress was made in reaching argeement on crisis cartels in sectors such as man-made fibres, although these arrangements have fallen foul of the Competition Directorate. Apart from the curbing of export subsidies within the EEC market little progress has been made in recent years in curbing sectoral aid schemes of national governments. An important exception has been in the shipbuilding industry, where generally accepted curbs have curtailed the competition in subsidies for new orders. A similar agreement has been secured recently in the steel industry also.

Ambitious schemes for Community involvement in promoting and restructuring advanced technology sectors such as aerospace and computers came to nothing in the face of national resistance. Since then the Community has found great difficulty in playing a positive role in this field. European co-operation in aerospace, for instance, has proceeded outside the Community framework, though of course with its support, as individual European countries accepted the necessity of collaboration. In this industry collaboration with American firms would have reduced European companies to a subcontracting role. In the computer field, where the technology gap was greater, collaboration with American firms and not other similarly placed European firms proved more attractive, for instance to the French. The Commission is currently seeking a role in promoting the area of communications equipment. With the growing interaction of telecommunications and data transmission systems within Europe involvement in defining common standards and developing a European data network may be the beginning of a useful involvement in advanced sectors.

The other important area where the Community has played a major part is negotiating trade agreements with non-member countries, such as the Multilateral Trade Negotiations, the Multi-Fibre Arrangement, and the Lomé Convention. A common negotiating position, while often difficult to achieve internally, has given the Community states a far greater influence in these negotiations. Where the Community can identify particular industrial objectives its commercial policy can be a powerful adjunct of industrial policy. A case in point is the way in which the UK and France, the leading advocates, were able to obtain far more restrictive conditions in the current MFA than would otherwise have been possible. If we are moving towards a greater degree of managed trade then this role will increase in importance in the future. In addition the Commission is developing a series of surveillance schemes for monitoring imports of textiles, footwear, paper, etc., and has acted in a number of cases to curb imports and prevent dumping. Britain, as a country particularly affected by such imports, has a strong interest in the rigorous operation of these schemes and in prompt corrective action. Surveillance schemes may be extended to monitor the growing number of buy-back agreements with the Comecon countries in the future.

It is clear that the major constraint on British industrial policy making arising from Community membership has been the removal of direct control over commercial policy. Because of the British desire to promote inward direct foreign investment, limitations on the ability to control this have not emerged as a constraint for Britain, though they certainly have been for countries such as France. Because Britain is the most vulnerable to import penetration from the newly industrializing countries it is in Britain's interest to see much more speedy and effective monitoring and control of imports in sensitive sectors. This should include the ability to impose countervailing duties on imports of goods with 'unfair' cost advantages, such as the artificially low prices of energy and chemical feed-stocks in the USA. This is a very sensitive area where careful judgements have to be made on the merits of each case. Likewise distortions in trade patterns because of strong political lobbies, such as the US textile lobby, have to be countered by the Community. Improved codes of conduct in international trade are the best ways of dealing with these potentially disruptive issues, though progress in this area will continue to be slow.

Britain and her European partners will clearly be extensively involved in assisting declining industries, in easing the adjustment process, and in providing a breathing space for firms in difficulties. While it is important to retain the domestic freedom to provide this breathing space, the need to justify these actions to the Community provides an important and probably beneficial check on these activities, which can otherwise degenerate into feather-bedding domestically or result in self-defeating competition to support national industries. Indeed because similar pressures are felt to a greater or less degree throughout the Community there should be a common basis for collective action to restructure problem industries. So far this common interest has not been mobilized in the Community, though the possibilities for doing so may increase in the future. The OECD has also begun discussing these matters in the steel and ship-building industries; though the extent to which such discussions in the EEC and OECD can be complementary remains to be seen.

Although competitive national support for advanced technology industries is also potentially wasteful it will be much more difficult to tackle this issue at a European level, though proposals in the communications sector may be a beginning. European backwardness technologically will continue to make collaboration with US and possibly Japanese firms more attractive than European solutions. Where external collaboration is not possible and governments have come to the conclusion that promoting a purely national presence in an industry is impossible or too expensive, there may be scope for promoting European co-operation. However, on past evidence this is likely to be done through direct deals and not through the intermediary of the Commission. Even in this situation the Community could provide a framework for discussions and act as a catalyst.

Finally membership of the Community ensures the maintenance of the pressure for change that is essential for progress in regenerating British industry. It also prevents the retreat to insular thinking characteristic of British industry and governments and increases the awareness of what is going on elsewhere. Despite six years of membership British industry has not yet begun fully to exploit the potential scale advantages of the European market.

The Treaty of Rome was drafted in fundamentally different conditions from those prevailing today, in a period of expansion and convergence rather than a period of recession and divergent performance. A major test of its continued relevance will be the ability to adopt new policies and develop a greater degree of flexibility to cope with these changes. Imaginative and bold stewardship from an upgraded Industrial Directorate will be necessary to tackle what are becoming central issues in the evolution of the Community.

References

[1] Allen, G. C., *The British Disease*, London, Institute of Economic Affairs, 1976.

[2] Barnett, C., *The Collapse of British Power*, London, Eyre Methuen, 1972.

[3] Freeman, C., 'Technical innovation and British trade performance' in Frank Blackaby, ed., *De-industrialisation*, London, Heinemann for NIESR, 1979.

[4] Hobsbawm, E. J., *Industry and Empire*, Harmondsworth, Penguin Books, 1968.

[5] Hodges, M., 'Industrial policy: a directorate-general in search of a role' in Helen Wallace *et al.*, eds., *Policy-Making in the European Communities*, Chichester, Sussex, John Wiley, 1978.

[6] Jones, D. T., 'Output, employment and labour productivity in Europe since 1955', *National Institute Economic Review*, August 1976.

[7] —, 'Industrial development and economic divergence' in M. Hodges, ed., *Economic Divergence and the European Community*, London, Allen & Unwin for Royal Institute of International Affairs, forthcoming 1980.

[8] —, and Prais, S. J., 'Plant size and productivity in the motor industry: some international comparisons', *Oxford Bulletin of Economics and Statistics*, May 1978.

[9] Landes, D. S., *The Unbound Prometheus*, London, Cambridge University Press, 1969.

[10] Marshall, A., *Industry and Trade*, London, Macmillan, 1919.

[11] Mottershead, P., 'Industrial policy' in F. T. Blackaby *et al.*, *British Economic Policy 1960–1974*, London, Cambridge University Press, 1978.

[12] Pavitt, K., ed., *Technical Innovation and British Economic Performance*, London, Macmillan, forthcoming 1980.

[13] Prais, S. J., 'The strike proneness of large plants in Britain', *Journal of the Royal Statistical Society*, Series A, 1978.

[14] Saunders, C. T., *Engineering in Britain, West Germany and France: Some Statistical*

Comparisons (Sussex European Paper no. 3), Brighton, University of Sussex, Sussex European Research Centre, 1978.

[15] Smith, C. T. B. *et al.*, *Strikes in Britain* (Manpower Paper no. 16), London, Department of Employment, 1978.

[16] Svennilson, I., *Growth and Stagnation in the European Economy*, Geneva, UNECE, 1954.

Comment
by D. K. Stout

I sympathize strongly with Mr Jones's view that, until Britain is well on the road to catching up industrially with the more successful members of the Community, she will not be able to influence EEC policies as fully as she would like. Of the several issues raised in his paper there are three on which I particularly wish to comment: the unusual policy problems that Britain faces because her manufacturing industry has lapsed so far behind its rivals; the growing interest in *horizontal* measures both here and in other member states; and the natural and inevitable limits to Community industrial policy.

Britain's Industrial Decline
Industrial 'adjustment policies', as defined by the OECD, are measures to help an economy to move more closely towards a market equilibrium which is itself shifting quickly as the environment changes. But Britain's performance gap is now so great that faster adjustment to immediate market signals may lead to even larger losses of industrial markets than have already been incurred. (In 1977 the ratio of manufacturing to total value added in Britain was 28.5 per cent – one of the lowest proportions in the EEC. In 1970 it was the second highest.) Left to operate freely, market forces would lead to the production of integrated circuits, for example, being concentrated within an already successful economy like the German. Similarly, the market would tend to lead to concentration in Britain upon

increasingly labour-intensive techniques and relatively low value-added products within each sector. Such concentration is a stage on the treadmill of low productivity growth, balance of payments difficulties, devaluation, increased concentration of production at the lower-priced ends of product ranges where technical advances are less relevant and world demand growth slower – a market-determined process which a poorly performing economy should resist and try to reverse rather than cause to happen more smoothly. The evidence I set out in chapter 8 of *De-industrialization* (1979), edited by Frank Blackaby, does not support Mr Jones' view that decline has been due to past concentration upon slowly growing sectors or geographical markets. Rather it has been relative failure *within* each sector and market. Britain would not do well to take her present relative performance as given. One of the central aims of industrial policy should be to catch up, by means of higher transitional growth of total factor productivity within each industrial sector, and not merely to change the distribution of resources *between* sectors.

For Britain, 'sectoral policy' cannot mean the choice of winner sectors to be encouraged and loser sectors to be eased into a peaceful decline. There are too many sectors that are losers on present trends. It means establishing the conditions, sector by sector, for making up, over several years, the ground lost over several decades. Therefore Mr Jones is right to emphasize the importance of conditions for the rapid application of new technology across each sector of engineering.

Horizontal Policies

The greatest scope for industrial regeneration lies in measures which speed up the continuous movement of labour and capital out of obsolescent processes and products and into advanced techniques and products early in their life cycles and with a large potential for growth. Some of the most helpful measures possible do not involve any detailed intervention or planning within particular sectors. As Mr Jones points out, Britain lacks in any case the institutions, the industrial structure, and the appetite for detailed sectoral planning. He emphasizes four supply-side measures that would help to increase the speed of adaptation and permit growth without bottlenecks: incentives to innovation; the provision of specialist education and training; improved industrial relations; and closer relationships between government and industry, between banks and firms, and between vertically related firms.

The industrial sector working parties have identified particular examples of the need for these measures: the technological lag in electronic consumer goods (behind Japan); the continuously falling unit value of British exports of many types of machinery (compared with values of competitors' products); the chronic shortage of particular engineering skills in machinery sectors; resistance to modernization in many potential growth sectors (because of shop floor fears that productivity increases mean fewer jobs but unchanged physical output, rather than product improvement and a larger market share); the loss of economies of scale through the proliferation of standards (in the heating and ventilation industry); and so on.

Industrial recovery entails the much faster movement of factors of production within industries and especially into those supplying newer product markets. Ignorance of new technology and new market opportunities is as much the enemy of industrial regeneration as was the old style of sectoral policy which subsidized the waste of labour and capital in a few heavyweight industries.

The UK has not been alone in supporting inefficient industries. France is enabled by the CAP to perpetuate an inefficient system of agriculture. Germany buys domestic coal at more than twice the price of imported coal. There is no case in the Community where the losses in steel-making and shipbuilding are not covered. And the rate of increase in imports of fibres is limited by Community commercial policy. The object in these industries is partly a social one, to allow a rate of decline less than the rate the market would determine.

What has to be avoided, in what may be a protracted period while inflationary expectations are painfully reduced by monetary and budgetary means, is the blasting of the rest of manufacturing industry, all of it making the same claim to be treated as a special case as did steel and ships before. The need now for horizontal policies to increase mobility and to encourage investment and research and development is sharpened by the global and the domestic economic environment. All Community members are increasingly relying upon measures to support investment and research and development, to encourage small and medium-sized companies, and to increase geographical and skill mobility.

Since 1978 there have also been signs of disenchantment with more

dirigiste single-sector policies. This is clear, for example, in the policy
guidelines of the Eighth French Plan and the growing criticism of
development contracts between selected firms and the government
as 'market-distorting'. And recent industrial policy discussions in
Italy, the Netherlands, and Belgium have been increasingly critical
of planning in the style of the 1960s. Nevertheless, sectoral policies
continue to operate for coal, ships, and steel in Germany and several
other states, for the restructuring of the machine tools industry in
France, for integrated circuits in Italy and Belgium, and for data-
processing in Germany. The trend towards sectoral disengagement
is actually running faster in Britain, which may soon be more closely
in line with what the OECD Industry Committee regards as the model
of 'positive adjustment policy' than perhaps even Germany, in spite
of a heavy incubus of sector problems.

Future European Industrial Policy

Mr Jones has provided an excellent account of the past fits and starts
of Community policy in this field and of its enforced retreat into the
defensive areas of proposing orderly capacity reduction in endangered
heavy industries where it has a clear Treaty responsibility, of
negotiating the limitation of imports of steel and man-made fibres,
and of setting limits to national subsidies for steel and ships.

The theoretical criteria for an extension of the responsibilities of
the Commission's Industrial Affairs Directorate into horizontal adjustment policies and into the harmonization of national policies affecting
high technology industries are probably fairly uncontroversial. I
should favour four: cases where economies of scale are such that
unco-ordinated national initiatives are unlikely to be able to match
the Japanese and American competition (in communications satel-
lites, for example, or very large-scale integrated circuitry); where
bidding and counter-bidding for investment location by multi-
nationals is internecine; where very different levels of national effort
or success would destabilize the Community in the way that Britain's
industrial weakness already threatens to do; and where the enlargement of the Community requires space to be made for the industrial
development of the new members.

In practice, such an extension is unlikely. Both the most successful
and the least successful members will resist any such extension: the

former because they believe they can stay in front working alone; the latter because, given their peculiarly severe industrial problems, they want to be free of Brussels in what they do about them. Also, there are few relevant powers or budgetary instruments of the kind that exist for agriculture, with the result that only coal, steel, and energy and the trade, competition, and regional aspects of industrial policy can be much affected. And there is a dearth of detailed information, within the Community, on national industrial structure and performance and on long-run trends and intentions.

Finally, many of the critical industrial development decisions affecting the balance of future specialization and advantage in Europe will be taken by a handful of very large companies according to their own lights. One possible development of industrial policy at the Community level is through closer and more frequent informal controls between such companies and the Commission to the benefit of the companies jointly or severally concerned, and by means of which the Community's interests will be represented. This may go a little way to meeting the first and the last of the four criteria I suggested.

7 The Transfer of Resources

by A. J. Brown

The main purpose of this paper is to inquire into the future possibilities of gain to the United Kingdom through transfers of resources among members of the Communities. The present position, as Mr Godley's paper makes clear, is highly unfavourable to the United Kingdom, and is becoming more so. He estimates that, in 1980, there will be a net transfer from Britain to her partners of some £1,203 million through the General Budget, to which must be added a trade loss through the Common Agricultural Policy (that is, a loss in terms of what might reasonably have been expected if agricultural products had been imported and exported at world market prices) for which alternative estimates of £127 million and £315 million are quoted; broadly, therefore, the net external payments by the UK are raised by something between £1,200 and £1,500 million – a sum approaching one per cent of GNP. Nor can it be argued that there is much compensation for this in the effect of membership of the Communities on the UK's gain from non-agricultural trade. The static theory of customs unions has never demonstrated that even the total potential gain to all parties together was more than very small in the European case; the element of increasing returns to scale (which is very powerful as regards manufacturing industry in, for instance, small developing countries) has relatively little to offer in Europe, where national markets are mostly large and production for markets outside Europe already highly developed. As for the potential benefits to Britain in particular, her less than sparkling competitive performance over the last three generations has certainly not suggested that she would become a main centre of manufacturing development once the barriers were down; and internationally tradeable services, important though they are, do not seem likely to redress the balance.

In short, the economic case for British entry into the Communities was never strong, and the prospect of membership becoming advantageous depends largely on the possible development of favourable budgetary transfers, in place of, or offsetting, the present highly adverse ones. Since the UK is one of the poorer members of the Communities, and, from 1950 to 1970 at least, had been growing in income per head more slowly than her present partners, this raises the question whether there is any prospect that the Communities will develop their functions in such a way as to achieve the kind of income redistribution between their members that is normally seen between the states of a federation – a net transfer from the richer to the poorer. To throw light on this, it will be useful to start by looking in turn at the degrees to which the various items of Community revenue and expenditure exacerbate or reduce inter-member differences in real *per capita* income at present.

The Present Position

A preliminary question must first be raised. Payments into and out of the budget are denominated in European Units of Account, the unit being expressed as a weighted average of the official national currency values. This seems appropriate for the purpose of our discussion because the immediate effect of an international payment or receipt is upon the country's command over international goods, to which the official exchange rates should be not too irrelevant. But average real income per head in a country relates to purchasing power over both domestic and internationally traded goods and services, and price ratios of the former to the latter can vary widely between countries. The question therefore arises whether comparisons of average income per head between countries should use current official exchange rates (as has most often been done) or rates that are designed to reflect the general purchasing power parities of the currencies. Since average income per head is to be used to indicate average level of material welfare, to which ability to bear tax burdens and to benefit from subventions are assumed to be related, it is clear that the latter course is the more correct.

There is some diversity of estimates of *per capita* incomes at purchasing power parity rates. Two estimates (admittedly for different years) and the average of them are given in Table 7.1, along with

Table 7.1 Grants and income

	Community grants 1979 Units of Account per head			Income per head (Community average = 100) (GDP)		
	Total excl. Agric. guarantee	Agric. guarantee	Total	1975 est.	1977 est.	Average
Belgium–Luxembourg	2.8	18.6	21.4	102	109	105
Denmark	4.2	61.3	65.5	109	117	113
France	3.9	21.9	25.8	115	111	113
Germany	1.9	10.9	12.8	110	116	113
Ireland	16.8	55.5	72.3	73	61	67
Italy	6.6	12.1	18.7	80	70	75
Netherlands	2.7	37.6	40.3	97	106	102
United Kingdom	4.1	10.1	14.2	96	90	93

Sources: For Community grants 1979, Commission of the European Communities [4], vol. 2, p. 455; for 1975 estimate of income per head, Commission of the European Communities [5], Table 10; for 1977 estimate of income per head, Table 4.5 above, adjusted to give *weighted* average of national figures = 100.

the *per capita* receipts of grants under the two main heads for 1979. The chief effect of measuring incomes at purchasing power parity rates is to narrow the range by about one-third; there are some minor changes in order among the four richest countries (France, Germany, Belgium, Denmark), but the Netherlands, the UK, Italy, and Ireland still come in descending order in the lower half of the list. The UK, while three-quarters of the way down the range in the market exchange rate version, moves up to about the middle when purchasing power parity is used.

Total grants from the budget are, of course, dominated by the agricultural guarantee payments, 70 per cent of the total, which show practically no linear correlation with income per head, however measured. Financially, the Communities constitute a club for agricultural price maintenance, with minor philanthropic side-shows. The benefits of the agricultural guarantee payments naturally go to the biggest agricultural producers, which are not uniformly the poorest within the Community. The five richest countries, with very broadly similar real incomes levels, show a wide range of *per capita* receipts under this head, from Germany at the bottom to Denmark at the top. Only among the three poorest are receipts (covering a similar wide range) in inverse order to income, and the United Kingdom, as already mentioned, does worst of all. The chief effect of including non-agricultural grants in this distribution is to put Ireland a little above Denmark.

As already mentioned, the CAP involves burdens and benefits additional to those traceable through the General Budget, because it causes member countries to export and import agricultural products from and to their fellow members at prices different from those at which they would presumably trade (with them, or with the outside world) in the absence of the CAP. Mr Godley's paper shows that these (positive or negative) 'trade receipts' are very substantial. For Ireland, the Netherlands, and Denmark they are about as large as receipts in agricultural support grants; for France nearly as great. For other members they are negative – in the case of Italy, the UK, and Belgium of the same order of magnitude as their gross agricultural support grant receipts. If, therefore, one takes the agricultural support grants along with these trade receipts, the result is certainly to exacerbate income differences; the only substantial effect in the other direction is the massive assistance to Ireland.

If, however, one looks separately at the smaller totals of grants, *excluding* those for agricultural price guarantee, a much clearer relation to income emerges: France does slightly better than the general pattern might suggest; there is a heavy concentration of benefits on Ireland; and Italy, at half her *per capita* value, comes in second place. Here is the outline of a rational pattern, with benefits per head doubling for each 13 per cent or so by which real (purchasing power parity) income falls below the general Community average. This is much more like the distribution of benefits found among regions in unitary states or among provinces in federations.

We come now to the revenue side (see Table 7.2). Once more, it is the agricultural elements (the levies) which produce the biggest departures from a simple relation to *per capita* income. France gets off rather lightly, but the big anomaly is the very large contributions of the Netherlands and Belgium. To some substantial extent this must be explained by the levying at the ports of entry (Antwerp and

Table 7.2 Revenue sources and income

	% 1979 budget shares (prelim. draft)				Shares of GDP	
	Agric. levies	Customs	VAT	Total	At purchasing power parity	At market exchange rates 1976
Belgium–Luxembourg	11.1	6.8	5.4	6.8	4.1	4.9
Denmark	2.1	2.3	2.6	2.5	2.2	2.8
France	10.8	15.1	24.0	18.8	23.3	25.0
Germany	21.5	30.5	32.4	30.0	27.2	32.1
Ireland	0.7	1.1	0.8	0.9	0.8	0.6
Italy	19.1	9.5	10.4	11.5	16.5	12.2
Netherlands	17.2	9.4	6.3	9.1	5.5	6.4
United Kingdom	17.5	25.1	18.1	20.4	20.3	15.9
Total	100	100	100	100	100	100

Sources: For 1979 budget shares, Commission of the European Communities [7]; shares of GDP at purchasing power parity calculated from last column of Table 7.1.

Rotterdam) of contributions on imports in transit to France or Germany, but one cannot say whether it is all explained in this way. A less extreme version of the same anomaly is displayed by customs duties, presumably largely, if not wholly, for the same reason. The incidence of both these classes of impost – and therefore of total revenue – between the member countries on the northwest European mainland is difficult to establish.

The third main source of revenue is that based upon Value Added Tax. Here, one would expect a clearer relation of *per capita* burden to *per capita* income; there are, however, considerable irregularities in the relationship. A recent Commission study [7] has shown that, on the basis of estimates for 1979, Ireland's VAT contribution is some 13 per cent high in comparison with GDP (at official exchange rates), while Italy's is some 19 per cent low, and the United Kingdom's nearly seven per cent high. To introduce any progressive element into the tax system, one would of course want the richer countries to pay more in relation to their income than the poor ones. Because of the tendency for domestic goods in rich countries to be dear in relation to international goods, this result is actually obtained if one relates VAT yield (at official exchange rates) to GDP at purchasing power parity rates. The three countries whose VAT contributions are small in relation to real GDP are then Ireland, Italy, and the UK, while for all the other members they are large. But the irregularities remain; Italy still pays much less in relation to GDP than Ireland; France much less than Germany, Belgium, or Denmark.

On the whole, there is very little progressivity in the present Community revenue sources – unless one relates what countries pay (reckoned at official exchange rates) to their GDP (reckoned in purchasing power parity terms). The Commission's study group on the role of public finance in European integration [4] assessed not only the progressivity of revenue sources, but also the redistributive power of the various heads of expenditure, defined as the percentage by which the expenditure in question reduced the differences between the *per capita* average disposable incomes of the member states. The Regional Development Fund and the European Social Fund each have a redistributive power of 0.25 per cent; the loans of the European Investment Bank and the Coal and Steel Community (treated as if they were grants) had a power of about 0.5 per cent. The Agricultural Guarantee expenditure also had a power of about 0.5 per cent (most of which would no doubt have vanished if trade effects had been taken into account). The total redistributive effect of all Community outlays was thus about 1.5 per cent. It is useful to point out here that the total public finances of the member states have a redistributive effect as between their component regions which varies about a mean of some 40 per cent: that is, they reduce interregional average income inequalities by about this percentage. Since national and local public expenditures are greater than those of the Communities in a ratio considerably greater than 40:1.5 (in fact, about twice as great), it may be claimed that Community finances have a greater redistributive effect, *pro rata*, than those of the component countries. But considering that payments no bigger than those at present made by the Communities could, if they had no other object, reduce the inequalities between member countries' average incomes by something like 15 per cent, the present pattern of outlays cannot be judged very effective in this particular connection.

The Prospect of Enlargement

The extension of the Communities' activities immediately in view is that which would follow from the foreshadowed admission to the European Economic Community of Spain, Greece, and Portugal. Its financial implications have been surveyed in Supplement 3/78 to the *Bulletin of the European Communities* [5], from which the following estimates are quoted. They relate to what would have been the effect on the 1978 expenditures and resources of the Communities if the three countries had already been fully integrated in that year.

The three applicants are poorer than the existing members. Whereas Ireland, the poorest of the latter, has a *per capita* income average (at purchasing power parity rates) some 27 per cent below the existing Community average, Spain and Greece fall some 30–33 per cent below it, and Portugal something like 55 per cent below. They are also, of course, heavily involved in structural change, with agricultural populations still large but rapidly falling, and these are precisely the conditions which properly entitle them to large benefits from membership. The Commission's estimate is that their accession might add something between one-ninth and one-sixth to total agricultural guarantee payments but that it would double agricultural guidance benefits, raise Regional Fund benefits by 70–75 per cent, and increase payments from the Social Fund by anything from one-third to a half. The total effect would be to raise Community General Budget expenditure by 20–25 per cent or some 2,400–3,000 million European Units of Account (EUAs). There would also be an increase in loans.

On the revenue side, assuming the VAT rate of 0.6429 per cent which would have been needed to balance the 1978 budget for the Community of Nine, the three prospective members would, if already admitted, have contributed only some 1,500 million EUAs. To achieve a balance, it would have been necessary to raise the rate of VAT contribution from 0.6429 to 0.77 per cent of the base amount; the total contribution from the hypothetical new members would then have been about 1,620 million EUAs. The net annual transfer to them from the rest of the Community through the General Budget would thus have been, in round figures, 1,000 million units, or 6.5–7 per cent of the budget total. The direct budgetary effect of enlargement upon the existing members would be measured by the VAT increase of 0.13 per cent of the base, which in the case of the United Kingdom would have meant an additional contribution of about 190 million EUAs, or some £115 million. In view of the nature of the transfer, in line with those that arise from the working of well-designed systems of public finance in general, this would be a less legitimate matter for complaint than many of the existing transfers within the Community.

The Longer Run

If one looks beyond these immediate prospects, what developments seem desirable or possible? First, is there any likelihood of a remodelling or expansion of the financial transfers for the explicit purpose of achieving a greater inter-member equality of incomes, as an end in itself? The Preamble to the Treaty of Rome characterizes the contracting parties as, *inter alia*,

> DESIROUS of strengthening the unity of their economies and ensuring their harmonious development by diminishing both the disparities between the various regions and the backwardness of the less favoured regions.

While it is 'regions', not 'member states', that are referred to here, one may argue that income equalization between regions implies convergence between member states also. This would obviously be so in the extreme – and impracticable – event of complete equality being obtained between regional average incomes. Short of that, it still follows so long as the countries with the poorest regions, or the greatest proportions of poor regions, are also the poorest countries on average – so long, that is, as they do not have other regions rich enough to redress the general balance.

This, broadly, is the case, though much depends on what is taken as the threshold of regional 'poverty'. If, for instance, any region with average real *per capita* incomes (properly measured, using purchasing power parities) below the Community average were entitled to some aid, then the whole of Ireland and perhaps the whole of Italy (certainly 80 per cent of it, measured by population) would be so entitled, while at the other end of the scale no more than 6 per cent of Germany (by population) would qualify. In between, over two-thirds of the UK, perhaps one-third of the Netherlands and Belgium, and probably rather less of Denmark would qualify also. France, where regions containing half of the total population might have a valid claim, would do rather well in relation to her place in the hierarchy of real *per capita* national incomes, but with that exception the order of average benefits per head of the total national population in such a scheme would be close to the inverse order of real national incomes per head [1] and [2].

If one imagines aid concentrated on poorer regions, say those with average real incomes at least 25 per cent below the Community average, the outcome would, of course, be different. All the Republic of Ireland, or perhaps all the two-thirds excluding the eastern (Dublin) region, would qualify, as would more than half (still by population) of Italy. In the UK only Northern Ireland would have a chance of qualifying; elsewhere, within the present Community membership, no regions at all. It is still clear, therefore, that benefits for 'backward' regions (if 'backward' means 'poor') would involve transfers to the poorest *countries* of the Communities in the order of their poverty.

Zeal for regional convergence *per se*, however, is not the only, or perhaps the most probable motive that might conceivably work in the long run towards convergence-promoting transfers in practice. Other objectives the pursuit of which might do this are: progress through a completely common market in goods and services to full economic and monetary union; central provision of those public services that are best so provided; and progress towards full political federalism. These objects are inter-connected, and so are the obstacles to their attainment.

Progress towards free movement of goods and factors of production, even without monetary union (and still more with it) creates strains because, in many circumstances, heavy outward migration, however beneficial to the emigrants, is unacceptable to the areas they leave, and it may progressively reduce the ability to provide standards of public services sufficient to hold their remaining population and industry, or to attract new industry. At the same time, heavy inward migration can create social tensions, and can contribute to the formation of excessively large aggregations of population and industry. For such reasons as these, assistance to member states (or parts of them) that are sources of heavy emigration may be deemed necessary to moderate outward movement, and may, indeed, be a condition of willingness to forego unilateral restrictions of movement on one side or the other – that is to say, of the existence of free movement itself. Such assistance is undertaken by all the member states in the form of domestic regional policies; where international movements are concerned, it should be a function of the Community.

In a similar way monetary union, along with freedom of trade, deprives member states of their power to protect themselves against falls in the competitiveness of their products by shutting competing products out or by devaluing their currencies; reduction of their consumption and domestic capital formation is thus forced upon them, except in so far as they can borrow externally to finance a deficit. Within either unitary states or federations, regions which experience such falls in their competitiveness are substantially protected by the automatic reduction in their national or federal tax liabilities as their income falls, while unemployment insurance and other relief benefits, which increase, are nationally or federally financed. Member states of the Community, all the more because they are accustomed to using trade barriers and exchange rates to moderate external shocks, are unlikely to forego them unless they receive, through external financial channels, some of the cushioning that is available to their own regions through internal ones.

The built-in stabilizers of a substantial Community public finance system, and its specific relief mechanisms, are therefore highly relevant to progress towards economic and monetary union. Both the Marjolin Report *'Economic and Monetary Union 1980'* [3] and the subsequent MacDougall Report *The Role of Public Finance in European Integration* [4] dealt with this point, the latter in considerable detail. Views may differ as to the benefits of further progress towards economic and monetary union in Europe, granted that we already have quite large and highly developed member states with strong external trade connections (both inside and outside the Community). But if that further progress is deemed desirable, then it can be argued strongly that a more integrated Community system of public finance, with powerful and largely automatic compensatory mechanisms built into it, is a condition of getting it – or of keeping it once it is attained.

The first problem with the Community, viewed as aspirant to eventual fiscal federation, is that it is doing things in the wrong order. In all existing federations, the federalization of defence preceded any high degree of economic integration. With a reasonably progressive tax system, the costs of defence and central administration can introduce a very appreciable built-in stabilizer into the economies of member states; not very powerful in relation to the expenditure involved (which in the Community is at least four times the General Budget total), but well worth having. Again, most existing federations were formed before the age of massive social security expenditure, and in all the principal ones the federal government has taken the major part in this activity largely because people are mobile within federations and will move to escape taxation and to seek benefits if these differ geographically. In the Community, national expenditures under this head are something like twelve times the total amount of the General Budget, and their stabilizing-power for any region is a powerful one, because they are specifically directed towards areas of need. This is a bus that the Community was born too late to catch; but all may not be lost.

The third major example of mistiming is, of course, to be found in the operations of the CAP, which as already noted swamp the other transfers in the finances of a special purpose club. In proportion to their size these finances have little compensatory power and produce some notably perverse effects.

If one is looking at the prospects of building up Community functions that would have stabilizing and compensatory effects, one must look both at taxation and at expenditure. As regards the former, the Community is approaching the limits of its existing resources and seeking new possibilities. Unfortunately, the fact that it is in some respects in a quasi-federal situation seems to have engendered some unhelpful attitudes. In the beginning the Community's revenue was derived from contributions assessed on member states' gross domestic products, the statistics of which are among the more reliable available to the Commission. This, however, was deemed to be an infantile phase, to give way to a more adult stage in which the Communities would have their 'own resources' – designated sources of revenue collected by member states on their behalf. The first two of these were agricultural levies and customs duties, analogous to classic federal revenue sources, and justified in such a role by the fact that, once internal customs borders are abolished, the attribution of these taxes between member states becomes impossible – one does not know where imported products are finally consumed. (An attempt to assess movements of imported goods between the territories of the old East African Common Market, for the purpose of dividing customs revenue between them, was a constant source of dispute, and would not have been worth considering on a European scale.)

The system of treating these as common revenues is not ideal, because one simply does not know who is paying. There is some presumption that taxation falls disproportionately on those – perhaps mainly peripheral – countries which for reasons of tradition or transport cost, or both, consume extra-European goods preferentially. But it is probably inevitable in practice; and one can also admit the contention that the apparent incidence (that is, point of collection) of these taxes should not be taken as a basis for any subsequent financial mechanism to equalize tax burdens. It is, however, unfortunate that VAT has been selected as the basis of residual revenue. As already noted, the way in which this basis performs at present, in relation to GDP, is unsatisfactory. Why should not a GDP-based assessment, preferably with some built-in progressivity (for example, average income per head raised to a power of more than unity and multiplied by population) be served on member governments, as assessments of personal income tax are served on individual taxpayers in member countries? Presumably because, as *Bulletin* Supplement 8/78 ([7], page 7, paragraph 8) makes clear, the Commission (and possibly the Parliament) would regard this as a regression to the Communities' more infantile stage. Sentiments of this kind should be excluded from serious business. Since the levies and customs dues are inelastic the residual source of revenue will become more important as the budget expands. It is important to get it right.

In most member states, however, the progressivity of the tax system normally makes a smaller contribution to the stabilizing function of public finance than does that of expenditure, though the contributions of particular heads of expenditure differ a good deal from one country to another. The MacDougall Report [4] reproduces a number of simulations of the effects of introducing various Community expenditures; first, those which might be introduced in a period of 'pre-federal integration' in the fairly near future, and second, those which, in the peculiar circumstances of the Community, might go with the early stages of federation itself.

The 'pre-federal' possibilities explored include the transfer to the Community of all the foreign aid schemes of member governments, the similar transfer of a basic layer (perhaps about one-third of the total, on average) of national unemployment benefit schemes – the project particularly commended by the Marjolin Report of 1975 [3] – and a number of further possibilities from which a selection might be made in the fields of regional aid, vocational training, and emergency assistance to weak economies. The total envisaged would involve something like a doubling of present Community expenditure, of which half or more would be a transfer from present national budget burdens; it is calculated that, within a Community of Nine, it might reduce inequality between national average incomes by some 10 per cent, or one-quarter of the amount by which inter-regional differences are commonly reduced by national finance. (The Study Group remarked that this was far too small an equalizing power to form the basis of economic and monetary union.) Within a Community of Twelve the extent of inter-member inequality, in the sense of the total transfer necessary to equalize national averages, would be about 50 per cent larger than among the Nine, with a 13 per cent increase in total real income. Even after allowing for the automatic increase on enlargement, therefore, either the budget would have to be further expanded or the degree of reduction in inequality would be perhaps only 7 or 8 per cent, instead of 10 per cent.

How would the United Kingdom fare from such an expansion of the budget? Without precise simulation on necessarily arbitrary assumptions it is clearly not possible to give exact answers, but some general presumptions are plain. Within the present Community of Nine, Britain stands 6–10 per cent below the general average of *per capita* real income. There is thus a presumption that measures calculated to reduce inequalities in a uniform manner will benefit her. Since, however, she is the richest of the members below the average, measures that – like most one can readily envisage – have a higher tendency to correct large income deficiencies than small ones will leave her either virtually unaffected or a small net contributor – ignoring, of course, the specially perverse factors in the existing financial arrangements which make her a very large contributor at present. My observations about the effects of concentrating aid on the poorest regions may serve to substantiate this. Enlargement to a Community of Twelve, by bringing the general real income average down to very nearly the UK level, would reinforce this presumption; though in either case the UK might do better than is thus suggested in so far as benefits were geared, say, to unemployment rates or to competitive weakness rather than to lowness of real income.

For the still longer run, in which some form of federation becomes a possibility, the MacDougall Report [4] proposed a system of largely special-purpose matching grants to member governments, designed to ensure the highest degree of reduction in inequality for the smallest federal budget – a system estimated to reduce inequalities within the Nine by some 30 per cent within a budget amounting to 7.5–10 per cent of GDP, including defence. The simulations based upon this, and on 1975 income data, show the UK a considerable net beneficiary – to the extent of between one and six per cent of GDP, on various assumptions; but this result is highly sensitive to the country's position in the average income hierarchy. In a Community of Twelve, with present income relativities, it is likely that, again, the UK would stand to gain little, if anything, by way of net transfer. But given a continuation of its slower real income growth, in comparison with other Community countries, that could alter rapidly; the Community of Nine result just quoted, based on 1975 income data, is to be compared with one based on 1970 figures which shows the UK in a virtually neutral position.

It should be noted that these projections assume a diminution of the effects of the CAP which recent trends do not foreshadow, though it is always possible that a rise in real world market agricultural price levels might work in that direction if rates of industrial growth rose. In the longer run, too, structural change in the Community should gradually diminish the pressure for excessive agricultural support. Considerations such as these serve to emphasize the fallibility of prediction in this field.

The general position so far as Britain is concerned can therefore be summarized as follows. The United Kingdom does singularly badly out of the present financial arrangements of the Communities, mainly because of the existence of the Common Agricultural Policy and its high price levels; but to a smaller extent also because of imperfections in the VAT base as a foundation for international assessments, and perhaps to some extent because of a higher than average reliance, for consumption and capital formation, on non-agricultural goods from outside the Communities. The prospective enlargement of the Communities will increase the net burden on the UK by perhaps one-seventh or one-eighth – though, since this is in a better cause than the CAP, one should not complain too much about it. In the longer run, the peculiarly unfavourable treatment of the

UK may be mitigated by the modification or the overshadowing of the CAP, and perhaps also by the substitution of some more satisfactory (and more progressive) basis for VAT in relation to the increasingly important residual revenue source: but it must be emphasized that neither of these outcomes can be relied upon to happen by itself. However, if a more progressive revenue system is developed, together with an expenditure pattern more strongly geared to general national needs (developments which will be required on a very substantial scale if there is to be progress towards economic and monetary union), then the United Kingdom would acquire not insubstantial compensation for continuing to make slower economic progress than her Community partners. It is not an inspiring prospect, but in the general atmosphere of pessimism about the British economic future, it could be worse.

References

[1] Commission of the European Communities, *Regional Development in the Community: Analytical Survey*, Brussels, 1971.

[2] —, 'Report on the Regional Problems in the Enlarged Community', COM (73) 550 Final, Brussels, 1973.

[3] —, *Report of the Study Group 'Economic and Monetary Union, 1980'*, Brussels, 1975 (the Marjolin Report), 2 vols.

[4] —, *Report of the Study Group on the Role of Public Finance in European Integration*, Brussels, 1977 (the MacDougall Report), 2 vols.

[5] —, 'Enlargement of the Community: economic and sectoral aspects', *Bulletin of the European Communities*, Supplement 3/78, Luxembourg, 1978.

[6] —, 'Preliminary draft general budget of the European Communities for the financial year 1979: general introduction', *Bulletin of the European Communities*, Supplement 6/78.

[7] —, 'Financing the Community budget: the way ahead', *Bulletin of the European Communities*, Supplement 8/78.

[8] University of Cambridge, Department of Applied Economics, 'Policies of the EEC', *Cambridge Economic Policy Review*, no. 5, 1979.

Comment
by Carsten Thoroe

The intra-Community transfer of resources can be viewed from a number of different aspects. The most familiar approach is to look at changes in national income which result from resource transfers – Professor Brown focuses on this aspect. He discusses payment and receipt flows of individual member countries in relation to gross domestic product and he gives examples of the transfer implications of the Common Agricultural Policy and the value added tax. In addition Professor Brown elaborates possible developments stemming from an enlargement of the Community, and he points to those areas where resource transfers might be urgently required in the future. The attention which is given to the distributional aspects of resource transfers may be understandable because in any organization net payments are broadly looked upon as disadvantages and net receipts as advantages of membership. Thus it may be disturbing for a country to realize that it has to pay more to the Community than it is getting out; this may even be considered unjust, if the country feels poorer than others who receive net gains from the common budget. But a word of caution is necessary as the common budget tells us little about the gains and losses of integration, and even in the field of financial transfers national payments to and receipts from the common budget do not always provide adequate evidence about the national financial burden [2]. As a matter of fact empirical research on integration shows that, for welfare in its broadest sense, the trade effects of integration are much more important than mere financial transfers, and, what is most significant, seem to be dynamic effects which bring together the various growth-stimulating changes in allocation.

Therefore I think it is worth while to look at the transfer problem not only from distributional but also from allocative viewpoints. Such a perspective is quite in line with the Treaty of Rome, where both a continuous improvement in living and employment conditions and a lessening of the differences between the regions in the Community are proclaimed as common goals. While it seems obvious that in the treaty allocative policies are referred to for achieving these goals, it would be hard to show that redistribution policies were also intended by the treaty. Moreover, if reducing *per capita* income differences among the member countries by income redistribution had been aimed at, this could have been reached more effectively by a Community-wide system of financial compensation than by the variety of common policies which has been introduced. Financial transfers may be important for income and even for employment in the short run; for long-run economic development, however, they would not seem to be promising. But what reasons are there for a redistribution between nations? The principles which apply to an income redistribution among persons cannot be applied without modification to redistribution between individual nations. Not wishing to draw any conclusions, I simply appeal to past experience, which shows that redistribution of income between the members has been a problem tackled only in the late stages of integration processes.

For these reasons I think that the volume of redistribution involved in a measure is not a good criterion for relinquishing national authority to the Community. The principles of 'subsidiarity' call for authority to be exercised at higher levels only if the assignment can thus be fulfilled .more effectively (because of economies of scale) or if homogeneity is necessary all over the Community [4]. I do not think, for instance, that social security is a good example of a task that ought to be carried out at the EC level in the near future. I agree with Professor Brown that there would be a need for more homogeneity in social security if there were substantial internal migration; and I presume that in this field solidarity within the Community could be more easily reached than in other areas of income redistribution. At present, however, we have wide differences in income levels and social security provisions between member countries, and only small internal migration exists. Even within a wider Community I would not expect large migratory movements for a long time. Prevailing systems of social security reflect social attitudes, which differ substantially from nation to nation; authority for social security at the Community level would require common standards.

Although the analogy is not completely correct, the Common Agricultural Policy provides a warning example of conflicts arising from a common income policy. This common income policy for the agricultural sector has resulted in tremendous financial burdens to tax-payers and consumers within the Community. Structural surpluses in many agricultural markets have provoked drastic measures of intervention aimed at reducing immense inventories or at destroying non-storable agricultural products. Moreover, EC agricultural protectionism with barriers to imports and export dumping has had severe repercussions on third countries. A radical reform of the CAP has been overdue for years; and Britain, demanding such a reform, has sound economic reasoning on her side. However, one should not forget that, in principle, all the problems which flow from the CAP were known when Britain joined the Community. Furthermore the most spectacular decisions on the level of common agricultural prices were taken after Britain was already a Community member. For years the United Kingdom did not resist the raising of agricultural prices which has brought about the negative effects for consumers and the distortions of factor allocation that are now cause for so many complaints. Instead, she requested compensation in other fields of common policy (for example, the regional fund), and she has chosen a national strategy of delinking from the common level of agricultural prices by Monetary Compensatory Amounts.

I agree with Professor Brown that trade in agricultural products in the Community causes welfare-reducing effects for Britain. But I wonder why welfare changes from intra-Community trade are discussed only in connection with agricultural products. Trade policy as a main area of common policy is not restricted to agricultural commodities. Protection for production inside the Community implies resource transfers by intra-Community trade in comparison with free-market solutions. Because of significant differences in protection for specific products, balance-of-trade accounts do not allow for judgements on welfare gains or losses for individual countries from intra-Community trade.

If we look at transfer problems from an allocative point of view, it becomes obvious that some of them are closely connected with Britain's low degree of integration in the Common Market, though the United Kingdom's share of intra-Community trade in total external trade has risen in recent years. Stronger integration into the Common Market would result in an intensified division of labour between the British economy and the economies of the rest of the Community, in more trade within the Community, and above all in higher growth rates in Britain – requiring, however, structural adjustment both in the United Kingdom and in the other member countries. More intra-EC trade would mean a lower share of imports from outside the Community and a lower share in customs duties. Faster growth would be accompanied by increased investment, and this, together with a higher share of exports, would reduce that part of the contribution to the common budget which is based on VAT in comparison with GDP. From an allocative point of view it is important to note that faster growth would be less hindered by VAT-based contributions than by contributions based on GDP, because VAT is a tax only on consumption. Furthermore, higher growth rates in Britain would contribute to stabilizing exchange rates. As calculations provided by the Commission show, yearly national contributions to the common budget in relation to GDP are very sensitive to variations in exchange rates [1].

Future developments of financial transfers within the Community will depend heavily on what happens to the CAP. It is now widely accepted that expenditure for the CAP cannot rise in the future at the same rates as in the past. Fundamental relief for Britain, however, could be achieved only if agricultural incomes policy were less directly controlled at the Community level [5]. If the CAP could be fundamentally reformed the problems left for the common budget would be reduced to minor dimensions. This would hold true even for an enlarged Community. But interests in the CAP, and in reforming it, are quite different between the member states. It therefore seems impossible to come to an agreement about a fundamental reform of the CAP if negotiations are limited to agricultural policy alone. It will be necessary to connect negotiations on other areas of common policies and on possibilities for future common activities with proposals to reform the CAP. Distributional and compensatory transfers will surely be of great importance in the process of political agreement, but the main criterion for giving additional authority to the Community should be that there are more advantages for these policies on the Community level than on the national level. What share of the financial burden would finally be borne by Britain depends largely on economic development in Britain herself. Here Professor Brown has a very pessimistic view of future growth prospects. He would consider it a success if the United Kingdom could acquire compensation for continuing to make slower economic progress than her Community partners. But why should Britain persist in slower growth?

British growth performance was less favourable than that of other member countries long before accession to the Community and even before the EEC was established. Already in 1962 Alexandre Lamfalussy argued that Britain's problems would not be solved simply by her joining the Common Market. He saw entry rather as part of a beneficial shock treatment that would lead public opinion in Britain to recognize the necessity of structural adjustment, of raising productivity, and of increasing the share of investment in the national product [3]. High or low growth rates are not an irrevocable fate. They are the result of the economic behaviour of people and the framework that is given to them by economic policy. Activities for growth in weaker member countries or regions can be strengthened by the Community, but they cannot be entirely provided by it. Something is already being done on the Community level. The financial volume of Community activities to assist economic growth has reached nearly 15 per cent of total Community expenditure. These activities are highly concentrated on the weaker members. Great Britain, Italy and Ireland, for instance, will in 1980 receive nearly two-thirds of the expenditure of the Community for structural improvements. However, if the transfer problems within the Community are examined from allocative viewpoints, it is clear that more could be done to improve the growth performance of the weaker member countries and that it could be done more effectively.

There may very well be good reasons for nations to choose slow economic progress. But equally there may be good reasons for other countries to opt for fast growth and rapid change. Given such a constellation, why then should faster growing economies compensate the slower growing ones?

References

[1] Commission of the European Communities 'Working Paper about Budgetary Questions', AGRA-Europe 39/79, 1. Oct. 1979.

[2] Henke, K.-D., 'Die Finanzierung der Europäischen Gemeinschaft' in D. Pohmer, ed., *Probleme des Finanzausgleichs*, III: *Finanzausgleich im Rahmen der Europäischen Gemeinschaften*, Schriftenreihe des Vereins für Socialpolitik N.F. Band 96/III, Berlin, Duncker und Humblot, forthcoming.

[3] Lamfalussy, A., *The United Kingdom and the Six*, London, Macmillan, 1963.

[4] Oates, W. E., *Fiscal Federalism*, New York, Harcourt Brace Jovanovich, 1972.

[5] Thoroe, C., 'Die europäische Agrarpolitik als Finanzausgleichsproblem' in D. Pohmer, ed., *Probleme des Finanzausgleichs*, III: *Finanzausgleich im Rahmen der Europäischen Gemeinschaften*, Schriftenreihe des Vereins für Socialpolitik N.F. Band 96/III, Berlin, Duncker und Humblot, forthcoming.

8 Co-operation in Macro-economic Policy through the European Framework
by J. C. R. Dow

This paper is concerned with one aspect only of the United Kingdom's membership of the European Economic Community: its value to the United Kingdom as a forum for co-operation with other countries on general economic policy. This involves some element of comparative assessment, given that such co-operation takes place also in other international organizations, most notably the International Monetary Fund and the Organization for Economic Co-operation and Development.

Part 1 distinguishes two types of international economic collaboration, the first (perhaps more important) concerned with maintaining a framework of international order; the second (the focus of interest here), with co-operation in respect of macro-economic policies aiming to maintain a 'state of balance' in each economy. How active a role one thinks there is for this sort of international discussion must depend, *inter alia*, on the role that is seen for discretionary macro-economic policy in general. *Part 2* seeks to define the general role of such co-operation – whose possible benefits, though not at all to be despised, are, it is argued, often overstated. *Part 3* describes the general development of international economic co-operation since 1945 – the context within which economic co-operation through the EEC has to be considered. *Part 4* discusses the utility to the United Kingdom of membership of the Community, in its present form, as a forum for economic co-operation. *Part 5* discusses what the Community might become, and how that might affect the question. Brief conclusions are set out in *Part 6*.

1. Two Types of International Economic Collaboration

International collaboration in the field of economic policy is of two broad types, which have to be distinguished. First, countries have felt the need to agree on rules restricting their freedom, in particular their freedom to impose restrictions on trade, and to set up a semi-permanent legal framework embodying these rules. Co-operation of this sort is concerned with maintaining a framework of international order and compares with laws relating to competition and restrictive practices in domestic legislation. Once set up, they are intended to stay in place and be revised only occasionally.

Such co-operation needs to be distinguished from co-operation between countries in what may be called macro-economic stabilization policies, that is, policies designed to affect total demand or prices so as to maintain a reasonable 'state of balance' in each economy. Since policy making in this field has, in the past, involved relatively frequent adjustment of policy instruments, co-operation in this field – unlike collaboration in the field of law and order – has had to be a fairly continuous process.

The great examples of the first type of co-operation are the Bretton Woods Conference and its immediate precursors which resulted in the ground rules for the International Monetary Fund, and later the General Agreement on Tariffs and Trade. Some aspects of the EEC arrangements resulting from the Treaty of Rome – especially for instance the abolition of internal tariffs and the establishment of a common external tariff – are plainly in this category.

International trade is not separate from internal trade. Thus, Community regulations relating to the production of steel or of agricultural goods can be regarded as very similar in principle to, though more limited in scope than, regulations about international trade. International agreements relating to income taxation or patents are other examples. By a further extension, EEC regulations standardizing the size of lorries, or the standardized OECD nomenclature for trade descriptions of fruit and vegetables (which in effect reduce barriers to commerce), may be regarded as helping to set the framework for international trade. The Common Agricultural Policy, affecting only one sector, may be regarded as a half-way case: its governing principles have remained broadly unchanged, though its application requires annual negotiations.

International action of the first sort, relating to the international economic framework, is more basic and quite likely more important. Countries have attached great importance, probably rightly in their own interests, both to the maintenance of a *stable* economic framework, and also to securing *freer* conditions for trade and to reducing tariffs and other trade barriers. The fundamental elements of such a framework need to be established world wide; and it plainly is through world-wide international organizations that its maintenance, extension, and improvement need to be pursued. It must also in general be true that, if low tariffs are an advantage, the advantage is greatest when world wide. But fairly complete freedom of trade was most readily available on a European basis and, as it turned out, through membership of the EEC. Moreover, within the Community, with its relatively small area and tight-knit organization, very detailed interventions to 'hinder hindrances' to trade have been feasible. Membership of the Community has not conflicted with membership of world-wide organizations but has been supplementary to it.

This paper is concerned chiefly to evaluate the EEC as a forum for co-operation on matters of general economic policy that aims (let us say) to maintain satisfactory economic growth and high employment together with reasonable stability of prices, employing as its possible instruments fiscal policy, monetary policy, and exchange rate policy – and (perhaps) incomes policies or, in the past, import restrictions.

This describes what has happened. To some it will appear an unduly Keynesian formulation. For a monetarist, the use of monetary policy alone is necessary, and that of other instruments harmful. Since the effects of monetary policy take time to accrue, what is needed is a monetary policy that can be set for the medium term, not altered every month. With much less active economic policies, there must be much less scope for countries to co-operate about them. Indeed, it must be doubtful whether to a monetarist there is scope at all for countries' getting together on this matter; and whether, to him, international economic collaboration is not confined to ensuring the basic framework of law and order.

Countries have differed greatly on their economic philosophy (though the differences may be lessening). Some countries have been explicitly Keynesian – most notably the Scandinavian; others have been, or have been near to being, explicitly anti-Keynesian – perhaps most notably Germany and Japan, and in between have been many shades of grey. In practice, however, all governments, without exception, have intervened. They have not left things to the automatic pilot but have acted, at yearly intervals or even less, to affect aggregate demand.

It would be difficult or impossible to write a paper like this without having a standpoint on these questions. Our way of talking about economic policy has changed a great deal over the period since World War II. At present, the possibilities and *modus operandi* of macro-economic policies are in the course of radical reassessment. The underlying view adopted here is that, despite the current disillusion, there remains an essential role for discretionary stabilization policy, even if a smaller role than has often been claimed. The corollary is that there is room for international co-operation between countries in respect of their stabilization policy – even though (as will be argued) the possibilities here too are limited.

2. The Role of International Economic Co-operation Defined

An international organization is a collective body of sovereign states and can do what its members agree on. It is true that a collective body has some momentum of its own; that it is difficult for a country once it has become a member of an international organization to leave it; and that international civil servants – like subordinates and servants in general – have a certain power, though stronger in some organizations than others, which is nevertheless weak when faced with strong opposition from member countries. Indeed, when there is a conflict between an organization and one or more of its members, the strength of the former is the strength of the permanent staff of the organization in loose alliance with most of the members – generally on an issue, however, where the concern of these members is weak and diffused, as against one or more members to whom the matter is typically of close concern.

The effectiveness of international co-operation is often discussed in terms of the effectiveness of international organizations in making countries do what, left to themselves, they would not have done. Disappointment is often expressed at the relative impotence of international organizations; or that they seem, when their achievement is couched in these terms, not to have accomplished much. This is to mistake what international organizations are. Since they are composed of independent states, their value ought surely to be assessed in terms of the benefit their members receive from being part of them. The value of their members must certainly be much broader than is illustrated by evident instances of conflict or by victory over a recalcitrant member on some specific issue; and even in such cases the value must in part be contained in the benefit, harder to pin down, which the other countries obtain from the upholding of the particular code of conduct which is the occasion of the conflict. The elements of benefit, though real and important, are hard to define: indeed I do not remember seeing an attempt at evaluation in these terms.

To assess the value of international co-operation from the viewpoint of individual countries, such co-operation has to be seen, as Clausewitz said of war, as an extension of the powers of normal instruments of policy. The question is: how far can a country pursue its interests more effectively by co-operation than by abstaining? There are some matters where, in the absence of collaboration, inconsistent action by different countries is quite likely, for example on exchange rates under a managed exchange rate régime: for one country's exchange rate is the obverse of those of its neighbours. Co-operation is likely here because compromise positions are possible and effective action is likely to be impossible without agreement.

But for most questions of general economic policy this is not the case. Starting with the policies of its neighbours as given, each country must do the best it can in its own interests. The policies thus chosen by different countries will be consistent in the sense that they are capable simultaneously of being put into effect. Moreover, countries can make their choices and decide their policies without having to enter into confabulation with their neighbours. If conferring nevertheless appears beneficial, that must be because countries think they can achieve their aims better this way.

An individual country could plainly do better for itself if other countries did what it wanted instead of what they themselves chose. Countries, however, each have fairly different, and fairly definite, ideas and priorities; they do as their situations and their priorities dictate; and do not change merely in response to the wish of another country. A country may in respect of its stabilization policy be more receptive to the wishes of another if it is dependent on the latter, for instance as regards defence or perhaps on energy questions or in current trade negotiations. But a country's stabilization policy is generally regarded rightly as primarily its own affair, with the result that any element of horse-trading can be neither overt nor far reaching. Within the strict confines of co-operation on stabilization policies, the opportunity for such mutually beneficial deals is even more greatly restricted.

The one exception is where a country in a weak balance of payments situation feels itself in need of official international financial support; it may then be ready to modify its economic policies to obtain that support. This is in accordance with the generally accepted rules about how the international monetary system, and the IMF in particular, should work; and the parties to the negotiation will normally be a single country and an international institution (such as the IMF). But in the background – not always so far in the background – will be the more powerful members of the international organizations whose assent to the loan is requisite; and the modification of the deficit country's policy will generally be in the direction which the surplus countries would desire. A supplicant does not relish being in this position; thus to some degree it can be said to arise only by miscalculation – miscalculations, however, to which some countries, whether by temperament or by circumstances, are more prone than others. Obverse pressures against surplus countries do not exist. Calls for financial assistance arose more frequently in the days when we had a fixed but adjustable exchange rate régime; but they can arise still – as, for example, in the case of the United Kingdom in 1976.

Except for such situations, it is unlikely that countries will modify their general economic policies in any fundamental way to please their neighbours. In the practical formulation of budget policy, for instance, I would judge that international reactions are rarely if ever taken into account. If this were all, one might indeed wonder why such a great deal of international consultation nevertheless persists.

The reason why it is so much alive is, I believe, that it is convenient for various purposes which, although important, are only of secondary importance. An opportunity may arise for collective action, as in November 1978, for temporary support of the dollar. Interest rate policy needs to be framed, if not in concert, at least in the knowledge of other countries' probable reactions. It is useful, in general, to know what other countries' policies are – which has to be learned, less from speeches than from private contacts. Since developments are continuous, rapid, and complex, keeping abreast of understanding is difficult; and discussion with others in the same position is helpful. One country's own policies or actions may be misunderstood or resented; and since unnecessary hostility is a nuisance, it is convenient to be able to explain. As an example of a typical agenda, a Group of Five ministerial meeting is reported to have discussed three things: the sharp world-wide rise in interest rates, the soaring gold price, and plans to dilute the US dollar's reserve role (*Financial Times*, 17 September 1979). Discussion of these matters will not alter any country's GNP perceptibly, or slow down or speed up the rate of rise of prices by as much as a single percentage point. But since we have to live closely with our neighbours it is sensible to talk about things with them. Discussion in international organizations (multilateral diplomacy) is an economic and effective way of doing so.

This may be true now. But at times there was perhaps more than that to international economic co-operation. It has certainly worked best when conducted with the active interest of a strong and benevolent super-power – notably in the Marshall Aid period and a few years following (1947 to, say, 1955); and the years of, and just after, the Kennedy Administration (1960 to, say, 1966). In these periods there may even have been the beginnings of a perception of an overriding world interest; and the beginnings of a readiness to subordinate national interests and to participate in the pursuit of common aims – easier if there is some promise that other countries too are doing the same. A similar sense of overriding common purpose is latent in the idea of the European Community, an aspect of it to which other member countries have as yet probably been more susceptible than the United Kingdom; and which would wax with time (see Part 5 below).

3. The Changing Background to International Economic Co-operation

Many aspects of economic co-operation can best be understood in the broad historical context. Since the Second World War there have been three broad phases.

(a) *1947–1958*. Until the major European countries adopted external convertibility in December 1958, the Bretton Woods system remained on ice. This was the great first phase of European co-operation, under the Organization for European Economic Co-operation, with the European Payments Union as a central achievement.

(b) *1958–1972*. With a world-wide system of fixed but adjustable exchange rates in operation, this was the heyday of the International Monetary Fund.

(c) *1972 to date*. This era ended with the general adoption of floating rates in 1972.

Though the first phase is now history, the traditions then established continue in the work of the OECD, and have influenced the style of both the IMF and the European Community. The second phase is in many ways the contrary pole to the world we now live in; however, it still illustrates current problems, since it constitutes an opposite to which we are continually tempted back.

The Bretton Woods agreements set out an international code of conduct which was in some respects hardened and simplified when it came to be put into practical operation after 1958. There were perhaps three main elements.

First, it was accepted without much question that the system was one of fixed but adjustable exchange rates; and countries accepted that exchange rate adjustments were a matter of international concern – principles spelt out in detail in the Articles of the IMF. Underlying these provisions was a fear, arising from prewar experience, of competitive devaluations. This particular manifestation of beggar-my-neighbour behaviour has, however, not in fact proved a pressing danger in the postwar years.

Secondly, countries' pursuit of their social and political aims, and perhaps most to the point, their aspirations to full employment, were not to be thwarted by balance of payments constraints. If countries were in 'fundamental disequilibrium', devaluation was to be allowed: this vague phrase has in practice been interpreted as meaning a situation such that a reasonably balanced payments position could not be restored without undue deflation of demand. The original philosophy of Bretton Woods implied a movable peg exchange rate régime. In practice, the rules came to be interpreted with a bias towards rigidity. It is also noteworthy that it was intended that in a situation of fundamental disequilibrium, resort should be permitted to quantitative import restrictions. (QRs, as they are called, were to have been permitted under the supervision of the planned International Trade Organization after consultation with the IMF. The ITO, however, was never born, and the links between the IMF and GATT never became strongly established.)

Thirdly, credit was to be provided to countries in payments difficulties on condition that they adopted domestic policies judged appropriate by the IMF. Payments difficulties could arise as a result of a fundamental disequilibrium. Credit would then be needed to tide over the period before a depreciation could affect trade flows – and an adjustment of domestic policies would in this case be needed in order to reduce domestic demand and make room for greater net real exports. If payments difficulties arose *without* there being a fundamental disequilibrium, they must (by definition) be due to an excess of domestic demand – which, likewise, called for an adjustment of domestic policies (which, it could be hoped, would avoid the need that might otherwise have arisen for a devaluation later).

The IMF was set up as an international lending body – not as an institution in which countries could confer on and co-ordinate their general economic policies. But the administration of the rules governing exchange rate adjustments and the provision of conditional credit involved discussion, and even negotiation, with countries about their economic policies. The IMF thus got into the business of discretionary macro-economic policy. But it retained something of its character as a 'minimum interference' organization. Though member countries were involved in discussing each other's affairs, the discussion was 'at a distance' – being conducted through their permanent representatives in Washington who constitute the Executive Board. Again, though countries had regular visits from IMF staff as part of the consultation routine, they were left in peace except on occasions when they had broken the IMF's rules or needed to borrow money from it; and it was only when they needed to borrow that the IMF had much leverage over countries' policies. What benefit countries derived from membership of the IMF, in the fixed rate era, was perhaps the promise of a stable background resulting from firm rules, and a strong institution to police them. It was not basically an organization which allowed them, in any very direct, detailed or forceful way, to put pressure on their fellow members or have pressure put on them in return.

The OEEC, and (since 1960) its successor the OECD, had always overtly engaged in the co-ordination of macro-economic policies. In the early days (till 1952), the availability of Marshall Aid provided a strong financial sanction to the attempt to co-ordinate countries' policies. Unlike the IMF, discussions in OECD have involved direct participation, not of permanent representatives, but of the senior national officials responsible at home for macro-economic policy. This form of discussion, especially that in Working Party no. 3 (WP3), probably ensured some influence by member countries on their partners' policies. On occasion, the OECD acted as an adjunct to the IMF. For the latter was at times dependent for finance on the General Agreement to Borrow, the parties to which were nearly identical with the membership of WP3, whose recommendations therefore carried the more weight with a country that was currently seeking to borrow.

The OECD was also influential, together with the IMF, in the negotiations preceding the Smithsonian Agreement at the end of 1971. This was probably the most complicated adjustment of fixed exchange rates ever attempted, since the devaluation of the US dollar – previously in effect the fixed point in the system – was liable to un-leash adjustments of other countries' exchange rates, which could have undone the US adjustment. The difficulties stemmed partly from the need for simultaneous agreement by many countries, but the way to agreement was undoubtedly eased by the technical calculations pro-vided (in part by the OECD, in part by the IMF). The Smithsonian Agreement was later regarded by the United States as not going far enough (a view, however, that could still be disputed); and because of the complexities of a second multinational negotiation, the United States espoused, in 1973, the cause of generalized floating as a way of securing further effective depreciation. The first devaluation of the dollar was nevertheless clearly crucial and opened a road, long blocked, for a better mix of national economic policies.

The move to generalized floating also owed much to the heavy current of (mainly academic and semi-monetarist) criticism of the workings of the fixed exchange rate system. Floating exchange rates have not of course become universal. Many small countries peg to the US dollar or the currency of a strong neighbour; and fixed rates have operated within Europe – to be discussed below – under the Snake arrangements and now under the European Monetary System. Thus 'floating' describes the relation between major blocs. Since this came to be the case, in 1972, the world has changed enormously (though not entirely as a consequence of floating rates) in three chief ways.

First, general floating has more or less removed the possibility of codes of conduct specifying the use of exchange rate adjustments. Attempts to get agreement on, and to enforce compliance with, specified permitted bands have not proved workable – mainly because of the difficulty governments face in controlling rates effectively in a floating world. It is true that most countries have practised 'dirty floating' and that interventions have at times been massive. But it is questionable whether interventions have been more than smoothing operations, moderating the results of market forces rather than implementing preconceived ideas of where exchange rates 'ought' to be. The mobility of capital has now become so great (partly indeed because of unstable exchange rates) that the implementation of an exchange rate policy is now very difficult with anything short of return to a fixed-rate régime. The exchange rate has, for this reason among others, almost ceased to be a policy instrument.

Secondly, inflation has become significantly worse – a trend which started before, but was assisted by, the OPEC price increases of 1973/4. The control of inflation by means of demand deflation is probably nowhere regarded as a perfect instrument. But, for lack of a better, all major countries in present circumstances are seeking to keep their economies growing at rates of expansion well below the rate of growth that would earlier have been thought sustainable. This is a major change in the bias of national policies. However justified, it represents a defeat: economic policies have failed to provide a reasonably satisfactory solution to this problem. This cramps the scope for international co-operation.

Thirdly, the trade effect of adjustments of fixed exchange rates was always liable to be eroded, to some degree, by the repercussions on domestic prices so provoked. But these repercussions seem to have become larger and faster: partly because faster inflation has made everyone more aware of it; partly because a fixed rate was an apparent discipline which made it easier for governments to restrain the domestic repercussions. For this reason, too, it has become more difficult to use the exchange rate as an instrument of policy – though not impossible with a fixed rate system, as EEC experience seems to show. With a floating régime, exchange rates stand primarily to be influenced only indirectly – by the stance of monetary and fiscal policies.

All these changes seem to have diminished the role that international economic organizations can play. Multilateral discussion clearly retains an undiminished and essential role dealing with the numerous second-order matters, many of great importance, that throng the agenda of economic diplomacy. But the scope for co-ordination of the overriding questions of macro-economic policy is clearly lessened – partly because the scope for, and ambitions of, national economic policies have themselves been diminished. The role of the IMF, formerly the most important international institution, has probably been most reduced. In form, it is now recognized (under the new Article 4) to have a greater role in the general monitoring of countries' economic policies. But in practice its role has inevitably been lessened, because the major exchange rates appear, for the time at least, to be only partially subject to governmental decision; and because countries are less likely to need to turn to it for financial assistance, now that deficits can be absorbed by floating exchange rates – or met, much more easily than before, by market borrowings. The role of the OECD has probably been affected less. The EEC's role in this field has probably been affected least, in part because of the retention within its membership of strong elements of a fixed exchange rate system.

4. The State of Economic Co-operation in the EEC

This part discusses how useful membership of the Community, as a forum for economic co-operation, now is to the United Kingdom; and the following part asks how useful in this way the EEC might become in future. In the case of the Community, however, it is difficult, without departing from even justice, to keep present and future distinct. For the aims of the EEC are potentially ambitious and evolutionary. It has aspirations that constantly point ahead into the future: and most developments are seen as capable of leading on to greater things, or even as containing an inevitable dynamism that will take its member countries along a road where their separate identities will fade away. Though hopefulness needs constantly to be distinguished from present reality, it is right that regard should throughout be paid not only to things as they are but to the seeds of development within them.

It is no doubt a reflection of this forward-looking focus that the EEC's manner of work differs in some important ways from that of the IMF or the OECD. In other international economic organizations meetings of ministers are relatively infrequent, thus formal speeches tend to predominate and the agreement of communiqués is relatively time-consuming. In the EEC, by contrast, the Finance Council meets monthly, except in August. Meetings of officials (in principle, as in the OECD, the senior officials from finance ministries and central banks) are also frequent. There has been a succession of attempts to establish ambitious institutional mechanisms for economic co-ordination (often involving exchange rates, discussed below). The thought behind such schemes has been that the involvement of member countries in them would, in a way not perfectly defined, lead to more closely co-ordinated national policies. In practice, however, the aims have been more impressive than the actual content of discussions in the EEC. Though perhaps less efficiently conducted, they have thus been similar to the kind of international consultation conducted by the IMF and the OECD. Nevertheless, discussions on economic policy in the EEC, very tedious though they may have been, have to a degree been taken seriously by member countries; and the *communautaire* spirit which inspired them has been alive, if not an immediately effective force. It is a tribute to a political ideal, as it would be to a religion, to be able to say as much as this.

As in other bodies, there are considerable differences of view and approach between the different members of the EEC. If they appear more evident in the EEC than in wider international organizations – of which the same countries are of course members – that may be because ministers meet more often and agreement is attempted on so very many matters, so that occasions for possible discord are more frequent. Many disagreements arise in the course of negotiations on relatively restricted matters where there may be straight conflicts of interest between governments (for example, on the width of protected fishing zones). How important are differences of national viewpoint on much broader policy issues?

National viewpoints plainly do differ on questions of macro-economic policy, and generally reflect differences of economic philosophy. They may for instance reflect different attitudes to nationalization; to controls and other interferences with the private economy; and to the possibility of enforcing tax and other laws. Probably of most importance are differences which reflect different priorities as to the goals of macro-economic policy. The differences among members of the EEC have probably narrowed very greatly in the last few years, as inflation has come to be seen as the overriding problem. But in earlier years Germany was typically most emphatic on the importance of controlling inflation, and least inclined to follow an expansionist policy; while the other members, each in a different way, had a somewhat different view – and certainly were less successful in controlling inflation. It is sometimes argued that such differences of viewpoint impede collaboration. So they plainly do on occasions when agreement is being sought on a joint policy to which all members must adhere. But for the most part the policies discussed in an international forum are national policies, applying to separate economic areas. In such a decision-making framework, a difference of view between neighbouring countries does not prevent each country from optimizing its position within the constraints imposed by the choices of other countries – which, in turn, are freely adopted, under similar constraints.

International discussion remains useful, even though argument is unlikely to close differences of national viewpoint. For the disputes are basically not technical, but about the ends of economic policy; and, as with oecumenism in the religious domain, the source of argument cannot be removed without one party or the other changing sides (or both parties shifting towards the centre). International discussion nevertheless plays an essential role. Partial compromises, or a degree of accommodation to the outlines of a general view, may be possible; and agreement may be possible on restricted matters. And even if not, the reasons for discrepant policies need to be explained. From this workaday viewpoint it is indeed precisely the differences of national interest that make international discussion desirable.

At present, as is clear, 'Europe' is far from being a world power. It is sometimes argued that the United Kingdom has now such little weight in world affairs that its voice will be heard only if it speaks in concert with its European neighbours. If all members of the EEC had the same view on a particular issue, that would be easy. More usually, the divergences are more important than the convergence. The formulation of a common policy (as opposed to harmonization of national policies) is precisely what the EEC is least good at – as is natural. There have been successes in setting up institutional arrangements (for instance the negotiations in GATT with non-EEC countries about changes in the common external tariff are handled by the Community; or the Lomé Convention); but much less as regards the ingredients of discretionary economic policy, and in discussions with the United States and Japan any agreement among the EEC countries will be (and will clearly be seen to be) very incomplete. Useful though it may be for Europeans to act in concert, this will hardly check the natural tendency for the United States to deal direct with the stronger member countries.

A persistent strain of thought within the EEC has been the predilection for a fixed exchange rate régime. At its most ideological, it has been seen as a way of forcing members to adopt policies, and thus create economic conditions, that would perpetuate such a régime – paving the way thereby to an indissoluble monetary union. But experience showed that tails do not wag dogs; and the idea never came close to translation into fact. Nevertheless, there has been considerable success in working a movable peg régime – the Snake was able to accommodate fairly numerous currency realignments – which has continued to operate a miniature Bretton Woods régime in the general sea of floating. The Snake was perhaps a German currency area comprising a group of smaller neighbours with close trade links with Germany. This involved difficulties for the smaller countries, where inflation tended to be faster than in Germany. But, partly indeed for this very reason, their attachment to it – and to its successor the European Monetary System – has been tenacious; and there is reason to think that the barrier of a fixed exchange rate has exerted restraint on wage developments in the smaller countries and thus provided a much needed extra degree of stability.

It is less clear how far a fixed exchange rate régime can successfully be extended to include not only Germany, but the other major European countries – even with the safety valve of an adjustable peg. The growing trade integration of European countries may provide the conditions in which a fixed-rate régime can succeed, even though present-day circumstances prevent its reinstatement on a world-wide scale. The greater exposure of the United Kingdom to strong flows of international capital, demonstrated by the weakness of sterling in 1976 and its strength subsequently, may be thought to make it difficult for the UK to adhere to such a régime. Nevertheless, the ebbs and flows might possibly have been less if the United Kingdom already had been securely part of it; and the pressures might then have affected the European bloc as a whole, not sterling in particular.

If successful, the EMS seems bound to entail consequences for the economic policies of its members, as did the IMF fixed rates. Membership of a movable peg system logically requires a willingness on the part of its members to subordinate, up to a point, the other aims of economic policy in order to maintain the exchange parity. Both this general requirement, and the more particular necessity to be willing to intervene on exchange markets to maintain the parity, probably imply that the aims of monetary policy can no longer be defined purely in terms of domestic monetary targets that do not comprehend an element of flexibility on this score. The co-ordination of members' economic policies inside the EEC may therefore have more cogency and bite than is now necessary (and is thus now customary) within the IMF. (Member countries may well, however, wish to retain access to conditional credit from the IMF rather than be entirely dependent on the EEC provisions.)

These corollaries might not, in themselves, seem advantageous to members: they must be judged as part of what is entailed in belonging to a fixed rate régime. On that question there will probably always be two views. But the balance of opinion seems to be moving back closer towards the classic compromise enshrined in Bretton Woods. Experience with floating rates has shown them to have greater disadvantages than it was fashionable to believe before they were generally adopted, and by now there has been a considerable revulsion against them. Reliance on market mechanisms has clearly allowed much instability – and what industry appears to need above all is a degree of stability in exchange rates; it has also permitted the continuance for significant periods of unsustainable exchange rates, which in these cases will have given perverse signals and prompted industry to adjustments that will later have to be reversed. The recent experience also suggests that – apart from a compromise based on geographical propinquity such as the EMS – there is no half-way house between fixed and floating; so that a floating régime seems to rule out any real control over exchange rates. The countries adhering to the EMS probably see its main advantage as the fact that, within Europe, and to some degree at least, the exchange rate has become once more an instrument of policy.

5. The Possible Evolution of the EEC as a Forum

Two reasons may be given for suggesting that collaboration in the EEC is likely to be closer than in other international bodies. The general reason is that the EEC, in however blind and groping a way, appears to have a dynamic which leads it to sponsor initiatives that constantly press towards a truly communal form of decision making. The second (perhaps only an important example of the first) is its strong predilection for a fixed exchange rate régime. But developments seem bound to be slow and gradual; and whether one welcomes or fears such a direction of events, it is useful to look closely at what seems feasible, and what not.

Enthusiasts for the idea of a fuller Community have hoped to see the development of a closer integration of monetary policies; and have sometimes seen this as a logical counterpart to trying to run a fixed rate régime. That may be a misconception. The running of a fixed exchange rate system requires appropriately *different* monetary policies in individual countries, not the development of a common monetary policy for the area as a whole. Thus what the 'average' monetary policy should be barely gets a conscious look. What is involved is the familiar sort of discussion, dominated by the surplus countries, of what a deficit country ought to do. The result is likely to be biased in favour of the creditors' views – up to the point where a realignment of exchange rates is seen to be necessary. If rates of inflation in different countries continue to differ, with each country faced with its own particular problems, member countries' monetary policies are bound to diverge at times from the average.

It has been an old dream that the Community should establish a monetary union in the sense of establishing a common currency; advocates of monetary union have seen it as a step that would be irreversible and that would impel the integration of countries' policies. But it is not clear that it would work in that way. For many years the fixed parity between the Republic of Ireland and the United Kingdom seemed unquestioned; and it would presumably have been quite possible for the two countries, sovereign though they each were, to have had a common currency if they (or more particularly if Ireland) had wished to do so. This stable relationship, ironically now shattered, does suggest that a common currency area is not, under certain conditions, an utterly remote possibility. It would appear to require only a long experience in which economic trends in the participating countries had been compatible with a constant exchange rate; but it presumably could not be created merely by an effort of will to maintain a constant rate in the face of divergent trends. (There might be more mileage in the parallel circulation of money denominated in terms of the European and national units of account – which might also facilitate the power of the Community to borrow on national capital markets.)

Strange as it may appear, there are at present no effective arrangements within the EMS for the co-ordination of member countries' interventions in non-members' currencies, that is, no arrangement for exchange market interventions to affect the average exchange rate of the bloc *vis-à-vis* the outside world. If the EMS survives this is a gap that may well have to be filled in one way or another. This would represent a considerable diminution – for as long as individual countries wished to remain within the scheme – of countries' effective power over the disposal of their reserves. And since exchange rates are as much affected by domestic monetary policies as reserve interventions, it would surely bring with it some sort of collective decision making about the 'average' monetary policy of the group of countries. This would be a less formidable advance than it might perhaps appear to be – since there are market pressures towards conformity – and might make membership of the EMS more advantageous. Without such an arrangement the determination of members' exchange rates *vis-à-vis* third countries (affecting, in the case of the United Kingdom, half our trade) would remain the result of a fairly random process.

The prospect of any important development towards Community decision making in the realm of fiscal policy seems, at the moment, fairly remote. Probably for that reason, there has not been much discussion of the advantages and disadvantages of such a development. Its possible ultimate advantages may, however, be stronger than such inattention might seem to suggest. If depressed areas require special treatment, this probably has to be provided by special schemes of assistance – of which there are elements in present Community arrangements – rather than by divergence as between the broad fiscal stance of different member countries. The 'leakages' are such that an independent fiscal policy in a small national area is now becoming quite difficult, and will become more so.

The interdependence of member countries is a factor that cannot be ignored in policy decisions and it may gradually, over time, lead member countries to press for, and accept, an increasing degree of co-ordination as regards their fiscal policies. This would in practice tend to reduce countries' ability to change fiscal policy at short notice; and might thus also reduce the flexibility of fiscal policy as an instrument. There is much discussion of the Community budget, but mostly about its distributive aspects, particularly its incidence as between nations. The use of the Community budget as an instrument for affecting demand does not now arise. For it to be capable of use in this way, Community spending would have to become much larger; and the Community would have to have power to decide within wide limits whether spending should be financed by borrowing or by revenue – in this case, transfers from member countries: neither condition is likely to be met in any foreseeable future.

Any integration of policy making in the field of general economic development thus seems bound to be a very slow and very piecemeal development. In so far as it does occur, it could be advantageous for the United Kingdom to take part in it. A more integrated type of policy making might help to produce a more stable environment for industry, the provision of which should be a major aim of macro-economic policy. It must be reasons such as this which explain why, in the United States, where monetary and fiscal policies are decided on a nationwide basis, these go unquestioned, and why New England, the mid-West, Texas or the West Coast do not each clamour to have their own separate monetary and fiscal policies.

6. Conclusions

This paper has touched on a variety of large issues, and it may be useful to try to summarize the general drift of the argument. The value one places on the EEC as a forum for economic co-operation appears to depend very largely on one's judgement on much wider issues: whether one believes that the EEC has within it a momentum that will lead to an increasing degree of integration, not only between the economies of member countries but also between the policies of their governments; and whether one believes that it would be advantageous to the United Kingdom to take part in that development.

My own view is that such a development, no doubt very gradually, probably will take place. Since European countries are close neighbours in a shrinking world it seems inevitable that they should increasingly be involved with each other politically; and that we should be worse off if we tried to exclude ourselves from this development. If one sees less of a growing role for the EEC, it would still appear to be one of the areas where our need to take part in multilateral economic diplomacy will continue. In either case, since our relations with countries outside Europe are also important we need to belong also to wider or world-wide bodies.

Comment
by W. A. B. Hopkin

Mr Dow's paper is concerned chiefly to evaluate the EEC as a forum for co-operation on matters of general economic policy. If I read him correctly, his evaluation of the EEC in this role is moderately favourable though it does not amount to keen enthusiasm. I want to develop some arguments that lead me to a much less favourable view, in spite of my agreement with at least four-fifths of the paper.

I do not think it is unfair to say that Mr Dow looks at the problem from a 'European' or even broader point of view, in the sense that most of the arguments he deploys are quite general. He does not concern himself with considerations that are of interest only or mainly to Britain. It seems to me that this is a rather serious omission, given the theme of the Conference. I want to argue that there are certain factors which severely limit the extent to which, in present circumstances, it would be appropriate from a UK point of view to intensify co-operation in matters of general economic policy in the EEC forum.

These factors fall under two headings: the continuing weaknesses of the UK economy; and the continuing features of the institutions and policies of the Community. It is the painful truth that the UK economy does suffer from continuing economic weaknesses. I would diagnose two in particular, not unconnected but more than merely aspects of the same thing. First, we have an unusually strong tendency to inflation because of pressure for wage and salary increases. These pressures come from a strongly organized labour movement, highly divided sectionally. Secondly, we have an entrepreneurial sector which in comparative international terms can be called 'low-achieving'. The reasons for this are far from clear, but whatever the causes, it is difficult to deny the evidences of weakness shown by low productivity growth, low investment, and failures to conquer newly opening markets or even to hold existing ones. Of course there are honourable exceptions but this seems to be a fair picture over a great part of the field.

The second group of factors includes features of the EEC which largely reflect its origin in an agreement between the Six to which Britain was not a party. These are the concentration of Community resources in support of agriculture, the design both of the CAP itself and of the system of Community finance, and a comparative lack of interest in problems of industrial weakness.

Both sets of factors have been at work throughout the period of British membership of the EEC and have inevitably had a great influence on the balance of Britain's gains and losses from that membership. What I have called the internal weaknesses have created a tendency to weak and declining international competitiveness. These are no doubt the reasons why – as it appears to me – the much advertised 'dynamic benefits' from the enlargement of the Community have accrued more to other countries than to the UK. If opportunities have been created, one can only say that the UK economy has not, on the whole, shown an ability to grasp them. So far from the dynamic effects of entry to the EEC offsetting the 'direct' cost to us, they have been fairly small, quite possibly negative.

The UK's situation in the Community is rather similar to that of a depressed area inside a unitary state. But the position of a 'depressed country' within the Community is very different from that of a depressed area within a country. The depressed *area's* lot is substantially mitigated, partly by the automatic operation of the country's fiscal system and partly by deliberate regional policies. The Community's regional policies are so far on a very small scale compared with the problem, and the fiscal system operates perversely. Absurd as it may seem, the fiscal transfer, on a very substantial scale, is *from* the depressed country towards other and mostly more prosperous countries.

The way in which the Community's finances are organized produces a pattern of net transfers which on any objective view is indefensible and from which Britain is the principal sufferer.

The recognition on the one hand of these basic weaknesses in the British economy, and continuing characteristics and tendencies of the Community on the other, should very greatly influence our attitude to different kinds of international co-operation and the institutions through which it can be carried on. This is not to say that any kind of international action can by itself provide a remedy for the weaknesses. For that, some considerable changes of our domestic habits, attitudes, and institutions are needed. In the period before such changes have been made (it would be agreeable, but to my mind not very realistic, to say that they were visibly under way) we should distinguish between those forms of international co-operation which can be helpful and those which are more likely to be damaging.

There certainly *is* a kind of international co-operation which would be very materially helpful to a country in the position of Britain if it were available. It is the kind that was offered by the American government in the immediately postwar period, under the European Recovery Programme (ERP). This programme provided to the West European countries generous financial aid without strings and accompanied by a liberal attitude towards protectionist and discriminatory policies. Co-operation of this kind is not available now to any countries except (in a degree) those of the Third World; and there are several reasons – some good, some bad – why it would be unrealistic to suggest in any international forum that it should be re-instituted in favour of such a country as Britain. The kind of international co-operative action for which the Community has so far stood has been in most ways the opposite of what was provided under the ERP. Protectionist and discriminatory policies are resisted (outside agriculture of course) and there is no financial support to be had, indeed Britain has to support others on a large scale.

We are here concerned with the limited though important question of co-operation 'in matters of general economic policy', which may be taken to cover the exchange of information about, and mutual discussion of, *national* budgetary policies, monetary policies, exchange rate policies, and possibly incomes policy. This definition *excludes* the CAP, Community regional and industrial policies, and the Community budget. But one can hardly form an attitude to policies of the first kind without being influenced by one's attitude to policies of the second.

My assumption about these is that from now on the UK ought to and will make a strenuous effort to secure changes in policy in regard to Community activities and financing. While the result of these activities is still in doubt, the guiding principle in regard to co-operation in 'matters of general economic policy' surely has to be that the UK should seek to preserve its present degree of independent control of these matters. We ought therefore to take a very reserved attitude to joining the EMS (which would limit our freedom of action in regard to exchange rates), to movement towards EMU (which would limit our freedom of action in regard to monetary policy), and to proposals – if any are made – that would limit our freedom of action in regard to budgetary policy.

Such a policy attitude would not prejudice continued co-operation of the kind that already exists in the exchange of information about, and mutual discussion of, general macro-economic policies. Such discussion can and should continue in the Community context. But the more important role in this field belongs to the OECD. We have as much interest in exchanging information and views on these topics with the USA, Japan, Canada, and Australia as with fellow members of the Community. There is also the field of co-operation in the provision of balance of payments support. Here again the Community has a role to play but the major role belongs and should continue to belong to the IMF.

The last word has to be, however, that any view about co-operation in matters of 'general' economic policy must be provisional and subject to the results of the more important discussion now going on about Community policies in the more specific sense.

Comment
by M. Emerson

Mr Dow's paper gives a panoramic, sober, and fairly sympathetic view of economic policy co-ordination efforts in the Community and the broader international organizations. Professor Hopkin gives a more critical view, arguing on the one hand that the United Kingdom risks an erosion of vital fiscal and monetary powers, and on the other hand that the Community pays insufficient attention – in general and in its macro-economic policy bodies – to the UK's industrial problems and to the issue of burden sharing on the budget.

In preparing a brief reaction to the papers I thought the most useful approach would be to describe three episodes in Community activity in order to put more flesh on to the concepts and to demarcate more precisely how or where the Community's efforts should differ from those of the OECD and IMF, and where they should overlap.

The first episode is the concerted budget policy expansion of July 1978, decided almost simultaneously at the European Council in Bremen and the Western Economic Summit in Bonn. In early 1978 forecasts through to 1979 were showing a mediocre outlook: little more than two per cent GDP growth in the Community, against a background of reduced inflation, better balance of payments situations, and still rising unemployment.

The European Council of March 1978 called for action to improve growth and employment substantially. It set in motion the series of monthly meetings of the Finance Council held in the following April, May, and June, each prepared by the Co-ordinating Group (high officials meeting a week before), which progressively worked out quantified budget policy moves by each member state. The Commission fed these meetings with working papers, which started from simple propositions about the amount of budget policy stimulus required to raise the growth rate by one per cent, taking into account domestic multiplier effects, foreign leakages (of demand) and the simultaneous foreign feed-back of demand. The practical logic of collective action was thus discussed: for example, that in the event of isolated action by individual member states national multipliers of between 0.8 and 1.2 (after a year, for small and large countries respectively) could be increased to 1.5 on average in the Community in the event of an identical, simultaneous stimulus for all member states. Various packages of differentiated measures by member states (ranging from over one per cent demand stimulus to zero according to individual countries' room for manoeuvre) were simulated and discussed, with increasing approximation towards what was politically feasible.

By the June meeting of the Finance Council the package reached the stage of a Commission proposal, with detailed figures for each member state: but agreement was not yet reached because Germany in particular had not decided on its contribution to the programme of action.

At the European Council on 6–7 July in Bremen, the Community decided on the principle of the action, but held back the detail. Ten days later, at the Western Economic Summit on 16–17 July, Germany announced its expansionary package of measures amounting to one per cent of GDP. On 24 July, the Community's Finance Council adopted the Commission's June proposal: with the German contribution now specified alongside that of other member states.

The combined stimulus probably succeeded in raising the Community growth rate by over a percentage point. I say 'probably' because the second oil shock arrived at the beginning of 1979, reducing the Community's growth rate to only a little over three per cent in 1979, compared to the 3.5 per cent or more that would have been reached if the oil shock had not occurred, and depressing the outlook for 1980 even further.

The main feature of this episode here relevant is the way in which the Community prepared its part of a global action rapidly and in operationally quite precise terms. It used its institutional potential for quick circulation of the dossier between the highest political level and that of officials to good effect. The Community's activity fitted constructively into the wider international system. Indeed the Community was not acting alone: the OECD had an important preparatory role, and the Western Economic Summit was the most decisive single moment in the episode.

The second episode is the negotiation and entry into operation of the European Monetary System. President Jenkins reanimated debate on European monetary integration with a lecture in Florence in October 1977;

Chancellor Schmidt and President Giscard d'Estaing advocated a new, major monetary initiative at the Copenhagen meeting of the European Council in March 1978; the European Council at Bremen in July 1978 decided in principle on the broad outlines of the system to come, and set into operation the relevant committees to define the operational mechanisms.

From August to November work was done in the Monetary Committee and Committee of Governors of Central Banks on the monetary mechanism, and in the Economic Policy Committee on the question of associated budget resource transfers. Progress was reported back and forth through the Finance Council.

The Monetary Committee and Governors argued out a number of issues: the concept of symmetry in the system, as related to the *numéraire* (the basket ECU, or the bilateral grid of exchange rates), the size and type of credit facilities, the automaticity or non-automaticity of intervention, and/or of other policy adjustments (leading to the Belgian compromise in the 'divergence indicator' with whose operation I shall not burden this text).

The Economic Policy Committee worked hard at the objectively very difficult question of what type or scale of resource transfers to the less prosperous member states should be part of the package. Most people agree that monetary union would have to be backed up by large-scale resource transfers (this had been convincingly demonstrated in 1977 in the report of the MacDougall Group, which incidentally was an interesting example of forward-looking policy research done together by Commission staff and a group of independent economists). But how far should a build-up of resource transfer mechanisms be graduated alongside different degrees of fixity of exchange rates? The conclusion of the European Council in December 1978 on this point was that for an EMS which included the 2.25 and 6 per cent fluctuation margins there would be 200 million ECU of budgetary grants plus one billion ECU of loans for each of five years, shared between Italy and Ireland. Ireland later negotiated additional sums on a bilateral basis. The UK for its part was, as we all know, dissatisfied and negotiated a special clause whereby it neither benefited from nor contributed to these transfers. However, the outcome was in the end obscured by the European Parliament's amendments of the 1979 Community budget. Skipping the procedural detail, one can say that the Parliament's own initiatives, aimed at increasing notably the Regional Fund, interacted with the Council's resource transfer negotiations; and the aggregate result was a much larger increment in regionally progressive resource transfers than those negotiated between member states.

As regards the functioning of the EMS, I would underline the following features. The concept of convergence (notably of inflation rates) has been sharpened by the EMS, and this is reflected in discussions in the Community bodies and in Commission documents, and in reality also perhaps in a more convergent response to the second oil shock (of which more below). The need for closer co-ordination of interest rate policy moves has been perceptibly increased. Concern to work out a Community dollar policy has been increased (the distinction between intra-Community intervention in Community currencies versus extra-Community intervention in third currencies is becoming more of an operational concept). As regards the difficult task of negotiating central rate realignments, the ice has been broken; those worried about excessive rigidity in the EMS may relax; those worried about insufficient strictness may still be worried. Work on the European Monetary Fund is proceeding in the Monetary Committee and the Governors' Committee, and this of course provides the opportunity for imagining more ambitious schemes for building up the European part of a better international monetary system.

The main feature of this second episode is that monetary policy co-operation in the Community is an operational as much as a consultative activity. Its workings account directly or indirectly for quite a lot of the time of committee and Council meetings. Links between macro-economic policy *co-operation* and monetary and budgetary *operations* have been established.

The third episode concerns the Community's reaction to the second oil price shock. The Community as a whole was not successful in managing the aftermath of the first oil price shock in 1973: it led to a bad 1975, with recession (1.5 per cent GDP decline) and high and widely diverging inflation (13 per cent average consumer price rise). Much attention has been given in recent committee and Council meetings to how to avoid the errors of 1973–5, whose ingredients included the diversity of policy strategy adopted in terms of compensating or not, with fiscal or monetary policy, the oil price deflation effect. Divergent wage behaviour was a further factor. The combination of circumstances further led to large exchange rate changes, which amplified inflation differentials and increased the uncertainty factor – to the detriment of growth in trade and investment.

In response to the second oil price shock the Commission has advocated, in its Annual Economic Report for 1979/80, (*European Economy*, Brussels, No. 4, November 1979) the following general strategy:

> The following three-pronged Community policy response is required:
> (i) in a first phase of policy incomes have to be constrained such that consumers absorb the increased cost of energy and secondary increases in inflation are avoided; meanwhile monetary policy should be kept strict, and budgetary policy should at this stage provide only very limited compensation for the effects of the oil price rise;
> (ii) as and when certain positive results are assured as regards inflation, then policy could eventually in the course of 1980 be adjusted into a more actively supportive posture, notably if also investment and consumption were found to be weakening significantly;
> (iii) energy policy must in any case be strengthened in all its aspects, since without achieving a deep change in past relationships between oil imports and economic growth, there is little prospect for the latter to progress.

This extract is from a long document explaining how, in the Commission's view, the policy of each member state fits in and also giving much supporting analytical information. The objective is, for the Community as a whole, to avoid in 1980 anything like the inflationary recession of 1975.

Whether we succeed or not remains to be seen. Throughout the autumn of 1979 there were extensive discussions on the basis of this document in the European Parliament and its relevant committee, in the Economic and Social Committee (bringing together employers and trade unions), as well as in the Council and its subordinate committees of officials. The attempt is being made to communicate a consistent policy approach to a common economic problem into the political and economic systems of the Community and member states; the situation is one in which, it is argued, divergences in the policy or behavioural response of individual member states would increase the risk of an unmanageable deterioration in the economic climate. This fits with the broad intention behind the Council's Decision of

18 February 1974 (74/120/EEC), which provides the statutory and procedural basis for the Community's economic policy co-ordination. To be sure, it is difficult to put life into, and get results out of these procedures, given the fundamental prerogatives of member states to decide their own policy moves when and how they wish, and given the immense political pressures that bear upon such moves back at home in national capitals. The underlying objective of convergence of economic performance – on low inflation and high productivity and employment standards – is still worth pursuing, even if its achievement is sometimes elusive and irregular.

A remark on overlapping activities. The field of short-run economic forecasting is so important and hazardous that it warrants several separate international views: EC, OECD, IMF, and so on. This work should be as transparently comparable as possible in technique and presentation, so that all players in the international co-ordination game, including those in national capitals, should be able to study and reconcile differences. Nowadays this is more or less assured.

In conclusion. I would like to signal disagreement with some of Professor Hopkin's specific points. I do not see that the Community risks impinging on national fiscal powers. I would suggest that the EMS provides a mechanism that can increase effective national powers to have a positive exchange rate policy, rather than take something away. I do not recognize in the Community the suggested caricature of a body devoted to untrammelled global free trade, unresponsive to severe sectoral or industrial problems of the UK's type (what about textiles, steel, ship-building?). I am not sure how industrial policy issues should enter into macro-economic policy coordination in some way that is implicitly suggested.

9 The Community as a Framework for British External Relations
by John Pinder and William Wallace

Britain depends on international trade for its living and on the Western alliance for its security. It follows that much of our diplomacy must be conducted multilaterally, within the framework of international organizations. But the choice of priorities among such organizations, in both economic and security policy, remains open to debate. All members of the European Community are more sharply constrained in external economic policy than non-member countries. The benefits lie in common bargaining strength and in the influence gained by concerting diplomatic efforts, the costs in the displacement of national objectives by those of the Community as a whole.

This chapter considers these costs and benefits as far as Britain is concerned. We ask how far British priorities in foreign policy have proved compatible with those of our partners; whether there remain distinctive British interests in relations with third countries that are not shared by our partners or accommodated by the Community; and whether British interests would be better served by more tightly limiting the scope of Community co-operation on external relations or by extending it further, either in economic matters or in security and defence.

Are British Interests Compatible with Those of Other Member States?

British foreign policy objectives and interests have rarely been precisely defined. In 1977 an official formulation identified four 'first-order objectives': 'to ensure the external security of the UK'; 'to promote the country's economic and social well-being'; 'to honour certain commitments or obligations which the UK has voluntarily entered into or cannot withdraw from'; and 'to work for a peaceful and just world' ([1], paragraphs 2.24–2.31). Such a broad formulation begs difficult questions about how these objectives are to be pursued: the choice of partners and allies, the relative weight to be attached to military, economic, or cultural instruments, and the expenditure to be allocated to each. Britain has, for example, remained ambivalent in its relations with the United States, recognizing the loss of its privileged status but at the same time assuming a closer identity of outlook and interest with the Americans than with its European partners. Ambivalence has also been evident in approaches to the 'commitments and obligations' represented by the Commonwealth, particularly in policies towards the Indian subcontinent. The question how far British interests are compatible with those of the 'Eight' has not been clearly answered. Ambiguous political objectives and uncertain economic priorities leave room for doubt as to where British governments have believed British interests to lie.

Since British forces were withdrawn from east of Suez in the early 1970s there has been little dispute within Britain about the central issues of security policy or the multilateral framework within which it rests. For its defence against the only threat currently perceived, Britain relies upon the allied forces in Germany to which the United Kingdom contributes, the local forces in Norway for which we provide a reserve, American aircraft flying from Icelandic or British bases, and the combined naval forces of the European and North American members of NATO. There may be disagreement about the severity of the threat and the size and shape of Britain's contribution, but the stance itself commands general consent. In security policy more widely defined, a similar consensus is evident: disagreement, perhaps, on the interpretation of Soviet intentions and on the details of Western proposals, but agreement that the pursuit of détente, the improvement of communications and of confidence between the two alliances, and the endeavour to limit force size and armaments are best conducted through the overlapping mechanisms of NATO and of European Political Co-operation. British objectives, thus defined, do not significantly differ from those of the Community's other members, present or potential. The formal distinctiveness of France and Ireland, as non-members of NATO's integrated organization, is of little account in this regard, though when it comes to the methods by which the broad objectives are to be pursued, France and Ireland become much more distinct. There are other differences of emphasis. Any German government must be preoccupied with the central front; Greece and Spain will bring into the Community their own geographical preoccupations. The most distinctive and difficult British concern in the security field lies in the budgetary and balance of payments costs of the commitment to the central front, which requires the stationing of sizeable British forces in Germany.

In their broad objectives the economic interests of Community members are also akin. All depend on a healthy international economy, with a steady growth of trade, stable international money, and secure supplies of materials. Before accession, Britain depended less than the other members on trade within the Community; but, as a proportion of British GDP, visible exports from Britain to the rest of the Community have doubled, to reach about one-tenth, similar to the proportions of GDP for Italy, Germany, and France. Although France exports somewhat less outside the Community than the other three, all have a strong interest in access to markets outside the Community. For all the member countries, protection of the trade-destroying kind experienced in the 1930s would be a disaster, disrupting production and reducing living standards, to say nothing of the political consequences.

In their preferred ways of achieving these broad objectives, the member countries differ substantially, though less than in defence. Germany stands out in its commitment to free trade and open markets, whereas France and Britain have espoused a degree of managed trade, though both have limited this to a policy for selective control of imports of some sensitive products from outside the Community – and the present British government shows signs of moving back towards the German position. But if its economic policies fail and the British economy remains weak in comparison with those of other Community members, a future British government might wish to control imports from them as well. While a French government could, in similar circumstances, reach a similar conclusion, the circumstances are less likely to arise, because they stem from the sharp divergence in economic dynamism between Britain and the other Community countries. Here, Britain has been the Community's odd man out.

In the divergence among rates of inflation, it is Germany that is exceptional. Partly as a result, Germany has borne the brunt of pressure from the outflow of dollars: hence the German interest in tying the other Community currencies more tightly to the Mark – to share the pressure and moderate the rise of the Mark in relation to other Community currencies. The French government accepted this policy, in line with the long-standing French desire to develop a European counterweight to the dollar, and with its efforts to bring down inflation. But if French inflation, which has been around 10 per cent a year for about a decade, does not decline to Germany's much lower level, the attempt to tie the franc to the Mark is not likely to serve French interests; and the French, like the British, will place more emphasis on Community credits and reserve-sharing than exchange-rate linking, in contrast to the German priorities. All the Community members share an interest in a dollar that is neither under-valued nor unstable, and in securing the influence that would help them to bring this about. But they differ, again, in their views as to how it is to be achieved.

Thus divergences in growth, inflation, and economic philosophy engender differing trade and monetary policies. In the case of primary products the problem lies in differing resource endowments: Britain lacking temperate foodstuffs which France produces abundantly; the other eight lacking sources of energy where Britain is net self-sufficient. In principle, interests ought still to converge. All member countries need secure supplies of most primary products other than energy or temperate foodstuffs, since the Community is generally poor in such resources; but there have been few difficulties in securing these supplies. Around the turn of the century Britain will rejoin the others in being short of its own supplies of oil; but two decades are a long time in politics. The common interest of producers and consumers in a sale at a mutually acceptable price is the basis of the market economy; but the enlarged Community inherits an agricultural policy and an institutional structure that make an acceptable price hard for Britain to secure, while the politics of energy have been too highly charged for a substantial Community interest to become embodied in policy. The reciprocity of relations between Britain and the continent in energy and agriculture appears to offer the basis for a bargain; but it has not been perceived as such by governments on either side of the Channel. Yet there is not a clear-cut dichotomy of interests in agriculture and energy between Britain and the continent. Germany's agricultural interests are in many respects closer to those of Britain than of France; and Britain and Germany have, bilaterally, reached a fair measure of understanding on long-term prospects for the supply to Germany of North Sea oil.

The third in the list of Britain's 'first-order objectives' is much more particular, representing primarily 'certain inherited obligations ... from which the United Kingdom cannot honourably withdraw', derived mainly from the Commonwealth connection. Of the other Community members, only France retains such post-imperial commitments. The web of convergent and divergent interests, benefiting Commonwealth countries in Africa, the Caribbean and the Pacific, harming in varying degrees New Zealand, Canada, Australia, and the Commonwealth countries in Asia, is shown in the sections on trade and agriculture below.

The fourth objective, of a 'peaceful and just world', is one which Britain shares in broadly similar form with the other Community countries. By the time of Britain's third and successful attempt to join the Community, successive governments had accepted that Britain alone could no longer have great influence on the international order and looked to the Community to supply the standing and resources that Britain now lacked. The question to consider here is how far the Community does apply its weight towards this wider objective.

The Record so Far

The Community's success in reconciling external interests has, naturally enough, been strongest in the economic field. It has had the greatest success with those policies, external trade and agriculture, where it possesses the most powerful common instruments.

Trade

The common external tariff has enabled the Community to play the leading role, alongside the United States, in international trade negotiations. For the most part, it has used this influence in a liberal direction. The bold proposals of the Kennedy Round (1963–7) were the American reaction to the appearance of a trading power of weight equivalent to that of the United States; and the Community's response was positive enough to secure cuts of about one-third in industrial tariffs. The process continued in the Multilateral Trade Negotiations

(1973–9), with the result that cuts of one-third were again agreed. This use of the common tariff in GATT rounds has been in line with the direction of British policy during the period. At the same time, the Community has allowed Britain and other members to maintain orderly marketing arrangements for imports of some products from Japan as well as from developing countries.

The common tariff was also one of the main instruments involved, along with the European Development Fund, in replacing the Yaoundé by the Lomé Convention. This was a major gain for British interests, as the tariff preferences and aid were extended from the francophone Yaoundé associates to all the Commonwealth countries of Africa, the Caribbean, and the Pacific; and the Community undertook to buy agreed quantities of sugar from the Lomé participants at the Community price level, and to support their exports of several commodities when prices are weak. These advantages would not have been obtainable for most of the Commonwealth countries without British membership. Since they tend to import more from Britain than do other developing countries, their new trade and aid opportunities are also of benefit to British trade.

The Asian members of the Commonwealth have, however, lost their preferences in the British market without gaining these advantages. Their competitive power in some branches of manufacture was a threat to those industries in the Community; and the French felt that the privileges of the Yaoundé associates would be diluted too much if they were extended beyond the participants in the Lomé Convention. The Asian Commonwealth has had to rest content mainly with such measures as the Community's tariff cuts in the GATT rounds and the Generalized Scheme of Preferences. One of the consequences of British membership has thus been a shift of concessions away from the Indian subcontinent towards the francophone states of North and West Africa; not one that a British government would have carried through on its own initiative.

British attitudes to the import of manufactures from Asia have themselves changed during the hard times of the 1970s. Britain, with France, led the Community towards a more restrictive policy in the renewal of the Multi-Fibre Arrangement in 1978 and in seeking agreement on selective safeguards in the Multilateral Trade Negotiations; and Britain has pressed for other restrictions on imports of Asian manufactures, with Germany as the main moderating influence.

Although the volume of trade has continued to increase, the Community has restricted imports of many agricultural and manufactured products from Eastern Europe (though much less so from the Soviet Union, from which it imports raw materials and heavy industrial products). While the CAP has upset some traditional flows of trade, Community quotas on manufactures have not been irksome to Britain; indeed the Community has largely incorporated the pre-existing policies of the member countries [3]. The grounds for concern are, on the contrary, that the Community has been unable to adopt a common policy which reflects the interests of the member countries better than their several national policies have done, thus failing to persuade the Soviet Union to negotiate with the Community on issues that are of real importance to the Russians.

Agriculture
While the Community's trade policy has corresponded roughly with British interests, at least in so far as these are defined by British policy, agricultural policy has not. It had always been clear that free entry for food imports would have to be replaced by a degree of Community protection, with some switch from non-Community to Community suppliers. The best that could be obtained in the terms for British accession was assured access for given quantities of products on which certain Commonwealth countries were most dependent: sugar from tropical producers and New Zealand dairy products. But it seemed reasonable to hope that, by the end of the 1970s, the degree of Community self-sufficiency could be reduced and access for overseas suppliers improved, with British participation in Community decision making and with the possibility of keeping down farm prices in a time of general inflation. But progress in this direction has been disappointing; and a sharp divergence remains between British interests and the CAP, in its external as well as its internal effects. Unless world food shortages become prevalent, the conflict between British and French interests about imports of temperate agricultural products from outside the Community will remain through the 1980s. But during this period German policy should move closer to British as financial and consumer perspectives counterbalance the small but politically powerful farm lobby; and the accession of Greece, Portugal, and Spain should bring Britain new allies. So Community policy is likely to move in a more favourable direction.

Energy

Attempts to form a Community policy for oil in the decade before 1973 were dogged by disagreements about the roles of state intervention and market forces. Thus the Community responded incoherently to the quadrupling of oil prices at the end of that year, and to the embargo on the Netherlands. Disagreements over relations with America were evident during the Washington Energy Conference, and were institutionalized when France refused to join the other eight as members of the International Energy Agency. When Britain, as an oil producer, demanded a separate seat at the Conference on International Economic Co-operation, it was supported neither by its partners nor by the representatives of OPEC, and had to express itself from within the Community delegation. During 1974–5 the Community initiated a 'Dialogue' with the Arab oil states, building on the member countries' common interest in a more stable relationship with the principal suppliers; but this was interrupted by the dispute between Egypt and its partners over policy towards Israel, and the alternative dialogue with the Gulf states, attempted during 1979, had not got under way by the beginning of 1980. At the time of writing, sensitive negotiations are expected to take place during 1980 between the United States and Euratom, for which the member governments have not yet agreed either their stance towards American demands or the future role of Euratom in controlling uranium supplies.

Britain has thus been neither much hampered nor helped in this sphere by Community membership. Bilaterally, a complementary relationship is growing up between suppliers of North Sea oil on the British side and importers of oil in Germany. But the French and other member governments have continued to prefer bilateral arrangements with Arab suppliers. The Community has not yet come near to developing a common policy that could embody the common interest of all member states in secure and stable supplies for the future. Agreement on such a policy would require greater awareness in Britain that we must prepare for the period beyond North Sea oil, and in France of the hazards of reliance on the Middle East. Unless and until the member states do reach agreement, they will remain largely free to pursue their national interests as they themselves define them.

Money

In money as in energy, external forces and differing views of external interests have impeded the creation of common Community instruments and the formation of common policy. Divergent attitudes towards the United States and the dollar stood for a long time in the way of common action by Germany and France; and when they did agree on the plan for Economic and Monetary Union that was adopted in February 1971, the snake which was at the centre of it was broken only a few months later when the floating of the dollar was followed by that of the guilder and the Mark.

By 1979 German irritation at American policy was one of the impulses behind the launching of the European Monetary System; and the German desire to spread the strain of the dollar inflow was decisive. Doubts about this German mood reinforced Britain's reluctance to become a full member of the System. Adjustments within the exchange rate mechanism in 1979, together with the continued divergence between German and French inflation rates, indicate that the EMS will work as an adjustable peg (or even a crawling peg) system, which will not of itself provide the solid counterweight to the dollar that the French have long sought. The move from the current arrangements with the European Monetary Co-operation Fund to the reserve pool in the European Monetary Fund, due to take place in 1981, could have more impact if the reserves are used collectively in the international currency markets.

While British and French suspicion of supranational solutions is a deterrent, both countries have an underlying interest in the sharing of reserves, where Germany has more to share and therefore less to gain. Britain is already a participant in the reserve-sharing arrangements of the scheme, and in principle committed to eventual full membership. If the EMS remains active it is therefore likely that British influence on the international monetary system will come to be exercised increasingly through common Community arrangements and actions rather than directly and independently.

Security and foreign policy co-operation

Security and defence considerations were part of the original impetus towards European integration. But the collapse of the European Defence Community proposals in 1954 removed the issue from the

European agenda. The rift between France and its partners on Atlantic policy, which led to French withdrawal from the integrated structure of NATO in 1966, only reinforced the reluctance to re-open the issue. But budgetary pressures and escalation in the cost of weapons have pushed European governments into extensive joint pro-grammes for military procurement, in many of which Britain is a partner; and the Independent European Programme Group, of which France is also a member, offers some prospects for further rationaliza-tion. Attempts by the Belgian Prime Minister and the Commission to bring procurement within the framework of the Community have so far been thwarted by differences over strategy and tactics, suspicion of the Commission's motives and capacities, and French insistence on national sovereignty. Defence co-operation thus remains part of the hidden European agenda, likely to be raised openly only when one of its major members decides that it is in its national interest actively to pursue it.

Foreign policy – and thus some aspects of security policy – have, however, been brought within the scope of European collaboration, through the mechanism of European Political Co-operation: outside the framework of the Communities, strictly defined, but with identical membership, linked to the Communities informally through the European Council. Political Co-operation proved its effectiveness, to Britain as to other member states, in the Conference on Security and Co-operation in Europe (CSCE), during the negotiations in Geneva and Helsinki from 1972 to 1975, and the review conference in Bel-grade in 1978. The ability of the Nine to work as a caucus, agreeing on common positions in advance and pressing them in the conference through the spokesmanship of the President-in-office, gave the Com-munity members a powerful influence over the shape of the Final Act – aided by American readiness to let the European partners take the lead. The gains to Britain's security from the CSCE have of necessity been indirect; but in the absence of active American leadership it would have been difficult to achieve as much within the looser frame-work of NATO's political consultations, let alone acting inde-pendently. Political Co-operation also served to support Federal Germany's *Ostpolitik* during its most active phase, thus helping to relax tensions in central Europe. Co-ordination of Western attitudes to the prolonged American–Soviet negotiations on the limitation of strategic armaments (SALT) has, however, been managed through the NATO framework, at the insistence of the Germans, British and others, as have discussions over the equally prolonged negotiations on mutual force reductions. Political Co-operation thus complements the NATO framework in the security sphere, rather than competing with it.

The Euro–Arab Dialogue, begun as a response to Arab demands for closer political relations in the wake of the 1973 Middle East War, may also have provided a useful, if marginal, contribution to Britain's security, as well as a loose framework for promoting European interests in the Middle East. It has enabled Britain and its European partners to resist more firmly the conflicting pressures of Israel and of the Arab protagonists of the PLO for a clearer commitment to either side, and to distance themselves to a degree from American diplomacy (and resist American demands for support). Whether the long-drawn-out manoeuvrings on the political content of the Dialogue, and the consultations on economic co-operation in its working parties, have created enough mutual understanding to influence Arab treatment of European interests in another acute crisis remains untested; but in the uncertain world of diplomacy an improvement in the context for relations is itself a substantial gain.

Britain has had only limited success in exploiting the framework of co-operation among the Nine to fulfil its remaining political commitments and obligations outside Europe. During the most acute stage of the Cyprus crisis, in summer 1974, Mr Callaghan as Foreign Secretary took the initiative in using the Political Co-operation machinery to support Britain's delicate position as a guarantor of the independence of Cyprus and a sovereign base holder – though opinions differ as to whether this made for a more positive European response to the crisis or enabled Britain to shelter behind the measured consultations with its colleagues. Active consultation on all aspects of the Southern African conflict, since Britain's accession to the Community, has ensured support for Britain's diplomacy over Zimbabwe–Rhodesia, though co-ordination with the United States has often been more important. It has also achieved a degree of commonality in declared policy and even action (as in the formulation of the Code of Conduct for European-owned companies) towards South Africa itself – although the distinctive attitudes of the Dutch, Danish, and French have sometimes been disappointing. Perhaps partly because of this, British efforts to resolve the status of Namibia have during the past two years been managed within the *ad hoc* grouping of the five Western members of the UN Security Council, leaving out the smaller member governments of the Community and bringing in the United States and Canada. Hardly surprisingly, the other members of the Community have not been very willing to share the burden and the potential odium of resolving such awkward post-imperial problems as Belize or Gibraltar; though here again continuing consultation has helped to create passive support.

The Community framework has also helped in efforts 'to work for a peaceful and just world'. Both governmental and parliamentary commitments to the restoration of democracy in Greece, Portugal, and Spain were strong. Between 1974 and 1977 the attraction of Community membership, and the associated political conditions, influenced the evolution of domestic politics in these three countries. Over Portugal, the Nine played an active role, persuading the United States that European influence was more acceptable than transatlantic in the confused conditions of Portuguese politics. Community instruments and other channels of financial support were used to exert influence over the evolution of Portuguese politics [2]. The Nine ensured a significant human rights dimension in the CSCE. The last Labour government proposed a human rights clause for the renegotiated Lomé Convention – with Amin's Uganda particularly in mind; this was blocked less by the lukewarm response of other Community members than by the opposition of the associated states.

The Balance of Interests for Britain

The record is thus mixed, but on balance favourable. Britain shares most of the underlying interests of its partners, in security, trade, international monetary stability, access to raw materials, and support for democratic values. There are differences among the member states in immediate interests and on particular issues. But these do not fall along any single fault line, to isolate British interests from those of the remaining eight. On selective protection in trade policy, Britain and France have found common ground, not shared by Germany and some other member states. In monetary co-operation, British interests are close to those of Italy and of other high-inflation countries. Agriculture and energy remain the most difficult areas, though here too there are convergent as well as divergent interests. In foreign policy and security, British interests have been served within the limited capacities of Political Co-operation; but Britain has shared with France a settled reluctance to grasp the nettle of sovereignty which further progress would demand.

The extent to which Community membership has affected Britain's external relations should not be underestimated. Bilateral relations with other Community members, with the United States and with other countries, both developed and developing, have been significantly reshaped. Commonwealth countries now look to Britain to promote their interests in relations with Western Europe. Such states as Nigeria and Ghana weigh their relations with Britain partly in terms of their attitude to the EEC-ACP association; Malaysia and Singapore see bilateral relations refracted through the prism of EEC-Asean negotiations. In a range of international organizations, from the UN General Assembly to GATT, Britain operates as part of a co-ordinated group which votes together and explains its position through a common spokesman; and indeed she is seen by third countries as one of the leading members of the caucus.

The alternative of a more independent foreign policy, on the model of Sweden or Switzerland, working within wider international organizations such as OECD and GATT but not within NATO, has been given little attention. It would free Britain from the constraints of alliance as well as Community commitment, at the cost of a loss of influence in both the security and the economic fields. By following the Norwegian example, with membership of NATO but not of the Community, Britain would retain some influence in defence matters, at least until such time as France and Germany might combine their weight through defence co-operation within the Atlantic Alliance. In security more widely defined, the Community members have already come to constitute an inner circle in international organizations. In economic affairs, European countries acting independently have little weight in negotiations that involve the Community and the United States; and the Kennedy Round, which took place when Britain's relative weight was considerably greater than now, showed that this applies to Britain as well as to smaller countries. It is difficult to avoid the conclusion that the gain of independent policy making on each issue would be unlikely to compensate for the loss of influence over our external environment, provided that the balance of interests within the Community and its outcome in Community policies taken as a whole do not diverge too far from British interests over the longer term.

The alternative offered by the Commonwealth has now been largely discounted, apart from some particular issues such as the negotiations over Zimbabwe-Rhodesia. A closer relationship with the United States (and perhaps also Canada) within the Atlantic system, rather than participation in that system as a member of the European group, still has its proponents, who argue that there is a coincidence of British and American interests in many economic issues, as well as a shared culture, and that Britain would gain more from American support in defence, security, and economic concerns. But this discounts the cumulative decline in American attentiveness to British interests over the last fifteen years, and the rise in attentiveness to Germany and France. It ignores also the uncertain capacity of the American political system to respond to second-order foreign policy concerns, given the shift of influence from the Administration to Congress and the susceptibility of Congress to domestic pressures. It also appears to exaggerate the extent to which British interests coincide with American, particularly in economic diplomacy, rather than with the balance of interests in the Community.

The development of Atlantic summitry, bringing together the United States, Canada, the leading European governments, and Japan in a concert of powers to attempt to lay down global priorities, might seem at first glance to provide an alternative. This forum has now been used to discuss international economic and monetary issues, East-West security, and the Namibian negotiations. It avoids much of the tedium of Community consultations, likely to become yet more tedious as three more members join the discussions, and avoids the formal constraints of the Treaty and the Commission-Council machinery. But it has severe limitations. It lacks the infrastructure which the Community and Political Co-operation have developed to prepare for high-level discussions and to implement decisions taken. It lacks the capacity for common action, which stems from the Community's common instruments and the continuing consultations provided by Political Co-operation. It lacks the common internal policies, which often provide a basis for common external action. Atlantic summitry may set a general context for international negotiations; it cannot cope with the hard technical details around which so many of Britain's interests in international diplomacy now revolve. It boils down, indeed, to a minor variation on the theme of a Norwegian or Swedish solution.

Even the present semi-integrated Community, with its limited capacity for external action and its half-developed network of internal policies, provides a valuable reinforcement for Britain's pursuit of its global interests. Whether a more integrated Community would provide a stronger support for British interests would, of course, depend upon the direction of Community policies. So far, the British have appeared to seek the benefits of Community solidarity in external relations without accepting a corollary of common internal policies and stronger institutions. British perspectives on the development of the Community and its policies have remained clouded. Successive governments have been preoccupied with the CAP and the budget as they affect Britain, reluctant to raise the delicate issue of sovereignty, and aware that a more active foreign policy would cost money which they do not want to pay. Thus the potential for concerting external interests through a more integrated Community has hardly been explored, let alone tested.

For Political Co-operation to become more effective, it would need a permanent secretariat and a commitment to common policies going well beyond the current commitment to consultation. In return for such a commitment, Britain might secure more active support for its distinctive foreign policy interests. The need to find common ground with the other member countries would unavoidably force Britain to adjust some priorities. The French attachment to independence in foreign policy would also have to be overcome. The gains would flow from sharing the burden of Britain's remaining extra-European obligations, and reinforcing Britain's weight in global diplomacy and in relations with the superpowers; the costs would be in the adjustment of priorities.

Trade policy has corresponded fairly closely with British preferences for a liberal international system with some selective protection; so unless Britain's view of its interests alters, no great changes are indicated. Stronger Community capacity to negotiate with the Soviet Union, based on such instruments as a Community export bank, would be in the interest of Britain as of other Community countries. The extension to India and other Asian Commonwealth countries of advantages like those of the Lomé Convention would help to expand British trade with them and strengthen political links. The really critical issues for Britain, and for the Community as a whole, would arise if British industrial recovery were thought to require a period of much greater protection. The Community has not yet contemplated internal trade controls, except as a short-term response to immediate difficulties. It would require a great deal of hard negotiation with the rest of the Community to win acceptance for such a major departure from the rules of the common market over the medium term. Since it would in such circumstances be essential for Britain, as a large net exporter of manufactures and services, to minimize any retaliation, such negotiations would in any case be a necessity with our major trading partners, of which the rest of the Community is by far the most important; while Community backing, once gained, would be of enormous assistance in any wider negotiations. But the difficulty of securing the co-operation of the Community and of other industrialized countries in any such policy, whether or not Britain attempted to work through the Community framework, must not be underestimated.

After the Community budget, the largest drain on Britain's resources in Europe arises from our contribution to the common defence. On the expiry of the last offset agreement, to defray the foreign exchange costs of the British forces in Germany a further round of negotiations with the German government will be needed in 1980 or 1981. Given the fundamental compatibility between British interests and those of its allies in defence and security, it would seem to be here that British gains from greater European integration would be most direct: at once enhancing Britain's security and reducing the budgetary burden. To set this as an objective would be ambitious. It would require the British government to create a coalition of interests strong and wide enough to overcome French inhibitions and the settled particularism of armed services and defence ministries. But such a British commitment would place the issue firmly on the European agenda, and might attract enough support within other governments to provide a basis on which diplomacy could build.

In agriculture, the promotion of Britain's international interests is bound up with the reshaping of the CAP. The direction of Community policy on energy and money remains relatively open; and a British government with clear objectives could exert considerable influence. In international monetary policy there would be ready support within other member governments for many of the objectives

Britain would wish to promote. In energy policy it appears harder to reconcile Britain's interests with those of its Community partners. Britain's position as the Community's largest energy producer is strong enough to ensure that no common policy will be adopted that does not respect its interests. The question is, rather, whether Britain will be able to secure a common policy that is sufficiently advantageous, for example through the Community preference for indigenous energy producers, or whether Britain and other member states would gain more from co-operating within the looser constraints of the IEA.

The argument of this chapter has been that the advantages and disadvantages to Britain of the Community framework for external relations depend, first, upon one's understanding of Britain's loosely defined foreign policy objectives, and secondly upon the strength or weakness of Community policies, internal as well as external – with the costs and benefits which they bring. If Britain can resolve the problems of agricultural policy and budgetary balance to its long-term advantage, then closer co-operation in external relations will compound that advantage. To a limited extent, the advantages which have accrued to Britain's foreign policy interests from co-operating through the Community framework have already offset the disadvantages of the CAP and the budget. There are no attractive alternatives open to Britain, so long as its governments wish to exert influence in international diplomacy and economic relations. There could be major benefits in greater European integration in this sphere; but their achievement would depend upon a much clearer sense of Britain's objectives both in security and in foreign economic policy, as well as upon the uncertain reactions of our present and future partners in the Community.

References

[1] Great Britain, Central Policy Review Staff, *Review of Overseas Representation*, London, HMSO, 1977.

[2] Leigh, Michael and Praag, Nicholas van, *The Mediterranean Challenge*: I (Sussex European Paper no. 2), Brighton, University of Sussex, Sussex European Research Centre, 1978.

[3] Pinder, John and Pinder, Pauline, *The European Community's Policy towards Eastern Europe* (European Series no. 25), London, Chatham House/PEP, 1975.

Comment
by Miriam Camps

So far as it goes, it is hard to fault the Pinder–Wallace paper. But the key words in that sentence are the first five: it does seem to me that the authors stop short of asking some critical questions. I share their view that if the UK wants to exert power and influence in the world it is more likely to be able to do so as part of a large grouping than it is by acting alone and that, today, neither the 'special relationship' with the United States nor links with the Commonwealth are real alternatives to the Community. And who could disagree with their cautious and well-hedged conclusion that *if* British objectives were clearer and *if* these were shared by their European partners there *could* be major benefits for the UK in working to maximize European integration in external policies? The analysis along the way is much more informative than that highly qualified concluding sentence might suggest, but, all the same, it seemed to me to pay too little attention to what I see as a central issue: will the further development of common external policies by an enlarged Community contribute to what I shall, for shorthand, call the needs of the global system, or is the development of a more coherent external policy by the Community likely to be at the expense of an improved global system? Does it matter to the answer whether the UK is in or out of the Community?

To take the last question first: as the paper makes plain, British foreign economic policies are rather ambiguous, and, in most respects, short-term calculations of immediate national needs are given a clear priority over longer-term, rather more diffuse, global needs. A Britain outside the Community would probably tend to be more parochial than a Britain within the Community. The reason is obvious enough. The Community carries enormous economic weight in the international economic system; its actions, or lack of actions, matter in a way that actions of the UK alone do not. Weight, or power, carries obligations which British governments, for all their preoccupation with their own problems, are still likely to recognize. It used to be said that British governments were much more likely to recognize these obligations than were other members of the Community and that the British would be a force pushing the Community to be outward looking. Not much is now heard of this argument; the heirs of Cobden are hard to distinguish from the heirs of Colbert. Nevertheless, the chances that the UK government would take the repercussions on the wider system into account seem to me rather better if Britain is in the Community than if it is acting independently. But the real question is the second, harder one. Are common Community policies likely to advance or to hinder the broader process of building, or rebuilding, a more orderly, more efficient and rather more equitable international economic system?

Clearly a large part of the answer depends on the nature of those common policies and one comes back to the various cross pressures and uncertainties discussed in the paper. There is also, of course, the prior question of whether an economic grouping of the size and importance of the Community, simply by introducing a counterweight to US power and another pole of attraction, makes the system as a whole more or less stable and manageable. I tend to believe in the usefulness of countervailing power; but it would take more than a short comment to explore that question adequately. However, the Community will continue to exist, whatever policy the United Kingdom pursues, and so will Japan; we live in a multipolar world – in the economic dimension if not yet, perhaps, in the security dimension – and there can be no going back to a system that worked rather well in the 1950s.

The question that does seem to me worth addressing is whether the dynamics of the European Community are such that the common policies that are likely to be arrived at, if a maximalist path were chosen, are ones that will contribute to or pull against the evolution of a less fragile, more efficient international economic system. In the early days of the Community there were heated debates between 'Europeans' and 'Atlanticists' about whether the lump of 'European sugar' would dissolve in the cup of 'Atlantic tea' if the common market tariffs were lowered. The question I am asking today is almost the reverse of this: will common Community policies, given the evidence one has of how they are likely to evolve, tend to strengthen or to weaken the arrangements that I, at least, think are needed to manage the global economic system more efficiently?

The evidence does not seem to be very reassuring. If one looks at the linked problems of trade and industrial adjustment, the signs point to a tendency to adjust within the Community with little regard for the impact on third countries. (I am not so concerned by the impact on the rich third countries, like the US and Japan, as on the poorer countries, although the spectre of the three largest trading entities increasingly ignoring the repercussions on one another as they pursue neo-mercantilist policies obviously has its own dangers.) Expansion of the Community to include three relatively poor countries will, I think, intensify this trend to adjust internally with scant regard for the repercussions on others. Accommodating to the trade of 'our' NICs will, I suspect, more than exhaust any willingness to accommodate to the trade of other NICs. In a somewhat similar way, although the Lomé Convention broke useful new ground (notably with the Stabex arrangement), it pushed Community policy toward LDCs in the direction of dividing up the responsibility for LDCs, with Africa assigned to the Community, Latin America to the US, and Southeast Asia to the Japanese. Wholly apart from the fact that this leaves the largest and poorest without patrons, it seems to me to be a wrong pattern of relationship between rich and poor countries; one that is not likely to be in the best economic interests of the LDCs and which carries undesirable political overtones.

As one looks ahead many of the categories in which we have been accustomed to think become increasingly absurd. Is Portugal, a member of the OECD, really a rich industrialized country and Brazil, a leading member of the Group of 77, a poor developing country? The reality seems to me far closer to that of a spectrum of states – with the relative position of the countries in the centre of the spectrum shifting rather rapidly – than it is to that of the familiar 'first', 'second', 'third', and 'fourth' worlds. As more states become industrialized and become more closely tied into the many networks that today link modern economies, the need for more adequate global management of certain kinds of problems seems to me to be bound to grow. Money clearly needs global level management and so, too, do the now necessarily linked problems of trade rules and industrial adjustment policies.

Community policies in both fields – money management and industrial adjustment – will I think be obsolete by the time they are in place, if they are shaped on the assumption that the Community level is, for these matters, the paramount one. Community policies can be useful, both to the members of the Community and to the broader system, if they are shaped with 'global needs' well to the fore. But this is exceedingly difficult to do. The Community today, and, even more, the expanded Community of tomorrow, confronts a far more difficult task in defining the boundaries of Community policies than the founding fathers ever imagined. Then one could draw strained but not wholly false analogies with a federal entity; logically there was no appreciable difference between fitting the Community, with a common tariff and a common commercial policy, into GATT than there was with fitting a large state, like the US, into GATT. Now the problems of fitting Community policies into broader frameworks in ways that strengthen the broader frameworks is far more complicated. That is only partly because even the most 'maximalist' Community that is today conceivable is likely to be far less supranational than the Community of the Six might once have become. More important, it is because many of the issues that now require action at the international level lie in the ever-widening blurred area where domestic and foreign policies overlap and intermingle and because for many problems there is no level of management to which a problem can, as it were, be assigned. Certain aspects of the management of money have to be dealt with nationally, others at the European level, others in concert with the US and Japan, others at the IMF level. This is true as well, I think, with trade and industrial adjustment policies, although for various reasons the awareness of the global dimension in this area is, today, rather weaker than it is in the case of money.

I am very conscious of the fact that anyone who has read as far as this will say I have strayed from our subject; that what this conference is addressing is not the extent to which there is a global economic system and the kind of institutional arrangements it requires but the far narrower problem of the extent to which British interests will be served by more or less in the way of common Community policies. My reply is that all states, and in particular all modern industrial states, have an increasingly strong interest in the efficient working of the global economy. For the first time we really do live in a closed economic system with important feed-back effects. The Community carries such weight in that system that it has an obligation to design policies in such a way that they will help provide the public goods of order, stability, and efficiency to the system as a whole. Whether the complicated decision making process of the Community is capable of producing policies that are informed with what might be called a cosmopolitan view, I do not know. It seems to me to be a question of great importance. Europeans have been loud in their complaints that the US has not, in recent years, given the 'needs of the system' the same priority in the formation of US policies as it has sometimes done in the past. I agree with that criticism. But Community policies must now be subjected to the same kind of test. And it seemed to me that this test was missing from the otherwise excellent analysis produced for us by John Pinder and William Wallace.

General Index